LANNING ROPER

AND HIS GARDENS

Henry
to Primrose
and Lanning
June 1953

JANE BROWN

LANNING ROPER

AND HIS GARDENS

RIZZOLI
NEW YORK

Frontispiece] Lanning Roper,
pencil portrait by Henry Lamb, 1953.

The quotation on page 7 comes from
The Land by Vita Sackville-West, 1926,
and is reproduced by kind permission of
Nigel Nicolson Esq. and Heinemann Ltd.

First published in the
United States of America in 1987 by
RIZZOLI INTERNATIONAL
PUBLICATIONS, INC.
597 Fifth Avenue, New York, NY 10017

LIBRARY OF CONGRESS CATALOGING-IN-PUBLICATION DATA
Brown, Jane.
Lanning Roper.

Bibliography: p.
Includes index.
1. Roper, Lanning.
2. Landscape architects—United States—Biography.
3. Gardeners—United States—Biography.
I. Title.
SB470.R66B76 1987 712'.092'4 [B] 86—22060
ISBN 0—8478—0787—8

Designed by Trevor & Jaqui Vincent

Filmset by Keyspools Ltd, Golborne, Lancashire
Colour separations by Newsele Litho Ltd
Printed and bound in Italy by LEGO, Vicenza

First published in Great Britain by
George Weidenfeld and Nicolson Limited
21 Clapham High Street, London SW4 7TA

CONTENTS

. . . foresight is the gardener's text,

And though his eyes may never know

How lavishly his flowers blow,

Others will stand and musing say

'These were the flowers he sowed that May'.

VITA SACKVILLE-WEST

INTRODUCTION

This book tells the story of a citizen of the United States, a staunchly patriotic American, who found his happiness making gardens in England. Lanning Roper was born in a small town in New Jersey and ended his career as garden consultant to the Prince of Wales. Put like that, his story seems like fiction – something Mark Twain would have loved. But the facts are that this American possessed an innate understanding of the best traditions of English gardening, and managed to perpetuate them into the unsympathetic air of the later twentieth century. If he could have encountered Capability Brown in the Garrick Club, he would have struck up a lively and sympathetic conversation on 'place-making', for he fully understood the language of landscape gardening; but Lanning also possessed a rare combination of sound practical horticultural knowledge, a love of getting his hands dirty and a restrained and educated taste in planting and garden design. He could adapt his skills to a large landscape or a small garden. If, in many ways, he could have stepped straight out of the eighteenth century, he never allowed himself to forget the limitations, and the costs, of the present time. His combination of past and present virtues, his belief in what he was doing, and his success on terms which he respected, all add up to a reassuring story.

Lanning was born in 1912 into a happy, secure family. He possessed good health, intelligence, a sunny disposition and a great capacity for friendship. To this he added a passion for flowers, a love of art and architecture, of the opera, of sailing and of good parties. New York in the late thirties offered him a life of uncommitted ease and much pleasure, and had America not been drawn into the war, things might have stayed that way. But the shock of his war made him realize that he had to try to make a success of what he most wanted to do – create gardens – despite being surrounded by the conventional professions of his family who were in banking, the law or farming.

On reflection, I feel that his seemingly strange decision to live and work in England was made in stages. As a charming and attractive naval officer at large in the euphoric, victorious air of London, he must have found the English more lively and welcoming than their chill reputation presupposed. It was fun to stay on, but when his first attempt at earning a living in London palled, he had to think again. Having made the decision to have a go at gardening, his 'landscape' and gardening soul asserted itself, and he became captivated with the landscape and gardens of England. The country was, after all, the home of his ancestors, the basis of his anglophile education, and blessed with a climate that was perfect for green and growing things. The English love of gardens was reviving after the war, and there were many gardens to be restored and made anew. Who would help the hard-pressed owners? The horticultural students that became Lanning's friends at Kew and Edinburgh Botanic Gardens would cultivate wonderful plants and work in grand gardens; the small English landscape architecture profession would reorganize itself, but its sights were set upon recognition for work in public landscapes, in parks, schools, hospitals and factories. Somewhere between these two there was a gap: whether Lanning ever precisely identified that gap and aimed to fill it, I do not know; but he did come to fill it, both usefully and successfully.

In the segment of American life that he rejected priorities differed and there was no place for him there. The university landscape schools were turning out keen and highly qualified landscape architects (Lanning had rejected both architecture and landscape architecture courses *before* the war) and the accent was on the ecological approach. There was no ingrained universal love of gardening, but there was a sudden rediscovery of America's magnificent and maltreated natural landscape which her people would ignore at their peril. The landscape profession was pioneering the living in harmony with nature, ironically led by a Scotsman, Ian McHarg. The alternatives were either in juggling with urban landscapes with the brilliant Garrett Eckbo or Kevin Lynch (demi-gods to the English landscape mind), or in the California-culture gardens of Thomas Church. To Lanning, California *was* a foreign country. But he never forgot his homeland, and though his work there and his American allegiances are described mainly in Chapter 6, America permeates all his work and, indeed, this book. In particular there was an American gloss, a perfection to his work, which shows in many of the illustrations that follow.

In other chapters I have tried to cover Lanning's work in such a way that his skills, which had many aspects, are most clearly illustrated. He had two particular loves: for flower gardens, and for the historic landscape gardens, especially those we call 'the Picturesque'. He was very happy at work in Ireland because he had the chance to do all his favourite things – flower gardens for favourite clients, the classical landscapes of Castle Ward and Castlecoole for the National Trust in Northern Ireland, and – his longest association of all – work in the 'American Picturesque' garden of Glenveagh Castle, in County Donegal, for his former Harvard classmate Henry McIlhenny.

These aspects of his work can be seen in Chapter 7, 'Georgian Gardener', where I have mentioned the majority of his important jobs in 'period' gardens and landscapes in England, for both private owners and the National Trust. Scotney Castle was the place which won his heart, and the garden was his constant concern from the time of the death of its owner Christopher Hussey in 1970, up until Lanning's death. However, in his own mind Stourhead's garden was 'the greatest landscape achievement in Britain'. He never worked there, but in a lecture to the Royal Horticultural Society in 1968[1] he analysed his enjoyment of the place while 'walking' it (as he 'walked' all his sites in fair weather and foul): his pleasure came through every fibre of his being into the enthusiasm of his words.

The words alone are all we have left, but they do illuminate the qualities of Stourhead. Lanning admired it because he could see how its maker Henry Hoare had understood his landscape, and lovingly set his lakes, his broad grassy sweeps and tree-clad slopes, and 'a long, winding path that circuits the largest lake' within it. Lanning's love of architectural conceits delighted in the temples, a grotto, the vases, fine sculpture, bridges and follies that were arranged around. 'Why is Stourhead so successful?' he asked, and concluded that it was the scale, 'the broad sweeps, the giant trees, the proportions of the details in relation to the whole, the width of the paths and bridges . . . all in harmony'.

'The setting is superb. . . . The vast expanse of sky with the hills and trees silhouetted against it is a constant joy. . . . The siting of ornamental features is another of the great achievements. . . . The view across the lake, with the bridge over the stream in the valley in the foreground, and the Pantheon on the distant hillside with a backdrop of trees, or the Temple of Flora under huge beech trees, with a beautiful stone urn on the lower slope by the lake. . . .' All superb. He knew of no other garden (and his experience was encyclopaedic) where there was 'such a series of delightful pictures, which compose and recompose so successfully' as one walked around. And then 'the element of surprise is brilliantly utilized . . . you are always led on to see what is around the next bend or behind the massed planting, or how the garden looks from the other side of the lake, or from the heights of the folly. . . .'

Lanning loved Stourhead at every season: 'in spring with the tender new greens of the beeches and oaks, the silvery greys of the willows and poplars' and drifts of daffodils pouring down the banks; the autumn colour was magnificent, and 'in winter I find Stourhead equally satisfying, with the bold stems of the huge trees silhouetted against the carpets of russet leaves or snowy slopes with deep blue shadows. . . . ' Though he loved rhododendrons, he did not feel the need of them blazing away at Stourhead: 'I, for one, love the simple green and blue landscape of grass, trees, water and sky, with ferns, wild flowers and waterside plants.'

I have included this rather large quotation from Lanning's lecture for it introduces the language of landscape, and the perception and appreciation of a lively mind which could translate that language for all to understand. Lanning's greatest talent was that he could make these discerning judgements of a landscape or garden from his own objective experience, and then, in all his work, create, correct, adjust and perfect the required image for that place and the particular person he was working for. This was both a mental and physical process, a straight-from-the-shoulder 'designing' in the way of the old landscape gardeners. It was not watered down or modified into plans and drawings, and was therefore direct and powerful. It was much more involved with places, and with people, than the abstracted doodling of 'design' on paper, and, of course, much more dependant upon a receptive client or landscape manager. Lanning's infinite charm, generosity of mind, and talent for making such an assemblage of widely differing personalities as pass through this book 'receptive', were not the least of his skills.

My own interest in the twentieth-century landscape arts gives me special admiration for Lanning's tremendous, and mainly intellectual, sympathy with modern buildings. This is the subject of Chapter 8, and I think this may well be the most important chapter in the book. He could unhesitatingly adapt the eighteenth-century landscape rules he knew so well to modern buildings and their 'garden' settings. This was exactly what the Modern Movement intended. He was absolutely certain that plants and green sculptured spaces could be manipulated to flatter the exuberant geometry of glass and concrete, and yet also make it possible for such large-scale buildings to be comfortable for the human-scale individuals who inhabited them. As I know of no other landscape designer who has approached this pressing and difficult challenge with even half of Lanning's sympathy, determination and skill, I hope that when modern landscape comes into its own, Lanning's pioneering contributions will be appreciated.

For many people though, his most attractive work was in flower gardens: for Chapter 9 I have chosen five relatively small, private gardens from the dozens in his list of commissions. He loved flowers and flowering shrubs, with very few dislikes; he loved colourings of soft pinks, mauvy-blues and silvers, or of yellows, creams and greys; blood-red roses on a stone wall, glossy green leaves, puffs of lavender or lavender-cotton, sweeps of autumn's russets and golds, and always the scents of roses and his aristocratic loves, lilies and tulips. He loved plants in abundance, but like a couturier or a master chef, he developed his 'signatures' and 'styles'. Many of the illustrations in the book, and particularly in this chapter, will invite the soubriquet 'Very Lanning'. I think that would have made him smile.

In my penultimate chapter I have scaled the heights of his international reputation without, I hope, betraying the discretion he so carefully tended. For, after all, no garden can be enjoyed without the peace and privacy that most of us can take for granted. My final chapter, like the first, is more about Lanning himself than his work, though by the end of the book the two have become almost inseparable. I have not dwelt on his final illness because he would not have wished it, but all his friends speak of his bravery, and it was inexpressibly sad how the letters, full of plans and planting ideas, poured forth from the Lindo Wing of St Mary's Paddington up until a very short time before his death on 22 March 1983. He had had so little time: from 1957, when he left the Royal Horticultural Society to start on his own, until 1982, when he became seriously weakened by illness – just twenty-five years into which to cram the beautiful gardens of a lifetime.

After his death, the executors of Lanning's will, Lord Normanby and Mr Humphrey Whitbread, saved his papers, and these were sorted by Lanning's devoted secretary, Miss Anne Terry. This collection of papers have formed the basis of this book, and they have now been deposited in the Royal Horticultural Society's Lindley Library. I am particularly grateful to Lord Normanby and Dr Brent Elliott, the Librarian of the Lindley Library, for their patience and kindness whilst I have been using the papers.

The Lanning Roper Papers consist of files relating to most of the gardens specified in the list of commissions set out at the back of this book. (The list indicates the material that has survived.) The files contain correspondence, garden reports, plant orders and invoices, and some plans by Lanning. Because Lanning did not draw well, the plans are comparatively unimportant, while an additional collection of miscellaneous plans and drawings from various hands only supply information of limited value. Some of these have been used in this book. There is also a collection of colour slides, mostly taken by Lanning, and as many of these as possible have been reproduced in the book too. There are scrapbooks containing all his *Sunday Times* pieces, over six hundred of them, from 20 April 1969 to 21 March 1976, with some additional cuttings from the *Sunday Times Colour Magazine* and other magazines.

There is a substantial collection of his *Country Life* articles, covering over thirty years of his contributions.

Apart from the Lanning Roper Papers, the other main source of material for Lanning's gardens is in the Harry Smith Horticultural Photographic Collection. Lanning had very definite ideas on how his gardens should be photographed, and Harry Smith, Ernest Crowson, and the present Curator of the Collection, Dr R.H.M.Robinson, all knew him well and photographed for him. This book is greatly enriched by many photographs from the collection, many of which have not been published before, and I am especially grateful to Dr Robinson, his partner Dr Anthony Huxley and his staff for their kindness and informative help. Mrs Sheila Orme, who now photographs for the Collection, has taken some lovely new photographs where this was necessary. *Country Life* magazine has been the other major source of photographs, and my thanks go to the staff of the Art Department for providing them for me; the *Country Life* pictures are mainly the work of Jonathan Gibson and Alex Starkey.

The final source is of course the gardens themselves, and the many owners and gardeners who are perpetuating Lanning's plantings and caring for his designs. So very many of his clients, colleagues and friends have answered my requests for information that I cannot name them here, but I offer my thanks to them all. Most of their names occur somewhere in the book. For myself, I would like to single out for special thanks Mrs Betty Hussey, Mrs Biddy Hubbard, Lady Berkeley, Miss Mary Lutyens and Mr Peter Palumbo. From America I received the greatest encouragement from Lanning's sister-in-law Mrs Laura Wood Roper, and from Mrs Janet Murrow. A cousin of Lanning Roper, Frank W. Roper, has given me invaluable help with the Roper family history.

I am also grateful for the patience and support of everyone concerned with the origination and production of my book, especially Michael Dover, Martha Caute, Annie Lee and Trevor Vincent.

I never actually met Lanning. A few months before he died, while I was working on my book about Vita Sackville-West, I wrote to him asking if I could come and talk to him about his memories of her. I received a courteous and cheerful reply saying 'yes', but asking me to wait until he felt a little better. So I never saw him, but I feel it was a rather nice twist of fate that I came to be asked to write this book, and I have enjoyed the privilege of getting to know him. I only hope that my work in some way fulfils the expectations of his many friends.

JANE BROWN

I

BEGINNINGS

IN MAY 1850 a young American farmer Frederick Law Olmsted (1822–1903) saw the home of his fathers, Mother England, for the first time. He had crossed the Atlantic in the sailing packet *Henry Clay* with two friends; they first glimpsed Holyhead looming in the fog, 'a great sublime mountain . . . its head in the clouds'.[1] When they landed, most of Liverpool was hidden in a pall of smoke, and they hastily left it to spend their first night in a country inn near Chester. There Olmsted rose at dawn and looked out of his latticed, 'woodbine-curtained' windows to a view of thatched cottages, flowering hawthorn hedges that sparkled with dew, some haystacks in small fields and sheep grazing on distant low hills. On this hilly horizon was the rising sun, lighting the clouds of the grey dawn. He wrote: 'Such a scene I had never looked upon before, and yet it was in all its parts as familiar to me as my native valley. Land of our poets! Home of our fathers! Dear old mother England! It would be strange if I were not affected at meeting thee at last, face to face.'[2]

Olmsted's susceptibility to the romantic and picturesque elements in landscape was partly responsible for his enthusiasm, but though he had not seen England before, it was a spiritual homecoming. As Laura Wood Roper has written in her biography of him, 'By background and tradition he was an Englishman; love of England was a rooted, almost an instinctive, sentiment with him.'[3] That first passion for the enchantment of the English countryside lasted throughout Olmsted's life; he went on to become the designer of Central Park in New York and many other parks across America, the saviour of the sublime wilderness of Yosemite for the nation and the champion of the American National Parks movement, the most prolific and influential landscape architect of his century. And he always found inspiration in his memories of English parks and gardens, and of the English landscape and its traditions.

I have begun with Frederick Olmsted for the sake of the close parallels, which cross almost one hundred years, with the feelings and sensibilities (though never expressed in so flowery a way) of a young naval officer named Lanning Roper. He stood on the deck of an American warship and gazed longingly at the ribbons of wooded valleys of the Cornish coast in springtime, wondering what 'garden glories' they concealed. He knew that he had little chance of finding out, for this was May 1944 and he was part of a convoy that had an assignment with what we now know was Operation Overlord, the Allied invasion of the Normandy beaches.

Lanning Roper was born on 4 February 1912 in West Orange, New Jersey, where his parents lived within commuting distance of Wall Street. He was the last of the three

Lanning Roper as a young man.

Florence Eveleth Roper
with her three sons –
Hartwell on the left, Crosby
on the right, and Lanning
on her knee, *c.* 1915.

Below] The three Roper
boys, Crosby, Lanning and
Hartwell, *c.* 1920.

sons of Willet and Florence Roper, who had married in 1902. A daughter, Catherine, had been born in 1905 but had died soon afterwards; Hartwell was born in 1907, Crosby in 1910 and lastly, Lanning.

Willet Crosby Roper was in the tenth generation of a large clan of farming families descended from John and Alice Ropear, who had left Buckenham on the Norfolk Broads for New England in 1637. The New England Ropers formed an association, and the saga of their lives, including surviving Indian massacres and fighting for independence against the English, was written and published by Ella Roper in 1904. The move from New England to New York State was made in Willet's grandmother's time; she was a remarkable woman, Adeline Whipple Roper, who was widowed during the move as was her sister, Harriet Whipple Lanning. They were left, each with a son to bring up in a strange place, and received a great deal of help and support from their brother, Andrew Whipple. Adeline's son, Frank Herbert Roper, was Lanning's grandfather, and Harriet's son, Willet Lanning, who became a well-known doctor practising in New York City, was the source of the unusual Christian names of both Lanning and his father.

Willet Roper had graduated from Harvard in 1899 and joined the firm of Brown Brothers, Harriman & Co., who were private bankers in Wall Street. He was a rather formal, kindly and gentle man, a stickler for his routine, and he served Brown Brothers loyally for all his working life. He joined their Quarter Century Club in 1948 and eventually became a director. His work and his family were his life; he was a gentle and loving father, and Lanning always remembered how happy he was in his garden at the weekends.

Florence Emeline Eveleth, Lanning's mother, was a small, strong and energetic woman, always going at top speed. 'I work till I'm exhausted, then I rest for twenty minutes,' was her constant riposte to her family's concern for her health. She also came of stout Pilgrim stock, and her ancestry traces back easily through eight generations to the marriage of John Smith and Sarah Hunt in Middlesex County, Massachusetts, in 1647. The John Smiths set up house in a building that survives as 174 Great Road, Maynard, ten miles west of the boundaries of present-day Boston. Florence, who was born on 9 May 1874, was very proud of her forebears who had fought at Concord and Ticonderoga and who had established the solid New England comfort she remembered from her childhood. In 1947 she longingly recalled the lovely old furniture and the big dining-room of the Smith house – and how 'we used to lie in the big four-poster bed and pick out the fruit we'd most like' from the paintings on the walls, done in the New England tradition. 'The horn of plenty of our childhood' was her phrase for such happiness. She was extremely intelligent and independent of mind – she had graduated from Boston University in 1897, five years before her marriage – and this lively intelligence was passed to her youngest son, though he was probably far more impressed to learn that her father was head groundsman at Harvard University.

The Willet Ropers were loving and indulgent parents, with discipline instilled by kindness and example, and a love of orderliness in living softened by a lot of laughter in the home. Consequently, Lanning's was a well regulated childhood, happy and uneventful. The Ropers moved their family to Closter, in the north-east corner of

The Roper home in Closter, New Jersey, where Lanning spent his childhood.

Opposite] Lanning as a schoolboy [*above*], and as a Harvard undergraduate [*below*].

New Jersey, where it meets New York State and the Hudson River. They had a large and comfortable house and garden, and Lanning remembered making gardens of his own and hours spent roaming the wooded slopes towards the Palisades of the Hudson for wild flowers. All three boys went to school in Englewood, and their holidays were spent at Lake Champlain, where the Adirondacks meet the Green Mountains of Vermont, or at Cape Cod. When Lanning was old enough he was sent to summer camp at Buzzards Bay to learn to sail.

Hartwell, the Ropers' eldest son, persisted in wanting to be a farmer (like generations of Ropers before him), but against his father's wishes; the wise parent relented and sent him to Massachusetts College of Agriculture, where he met and married a strong, handsome girl and they settled down to farm in Lancaster County, Pennsylvania.[4] Crosby, the second son, was equally sure of himself. He graduated from Harvard Law School in 1931 and became and remained a respected lawyer, eventually working for Covington & Burling in Washington DC. In 1940 he married a Vassar girl and a Southerner, Laura Emily Wood; she would later write the brilliant biography of Frederick Law Olmsted which I quoted on my first page.

Lanning, in contrast to his brothers, was uncertain about what he wanted to do. That is to say, he knew really – deep down – that he had a passion for gardens and flowers (as well as for sailing), but did not know how this could be transformed into earning a living. He graduated from Harvard with honours in Fine Arts in 1933, intending to follow on to study landscape architecture. The profession was well established in America, having been founded in 1899 by a group of eleven, which included Frederick Law Olmsted's sons and Edith Wharton's niece, the remarkable Beatrix Farrand. Landscape architects had earned good livings, but in the penultimate depression summer of 1933, with the unemployment figure over 13 million, Lanning heeded the warning that it was an eminently dispensable profession. There was, however, the argument that people still must have houses, shops, factories, even cinemas ... and he was convinced. In the autumn of 1933 he enrolled for the architecture course at Princeton. His architectural career was to be short-lived: 'not as the cynics and the loyal Harvard alumni will say, because I chose the wrong university, but because my real interest was in landscape gardening with emphasis on the gardening'.[5] By the end of his first year he had had an 'elegant sufficiency', which did not really surprise him – 'even as a child I had spent my allowance on bulbs and seed packets and shown little inclination towards bricks and mortar'. One imagines he skipped sessions on drainage and pipework and retreated to contemplate the filigree domed pavilion on the lake at nearby Drumthwacket, wandering among the statuary and flowers of that beautiful, romantic garden.

After Princeton, Lanning organized his life very pleasantly for the next six years. If there were disappointments and frustrations, he did not seem to remember them. In the autumn of 1934 he became a schoolmaster, teaching English and Latin at the smart Buckley School on 73rd Street in New York. He continued to live at home with his parents at Closter, gardening at the weekends, but also making full use of the city theatres and galleries and opera at the Metropolitan. The opera was to remain a lifelong passion.

In the long summer vacations he took tutoring jobs, which allowed him to indulge another passion – for sailing. He was careful to choose families with yachts, even the ocean-going variety. His first summer was spent around the coast of Florida, and there were later summers at Newport, Rhode Island, where he was in his element with the mixture of racing and grand gardens to be explored. Those legendary Newport palaces – Belcourt Castle, The Breakers, The Elms, Beechwood and Rosecliff – with their grand and formal gardens hybridized from Fontainebleau and Villa Gamberaia, with Victorian carpet bedding still planted out by expatriated Scottish gardeners, were an education in themselves. But I think Lanning would have been more enchanted with the good Newport gardens that were still mixed with the magnificent: pictures taken in the 1920s show Chetwood, with its highly individual use of ivies, glossy and variegated, draping over vases, balustrades and steps and around the stone edges of pools. At Mariemont there were long borders with flowery drifts of blues, mauves, pinks and whites, classical columns draped with flowers, and vases overflowing with more flowers. Ground coverings and garden ornaments – and his fine taste for both – were to become strong themes in his gardening.

Those Newport summers, the opera in New York, his first serious girlfriend – an elegant and intelligent lady, Dorie Foot, who worked for Lenthéric in Fifth Avenue, whom he took for teas at the Ritz – all these were aspects of his life that were about to be changed. As an Anglophile and a New Englander by descent, Lanning shared the concern of many of his friends that America had not gone immediately to Britain's aid at the outbreak of war. He joined the New York National Guard as a private in

Lanning's first command,
LCI(L) no. 412, at Omaha
Beach on the afternoon of
D-Day, 6 June 1944.

January 1941 but absolutely hated the drilling. In the following December the
Japanese attack on Pearl Harbor brought America into the war; on 16 March 1942
Lanning accepted a commission as an ensign in the Naval Reserve, and four days later
he reported for active duty as a communications watch officer on inshore patrols. For
the rest of 1942 and the whole of 1943 he was either on these inshore patrol
operational duties or attending naval courses, which included a two-month
indoctrination course at the Naval Training Station at Newport. The training and
experience turned him out as a commanding officer for a landing craft – officially
called Landing Craft Infantry (Large) no. 412 – and he picked up his charge at
Lawley's Shipyard in Boston on 31 January 1944. He imagined he would be sent to
the Pacific, but a month later the LCI(L) was moored among others at Lambert's
Point, Norfolk, Virginia, her original green paint changed to grey, provisions on
board for six months, fuelled to capacity and ready for sea. Only the order to sail
was awaited.

Lanning has wryly noted that it took his lumbering convoy longer to get across the
Atlantic in the spring of 1944 than it had taken Columbus. He was rather shocked to
discover that he hated this kind of 'sailing'; the journey from Boston to Virginia had
been a terrible strain, and the Atlantic crossing turned into a nightmare. To actually
make landfall at Plymouth and to make contact with that healing Devon countryside
became his priority. At the first opportunity he rushed off, out of sight of the
dockyard and all ships and evidences of war, and eventually returned with large
bunches of primroses for the mess tables. This was not, he always grinned as he
remarked, 'a typical naval custom' but it was a welcome relief to him and his men all
the same. For Lanning, as probably for so many others, the war was to make it

impossible for him ever to associate being at sea in a small boat with pleasure or 'fun' again.

On the morning of 6 June, D-Day, he was in charge of a division of landing craft (division no. 67) carrying the troops of the United States 115th Infantry Regiment to Omaha Beach. They arrived after the first disastrous wave of attempted landings of tanks and men on to what was thought to be an undefended coast; a pall of smoke and dust hung over the beaches, obscuring landmarks and making controlling impossible. The citation for the award of Lanning's Gold Star Medal for his work that day tells the rest of the story: 'He beached the LCI(L)s and all troops aboard were landed safely. Enemy artillery, machine gun and mortar fire were continuous, and the waters near the beach were cluttered with obstructions, wreckage and mines. In spite of all these difficulties, Lieutenant Roper completed his mission successfully and on schedule.'[6]

After the D-Day operation Lanning was assigned as a group commander and operations officer for LCI(L)s in Flotilla 12. It was this duty that took him to, of all places, Exbury House, Lionel de Rothschild's 'ante-bellum' English mansion set in the New Forest and surrounded with magnificent rhododendron woods. The Admiralty had turned it into a 'stone frigate' called HMS *Mastodon*; in *Requiem for a Wren* Nevil Shute describes beautifully what Wrens Janet Prentice and May Spikins found when they arrived exactly a year before Lanning:

> All afternoon the two girls wandered up and down woodland paths between thickets of rhododendrons in bloom, each with a label, with water piped underneath each woodland path . . . they found streams and pools, with ferns and water lilies carefully preserved and tended. They found a rock garden half as large as Trafalgar Square that was a mass of bloom; they found cedars, and smooth, grassy lawns. They found long ranges of greenhouses . . . they learned with awe that the staff of gardeners had been reduced from fifty to a mere eighteen old men . . . they found the Beaulieu River . . . and the sea, with the seagulls drifting by upon the tide.[7]

How much more must Lanning, who knew well how to appreciate gardens and rhododendrons, have wondered at what he saw? The rhododendrons were much better than any he had the opportunity of seeing at home, and there were also – though he might not have been able to name them – nyssas, eucryphias, nothofagus, Japanese maples and plantations of cotoneasters, kalmias, pernettyas, hydrangeas, pieris, camellias and philadelphus, with roses, wisterias and vines climbing everywhere. Neglect only added to the profusion. The wonder of Exbury at that particular time never left him; if he had moments to think as he wandered through the glades, and ponder what he might do after the war was over, then Exbury made a very important point.

Lanning finished his war with six months' intelligence duties with the Combined Intelligence Objectives Sub-Committee at the headquarters of Naval Forces Europe in Grosvenor Square. He had to work very hard and was highly commended for his quickness and efficiency. He apparently showed considerable ingenuity in devising systems for collecting and disseminating a massive amount of information through a tiny office with an inadequate staff. But, when he did have time off, London in the aftermath of victory was a pleasant place to be and there were parties galore within a short walk of Grosvenor Square. All the young officers frequented Constance Spry's shop in South Audley Street for their flower offerings, and Lanning much admired her way of doing things. He met Walter Fish, the ex-editor of the *Daily Mail*, who had been doing war work for the Ministry of Information from his home at East Lambrook Manor in Somerset – Walter's wife, Margery, who was making her lovely garden, became a firm friend of Lanning. He also met Herbert Agar, an American historian who was Counsellor at the Embassy – a very important meeting of which more later. Lanning was in a position to make many friends in the euphoria of victory, and so many of his American and English connections go back to this time, including John and Nancy Blakenham, Patrick Leigh Fermor, Cecil Beaton and Malcolm Bullock, all of whose company he enjoyed in later years and many of whom are encountered in his gardening. But the most important of these early friendships was with Oswald, the fourth Marquis of Normanby. Lord Normanby and Lanning were exactly the same age, they both had wars that they wanted to forget as soon as possible, and they had many interests in common. For Lanning this was to be one of the strongest friendships of his life, and right from the start had an important influence on his life. Oswald Normanby introduced him to the kind of English life that he found most intriguing – a quiet permanence pervaded his world that was balm to war-torn nerves. During 1945 Oswald Normanby was Lord in Waiting to King George VI, and it was on a triumphal royal occasion, at an excited gathering to greet the King and Queen on the terrace of the Houses of Parliament, with fireworks and Handel's 'Water Music' completing the atmosphere, that he met Lanning for the first time. He took him back to see Mulgrave Castle, his home between the moors and the sea, north of Whitby in Yorkshire. From there Lanning pondered upon a way of life that kept a person in one place for a lifetime, families there for centuries, so that the making of a garden was really worthwhile. He wondered even more at the balmy and kind climate of England, which encouraged green and growing things so much, and dispelled the recurrent heartbreaks that he knew of that bitter east coast and the New England winters and late springs. And he considered the philosophy of life that made gardening so important to so many English people, even though they were busy with politics and business, farming and writing, and other things. Mulgrave added impressions to those made by Exbury, which settled into the corners of Lanning's mind.

He finished his intelligence duties in Grosvenor Square on 15 November 1945, and he was released to inactive duty two weeks later. Now he was free to go, but where? In his heart he knew that he wanted to make his living in England, but he was also sensitive (to a fault, I'm told) over the feelings of his parents. The sequence of events over the following months is hard to piece together, but there were some definite points of reference. He knew that he did not want to go back to teaching. However, he returned home to see his parents and Dorie Foot, his girlfriend of before the war. They had, at some time, taken a mutual decision that they were not right for each other in marriage, but they vowed to, and did, remain firm friends. Dorie married an Englishman in 1946, and when she subsequently found herself in England and in need of a friend, it was Lanning who helped her; she continued to see him on occasions for the rest of his life.

Lanning confided his doubts about what he should do to Dorie. Oswald Normanby went over to New York, met Lanning's parents at their home in Gramercy Park, and encouraged Lanning to speak out. When he did 'confess' to them that he wanted to return to live and work in England, Willet and Florence Roper made it very easy for him, and sent him on his way with their blessing. But what was he to do? He had met some old New York friends, Dick and Connie Rheem; Dick Rheem wanted to expand his company into the manufacture of oil drums for the Middle Eastern oil market, and he suggested that Lanning take on the London end of this operation. It seemed a wonderful opportunity and Lanning returned joyfully to London, with a job. However, even though it was a kind of commercial intelligence operation and he enjoyed the 'intelligence' part of it, the problems of steel and furnaces did not entrance him and he lasted less than a year. He returned home once more, to consider the matter. On this trip he confided to Dorie that he was going to give himself one more chance, and at least he would set out to learn 'how to garden and grow things'.

Lanning in uniform, *c.* 1945.

2

ENGLISH ATTACHMENTS

The garden at Chevithorne Barton, as Lanning would have seen it.

Opposite] Chevithorne Barton, the woodland garden.

N O ONE realized more than Lanning himself just how much he had to learn if he was to make gardens as a career. He was already thirty-four, rather old for a student, and yet a student he must become; his enthusiasm for England and for plants carried him along, he learned fast and was prepared to make the most of every waking hour, and in this way he built up his knowledge.

His first visits to Margery Fish at East Lambrook Manor were made while he was still in uniform. Walter and Margery Fish had bought their little manor house just before the war, and Margery had been busy learning as she gardened. She has told her story in the book *We Made a Garden*.[1] Lanning had a tremendous respect for her cottage planting, and he learned a great deal from her in the course of a friendship that lasted until her death.[2] It was Margery who introduced him to that Somerset coterie of good gardens – Montacute House, already owned by the National Trust, the Lyles' Barrington Court, with its series of garden rooms originally planted by Gertrude Jekyll, and the Reiss's Tintinhull. He was greatly impressed by the dignity and unity of Mrs Reiss's smallish garden, the integration of the exquisite Queen Anne manor house and the complementary spaces of the garden, with self-contained vistas and wonderful use of texture and form in planting. He visited Tintinhull time and again, and eventually wrote about it in *Gardening Illustrated*,[3] noting especially how she used bergenias, hostas, lavender, *Iris pallida*, *Senecio greyi*, *Rosa rubrifolia* and catmints, all adopted as his favourite plants in due course. He also noticed how the plantsman's natural desire for novelty was not allowed to interfere with the essential harmony of Phyllis Reiss's planting, and she was not afraid to repeat a plant if it was the best plant for that position.

Margery Fish proudly told Lanning that her orchard and outbuildings were called a *barton* in Somerset and Devon terms; he soon found Chevithorne Barton, near Tiverton, on a rather larger scale but the same principle – a lovely, mellow house with a large land-holding attached, where Mrs Ludovic Heathcoat Amory was the gardener.[4] Lanning came to regard Chevithorne as his ideal garden, and it occupied a very special place in his early discovery of England. The gabled house was covered with wisterias, vines, clematis and figs; pots of agapanthus and clumps of iris, crinums, nerines, artemisias, woolly-leaved helichrysums and small lavenders crowded the paved terraces; the orchard was 'a primavera' of cardamines, primroses, celandines, bluebells and pale yellow daffodils; in dappled woodland were tender, heavily scented rhododendrons, the weeping *Mahonia bealei*, daphnes, viburnums, philadelphus and honeysuckles, with clumps of hostas, forget-me-nots, scillas and columbines at the wood edge, left to their own devices and looking entirely natural.

24

The wilder garden also sported drifts of white, blue, silver and mauve anemones with scillas and honesty. The kitchen garden was 'a masterpiece of neatness', and finally there was, everywhere, the water – cascades, rills, streams and pools, golden kingcups and candelabra primulas. The spirit of Chevithorne Barton was of controlled abandon – a phrase Lanning later converted to 'careless rapture', which became the prime inspiration of all his gardening.

Lanning was a strongly practical person, and he realized from seeing these gardens that he had to learn to do the job properly. The well-worn path for so many of the 'working' gardeners whom he knew in England and America was via the Royal Botanic Gardens, first at Kew and then in Edinburgh.

He became a voluntary student at Kew, possibly in late 1948 – he was certainly there during 1949. As a voluntary student he worked in the garden for three or four days a week, attended lectures and field study expeditions, and had the use of all the library and research facilities. The Kew that Lanning knew was under the directorship of the great botanist who pioneered the ecological approach to gardening, Professor Sir Edward Salisbury. His book *The Living Garden*, first published in 1935 with a sub-title 'The How and Why of Garden Life', had an almost revolutionary impact in Lanning's day; here was this eminent and broad-minded botanist explaining plant communities, micro-climate, the habits and characteristics of familiar and not so familiar wild and garden plants, in terms that mere gardeners could understand. *The Living Garden* made what William Robinson and Gertrude Jekyll had rather airily referred to as 'respect' for plants a practicable reality; Lanning could have had no better start. Two more people made Kew extremely worthwhile for him – William B. Turrill was Keeper of the Herbarium and Library and he took the students on long-remembered botany expeditions; and Charles Raffill was still teaching (he was to die in 1951 at the age of seventy-five), a fountain of knowledge on rhododendrons, lilies, irises and fuchsias. These, in particular, remained Lanning's favourites.

Kew, like everywhere else, was recovering from the war. The rebuilding of the whole rock garden in Sussex sandstone was re-started in 1949 (to take the next twenty years), and Lanning worked on this. He found the physical labour very therapeutic after his war experience and after the long period of indecision about his future. The replanting of the rock garden gave him a thorough knowledge of plants for wet and dry conditions; that wonderful rock garden at Exbury and the rocky flower-strewn cascades of Chevithorne were no longer mysteries. He also worked in Kew's nursery on plant propagation, soil preparation and actual planting techniques, and further solid background knowledge was acquired.

In the early autumn of 1950 Lanning arrived, also as a voluntary student, at the grey portals of Edinburgh's Royal Botanic Garden, on the Inverleithen Road. It must have felt like a step back into another world, for Edinburgh was still in the *ancien régime* of William Wright Smith, Regius Keeper and King's Botanist since 1922. He strolled in the garden every morning, coming 'down' from the Keeper's House at 11 o'clock sharp, in immaculate morning coat and winged collar, striking terror into the hearts of every lesser mortal. But the 'Botanics' was also full of warm-hearted, welcoming Scots, and Lanning was extremely happy there. Wright's deputy was John Macqueen Cowan, a son of the manse who had explored and collected in the

Opposite above] East Lambrook Manor, Margery Fish's garden, photographed by Lanning on an early visit.

Opposite below] Chevithorne Barton: the spirit of controlled abandon or 'careless rapture'.

forests of Bengal and the high pastures of Sikkim and had been at the Royal Botanic Garden in Calcutta. He was the greatest expert on rhododendrons, for which Edinburgh was so renowned; Calum MacRitchie was then in charge of the propagating department dealing with softwood cuttings, where Lanning worked, and he still remembers how Lanning was 'thirsting for knowledge of rhododendrons'. Calum MacRitchie went on to become Parks Superintendent at Windsor Great Park in 1952, and continued to encounter Lanning in later years, though he felt he viewed him from afar. Like other friends at Edinburgh, he found Lanning very bright, and loved his soft American drawl and his kindnesses – 'you can imagine the delight when Lan produced a pair of nylons as a prize'[5] – but they were all aware that the war had matured him beyond their ways of thinking, that he went off to London to get his hair cut and slipped away quietly for long weekends in the kind of houses where they might hope to find gardening work in their vacations. Calum MacRitchie now grows lilies in the Highlands – and Lanning developed his passion for lilies further while he was at Edinburgh, another aspect that warmed their relationship; another colleague, Dorothea Purves, who was in charge of the library at that time, remembers how Lanning was always researching the genus. It was also most usual for Lanning to share a lunch table with her and William Lauener (who still 'works' at the Botanics, even in 'retirement'), where they enjoyed three courses for a shilling.

In a way Lanning's encounters at Kew and Edinburgh and the affection he won, particularly at Edinburgh, were the best possible education in the nuances of the social system that he had entered. No one is more sensitive to the proprieties of 'knowing his place' than the old-style professional gardener. The old system would rule much of Lanning's working life, and it is only very recently, with the advent of the university-educated working professional, with degrees in botany and ecology and a middle-class background, that the system has begun to break down. It was rather typical of Lanning that he learned best through kindness and friendship, and throughout his working life it was working gardeners who would always remember him with the greatest affection, as well as with respect.

His Edinburgh friends were also conscious that the war had not left him completely unmarked in the physical sense. He loved the practical work even more because he hated taking notes or writing in any way, even such trifles as plant labels, and any kind of drawing was completely out of the question. Some injury had so damaged the nerves of his right arm that he had great difficulty in holding a pen; later, when he attempted to write with his left hand, he fared no better. He clearly had a great design ability, so this was a real tragedy, though he would never have admitted anything of the kind. It was, however, to be the underlying reason for the way he worked throughout his career; he liked to be called a gardening consultant, not a designer.

Being at Edinburgh introduced Lanning to Crathes Castle and Inverewe, to Benmore and, especially, to Logan. 'Wait until you have seen Logan' was a phrase that greeted him on every side when he arrived. He fretted through an interminable winter, which only made the Logan legend grow, and finally paid his first visit in late April 1951. The garden made by the MacDouall family on the Rhinns of Galloway was then looked after by R. Olaf Hambro (it is now an out-garden of Edinburgh

Logan, the garden Lanning became so impatient to see while he was at Edinburgh Botanic Garden, and which did not disappoint him.

University); it did not disappoint him, and he went again and again.[6] He was seeing a full-blown miracle of a garden, warmed by the moist airs across the Gulf Stream and protected from major gales. He saw the avenue of exotic dracaenas, and an equally surprising avenue of *Chamaerops excelsa*, palms from North Africa; the cordylines (*C. australis* and *C. indivisa*), embothriums and other tender plants on the old castle terraces; the New Zealand flax (then a stranger here) and *Strelitzia reginae*, the bird of paradise flower now familiar from Canary Island holidays. Familiar plants grew to enormous size – shoulder-high candelabra primulas lining a path through the woods, hydrangeas grown to tree-like proportions, especially *H. villosa* and *H. sargentiana*, and giant olearias; *Pittosporum dallii* in flower in June, rhododendrons in profusion, with leaves two-and-a-half feet long of 'unblemished perfection', huge-flowered delicate hybrids Lanning had never cast eyes upon before (Damaris 'Logan', a delicate yellow), and peat banks specially constructed as home for masses of dwarf rhododendrons. And finally, among these unbelievable sights, came 'one of the most delightful combinations of flowers that I have ever seen':

In June there was a mass of *Calceolaria violacea*, which was at least 5ft tall, and completely smothered with little bells, mauve without and spotted with violet within . . . . Against this mauve background were fine blue *Meconopsis betonicifolia*, candelabra primulas, in all the shades of pink and mauve, a particularly fine, rich, wine-coloured one known as 'Logan's Purple', a film of mauve thalictrum, *Polemonium alba* and the clear apricot and strong wine-purple of violas.[7]

Exbury Garden in
Hampshire: the view across
the middle pond in the
Home Wood to the
Winyatt Bowl.

While Lanning was at Edinburgh it was convenient to spend a good deal of time at Mulgrave, where he gardened at weekends. In 1951 Oswald Normanby married Lord Moyne's daughter, Grania Guinness; Lanning was best man at the wedding and, eventually, a godparent to their first daughter, Lepel, some two years later. Lanning always stressed that he did not give 'advice' on the garden at Mulgrave, but worked there happily in perfect harmony with his friends. Geoffrey Jellicoe had helped design a walled garden for the castle immediately after the war, and Sylvia Crowe also worked there some time afterwards. At Mulgrave Lanning met both these landscape architects for the first time; they remained friends and will appear later in his life.

Also from Mulgrave he made the excursion to the Hon. Robert James's garden at St Nicholas, Richmond, in North Yorkshire. Bobbie James was a wonderful amateur plantsman, a perfectionist of fastidious tastes, and he had made his garden around his mellow stone house of monastic origins in a series of walled, beech and yew hedged enclosures which provided necessary shelter. Lanning noted that Bobbie James's garden was devoid of bright yellows – he felt that this and all autumny colours were garish and did not suit his northern light, whereas blues, mauves, magentas, pinks, reds and purples looked their best . . . . 'Viola cornuta creeps through the border like a breaking wave of mauve, grey and silver foliage are a foil for deep crimson and cherry sweet williams . . . .'[8] Here also he learned tricks – 'labour-saving' meant a double herbaceous border cleverly planted to need the minimum of staking, 'interplanting' was the wonderful way a white rose clambered through philadelphus, the two shades of white and the differing textures each emphasizing the beauty of the other.

Also in the north, Lanning visited Howick Hall, where azaleas, rhododendrons and eucryphias had been persuaded to grow by Lord Grey's uncle, Sir George Holford of Westonbirt Arboretum fame – the latter was another place that Lanning learned to haunt.

In the spring of 1950 he joined a Royal Horticultural Society tour of the Cornish gardens and so made good his wartime promise to himself. He was not disappointed in the treasures of Trewithen, Caerhays, Lanarth and Trengwainton: his favourite magnolias were there, Rhododendron macabeanum, 'in a state of perfection that lovely sunny afternoon', with huge leathery leaves and enormous yellow heads. He found Acer griseum with magical peeling bark, a grove of Myrtus luma (apiculata) with paling cinnamon bark at Lanarth, and future favourite camellia hybrids 'Donation' and 'Cornish Snow' were met for the first time. The war had not interfered with the tradition of Cornish cream teas, he was glad to note – 'but camellias and magnolias did, day after day'.[9]

The article Lanning wrote after the Cornish trip, 'Spring in Cornish Gardens', which appeared in Country Life's stable companion Gardening Illustrated in June 1950, seems to be his first published gardening article. His gardening knowledge was growing and so were the numbers of his gardening friends; he had met the lily expert James Platt at Edinburgh (and he was now with the RHS), he knew nurserymen James Russell at Sunningdale and Alan Bloom at Bressingham. Most of all he admired the doyen of gardening writers, then in his still active eighties, Edward Augustus Bowles, and his garden at Myddelton House in Enfield, Middlesex. In Bowles's quiet and scholarly determination to make his mark on the gardening world, despite all kinds of frustrations and handicaps and with no formal training, Lanning found particular inspiration. From Bowles he learned wit and encouragement as the secrets of good gardening writing, and he admired his drawings for his books on crocuses and narcissi, made despite having the sight of only one eye. Lanning was to become passionate about botanical drawings, and I think that his inability even to attempt such things became a small but very deep regret in his life.

In the late summer of 1951 Lanning joined the staff of the Royal Horticultural Society in Vincent Square as assistant to the editor, Patrick Synge. Synge was editor of the monthly journal, the four specialist year books, the plant registers and the Dictionary of Gardening and its supplements. He had joined the RHS in 1945 after a plant-hunting youth in Sarawak, East Africa, the Galapagos, Ecuador and Kashmir; he enjoyed writing and was happy immersed in the technical minutiae of the Society's plant expertise. Lanning, being more of a generalist, energetic and enthusiastic, made an ideal assistant to go out and about for the Journal; in turn Lanning became very fond of Patrick Synge, who was never too busy to help and was always tolerant and patient, despite his seemingly terrifying workload.

Now that he had arrived in the English gardening world Lanning felt able to start drawing on his American knowledge. He was to bring many good American ideas into English gardens, and his first significant step was an early article for the RHS *Journal* on 'The Phenomenon of Autumn Colour'. He saw English planting through the eyes of one familiar with the New England fall. He stressed his admiration for Sheffield Park and Westonbirt – especially Sir George Holford's glade of acers at Westonbirt – which he felt were as fine as anything he had seen at home. He searched out and emphasized his favourites – *Nyssa sylvatica* (the black gum), *Photinia villosa*, *Parrotia persica*, red oaks, maples of course, the hickories (*Carya*) in Windsor Great Park, vacciniums and gold and white birches. These trees and shrubs, once he had identified them in England, were gladly added to his repertory, and later he would plant them wherever he could.

Once he had settled in at the RHS he ventured farther, and began writing for *Country Life* at the instigation of Christopher Hussey, who was architectural editor of the magazine. His early articles were infrequent, but they were interesting – they carried the tone of after-dinner conversation or discussions, and clearly he was reviewing his situation and 'writing out' some of his conclusions about England, and Scotland, and gardens.

In 'Colour in Garden and Landscape'[10] he certainly gave the impression that he had been moving around with critical eyes wide open, and an observance heightened by enthusiasm. He analysed the blue haze of the English light that melted into mauves and purples in the distance, whether it was across the Hog's Back in Surrey, or across the Snowdon ranges seen from the terraces at Bodnant; he appreciated Lord Aberconway's planting of the Pin Mill Terrace borders with blue and purple flowers, 'for he sensed that the blue of the canal and the flowers in the foreground would enhance the blues and purples of the distant landscape'.[11] Lanning noted blues and purples – in bluebell glades, in sea lavender and blue-green rushes on the Suffolk marshes, along the shadows of a woodland ride in the New Forest, in willow herb on a London bombed site. He realized how autumn changed that predominance for only a short time, how scarlet poppies in cornfields and golden gorses and brooms had their brief blazes, how rich butter yellow was as much as the blue light could take and orange was no colour at all for the English landscape. So this was why the orange and flame hybrids of azalea and rhododendron were so difficult to place; except in the cause of autumn colour, a separate matter, he rather 'edited out' several berberis, chaenomeles, *Campsis chinensis*, *Fremontia californica*, climbing gazanias and embothriums and certain rather fashionable roses – 'Independence' (flat dazzling colour), 'Spek's Yellow' (too deep) and 'Fashion' (slightly artificial). He had read Gertrude Jekyll, and agreed with her that flame reds and oranges excite us too much and must be used *very* sparingly, for they are the exception, the flamboyant excess of some brilliantly individual gardener like Lawrence Johnson at Hidcote Manor, rather than the rule. Conversely, Lanning realized that he had disliked purples, mauves and magentas in gardens at home because the clear New England sun did them no service, whereas in this blue haze of England they blended to perfection.

The 'Problems of Garden Ornament' were already considerable when he wrote about them in 1954[12] – 'the horrors of gnomes, storks, monster frogs, miniature boys with fishing rods and giant toadstools' in highly coloured glazes, and rustic flower stands in a Georgian London square. There was a great lack of good modern sculpture at affordable prices; Lanning suggested plain cement urns, balls, finials, seats and bird baths. He applauded the figures by Siegfried Charoux, set in Brenda Colvin's informal landscape for David Astor at the Manor House, Sutton Courtenay. But he loved best of all the Russian gamekeeper, with his skates and ducks hanging by his side, in the garden at Howard's House, Cardington (Bedfordshire), belonging to his friend Humphrey Whitbread.

These expressed tastes in colours and ornaments, both the tools of his art, were becoming sorted out in his mind. He wrote with foresight of one-colour planting schemes[13] and 'Mystery in Garden Design'.[14] In 'What Makes a Good Garden?' he rushed in where angels fear to tread; after airing the merits of site, size and location, of whether it was a plantsman's garden or not, of divergencies in personal taste that could label the serenity of Stourhead (out of rhododendron time) as dull, Hidcote Manor's hedged rooms as fussy and claustrophobic, and Sissinghurst's profusion as untidy – what makes a good garden?

> It is a matter of neither time, nor the size, nor the site, nor the geographical location, nor even the plants. All these are variables, playing greater or lesser roles. All good gardens have one thing in common – the gardener who envisages, creates and cares for them. Each person must visualize what he wants his garden to be. If it fulfils his needs and hopes, it is a good garden for him, although on purely aesthetic grounds it may leave something to be desired. What other people think is bound to vary. What should interest every gardener is whether he can hand down the verdict of a 'good garden' on his own handiwork.[15]

Thus he set the parameters for his working life. Could he really be a purveyor of dreams?

The thoughts of these last few pages, which still seem fresh and debateable as I record them, must have come as a breath of fresh air into the tight little horticultural world of post-war Britain. Lanning had made himself enough of an expert to mix with the experts; but he retained, from his liberal arts education, from his American background, from his ability to use his own eyes and judge as he found, a kind of naivety that is inseparable from enthusiasm, and from the really creative mind. His willingness to see the other point of view, as well as his winning and frequent smile, made him something of a mediary between the aristocracy of Vincent Square and the outside world. His bright achievement seems to be symbolized in his first book – a slim picture book, *Royal Gardens*,[16] published in Coronation Year, 1953, with a foreword by Geoffrey Jellicoe (who had been working at Sandringham and Royal Lodge, Windsor, as well as at Mulgrave Castle) and brief commentaries on the gardens by Lanning. He had help in publication from Margery Fish's contacts and the blessing of Eric Savill, who was in charge of the new Queen's estate at Windsor and was a Council Member of the Royal Horticultural Society.

3

PRIMROSE

WHILE he was in London Lanning had lived in a flat shared with Oswald Normanby and, at one time, an old Harvard friend, George Dix. After Lord Normanby's marriage in 1951 this had to change; it was because Lanning was in need of a home that mutual friends introduced him to Primrose Codrington, who had a studio flat to spare at her home in Onslow Square.

Primrose was the younger daughter of an eminent physician, Dr Vaughan Harley, and his wife Mary, the daughter of an Anglican canon. They lived at 25 Harley Street, and in the country at Walton Hall in Buckinghamshire. Dr Harley's professional life was concerned with intestinal diseases, and he was a teaching professor at University College Hospital. At home in Buckinghamshire he was squirish and kindly, and beloved of the local community. His pride was his herd of pedigree cattle and his farm, where he liked to spend at least two days of his week. He had died of a heart attack in May 1923, when Primrose was just fifteen.

In 1931 Primrose's elder sister, Diana, had married an army officer, a hero of the First World War, Brigadier Eric Earle. Diana had inherited the Walton Hall estate on her father's death, and her husband brought with him four sons by a first marriage. Primrose, who wanted to be an artist, and was fiercely independent anyway, escaped from the alien invasion to a studio flat in Seaforth Place, between Victoria Street and the Wellington Barracks. There she met John Codrington, a captain in the Coldstream Guards, the younger son of a family whose name is inseparable from the military and naval history of England. He was thirty-eight, and had spent most of his army time abroad in Smyrna and Syria; he had just come home from India. In many ways they shared a burden of family expectations, and yet they both knew that a streak of rebellious artistry in their souls had to be taken into account. They could clearly help each other out, so Primrose did the expected thing and married a soldier, a music, painting and flower-loving soldier with more than a streak of wanderlust. They had a grand wedding, with eight bridesmaids; Primrose was given away by Brigadier Earle, in the Royal Military Chapel of Wellington Barracks on Monday 21 December 1936. They just had time to enjoy living in Vienna and Paris before the war brought them home, to their London house in Onslow Square.

Primrose had actually found Park House. She had known it since she was about eighteen, when she had taken a friend's painting to be restored at Major Rollo's, and found him living in a left-over corner of rurality that had somehow survived the building of the early nineteenth-century terraces of Kensington. Major Rollo lived in an eighteenth-century cottage surrounded by leafiness; it had once been a farm, and it occupied a left-over patch at the end of the gardens of Pelham Place, Pelham Crescent

One of Lanning's own pictures of the garden at Park House.

Opposite] Park House – a country garden in the heart of London; photographed by Valerie Finnis.

35

Park House – the pink-washed eighteenth-century cottage off Onslow Square – from the courtyard garden.

and Onslow Square. She had said, as one tends to, that she would like to live there; when she and John house-hunted after their marriage they found that it was on the market and bought it. It was approached through an arch in Onslow Square, down a lane equipped with a triple bar and brush fences. Primrose's patch of rurality was a jumble of odd buildings, two hard tennis courts and a yellow stock brick cottage with the remains of a formal garden, all adding up to nearly an acre.

They set to work with slim resources and endless ingenuity. They painted the house pink and planted vines, wisteria and jasmine against its walls. They cleared the formal garden, which was actually in a courtyard, keeping an old but fruitful pear tree and a laburnum which played host to *Rosa filipes*, and made a sitting and eating out area planted with hostas, lilies, lilacs and mints, chives, thymes, tarragon and parsley crowding the pavings. Out in the garden proper they dug up one tennis court (re-using chunks as paving, for this *was* war-time) and tipped spare soil on to the other, thus making a lawn on two levels. At the far side of the lawns they made a pool, lined with asphalt and retained with a low concrete wall, and planted rheums, ferns, iris and more lilies. They planted a precious *Catalpa bignonioides* on one side of the pool and a

paulownia on the other, and with the help of more commonplace willows, elders, limes, laburnums and cherry trees the Park House garden soon became a little green jungle in the heart of the city.

In 1942 Primrose and John Codrington decided to go their separate ways, he to Gibraltar and she to the Suffolk countryside to work as a war artist. She painted murals for hospitals, and helped with camouflage and dummy tanks in preparation for D-Day. She made many friends, including John and Christine Nash, Cedric Morris and the architect Basil Spence.

At the end of the war she returned to Park House and set about retrieving the garden from neglect. She picked up the threads of a very happy life – painting busily, including commissions for large murals (one for the British European Airways offices then in Dorland House, Lower Regent Street, another for St Michael's Church Walton, her old home), and she added to her painting friends – Henry Lamb, Mary and Kenneth Cohen, Freddy Mayer of the Mayer Gallery – and at one time let her studio to Augustus John. But most important of all, it was Rubus the cat who ruled Park House and its garden.

The studio and its terrace at Park House.

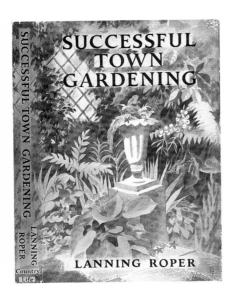

The dust-jacket of *Successful Town Gardening*, from a painting by Primrose Harley of the garden at Park House.

Right] Philip Reinagle's auriculas, one of Lanning's favourite plates from *The Temple of Flora*.

Opposite] Primrose Harley's painting of the white lily, in the style of *The Temple of Flora*.

Into this Alice in Wonderland world came Lanning – he must have found it difficult to believe his eyes. Beyond the perfectly comprehensible world of Onslow Square, predictable and urban and smart, he found himself in a gravel lane shaded with hazels and mock orange, where blackberries, old man's beard, bluebells, ferns and wild roses all grew. From this boskiness emerged a little pink house, with graceful vases filled with bright pelargoniums at the classical front door with its broken pediment and frame of jasmine. It was so pretty, yet had an architectural quirkiness that made it a little unreal, like a stage-set, with that touch of the picturesque, even sublime, that always intrigued him.

Inside the door was the glass-roofed verandah that linked what would be 'his' studio with the house. There was a small entrance hall, duck-egg blue with a glossy reflective ceiling and an exquisite small chandelier; two alcoves with a painted trellis each held a treasured piece of furniture – a child's piano and a Sheraton card table. Primrose's sitting-room – in memory of her flat in Vienna – had dark red walls, crimson brocade wallpaper, crimson carpet, pale apricot ceiling and tomato red velvet curtains. It was furnished with an interesting mixture – a Regency *chaise-*

longue, a French eighteenth-century gilt chair, a lovely large Georgian cupboard, a pretty gilded mirror, and comfortable plain settees and armchairs. Over the mantelpiece was the portrait, once thought to be a Lely of Nell Gwyn, that Primrose had been bringing to Major Rollo for re-framing when she discovered the house.

Predictably, Lanning settled in happily as Primrose's tenant and they became firm friends. They had people and gardening in common, they both loved cooking and entertaining, they happily looked at pictures and went to concerts and the opera together. Lanning was amusing, charming and irresistible company. Primrose

Primrose with Rubus the cat.

Wedding day,
Primrose and Lanning,
19 December 1952.

fulfilled even his high standards of intelligence and elegance, and she embodied almost all the things he loved about English life. They fell in love, and though Primrose might have been happy with such a status quo, Lanning would not have seen it that way. For him, marriage was the only course, and they were duly and happily married quietly on 19 December 1952.

Lanning used to say that theirs was a partnership in which he grew the flowers and Primrose painted them. A very good basis indeed for happiness, but he knew that it wasn't really as simple as that. During the 1950s Park House and its garden became celebrated in newspaper and magazine articles as well as by those who knew it, and was photographed for *House and Garden*, *Homes and Gardens* and *Country Life*, and by Cecil Beaton. It was not just the garden – the attraction was also in Lanning and Primrose themselves, and Lanning was always careful to give Primrose the credit for the garden, though he worked hard in it himself. But everyone expected a gardening writer to have his own garden, and now Lanning had such a base and reference point for all he wrote. He celebrated Park House and explained it to an eager public, for the garden did have things to say that were new in the fifties, and it was immensely important in encouraging the revival of town gardening in a city wrecked and neglected by war.

First of all there was the recognition that wildness could be beautiful. From the drive down the 'country lane', the pink house was approached across a patch of paving still surrounded by rubble from bomb damage, rubble that too many others still had, rubble that nature had taken over with a carpet of bluebells followed by rosebay-willowherb, evening primroses and heracleums, the common giant cow-parsnip, with ixias, flag irises and wild strawberries added by Lanning, haphazardly. Forsythia, followed by sweet rocket, bloomed by the front door. Here was the opportunism of nature come to town, and from inside the house the view of the spire of St Paul's, Onslow Square, was a country view. Though the expert in Lanning felt this haphazardry needed some evergreen reinforcement for screening in winter, he was careful not to spoil its naturalness. And visitors must have been amazed that clouds of Queen Anne's lace and old man's beard – just the things Mrs Spry was importing for her smartest and most mouth-watering decorations at that time – could find a home in London after all.

In the courtyard, Lanning's and Primrose's shared interest in cooking meant that they elaborated the supply of herbs in the pavings; they added festoons of vines, jasmine and laburnums, and masses of hyacinths, Lanning's favourite spring flower, with white periwinkles, grape hyacinths, dwarf narcissi and clumps of London pride, bergenias, hostas and *Lilium pardalinum* across the paving. Luxuriance of planting, the abundant growth of plants that could cope with city conditions, was the order of the day, and came to be Lanning's philosophy for success in a town garden. Good greenery was the first essential; in the courtyard high summer was brightened by Primrose's pots of pelargoniums, wonderful clashing reds, magentas, pinks and scarlets such as only a painter could control, mostly brought back from Spain and Portugal as gifts from friends and holiday souvenirs. The only difficulty with the courtyard was that it became too hot and dry in summer sun. Lanning hosed it down on these occasions, and then added a small pool in the shade of the laburnum and *Rose*

The studio at Park House.
Two of Primrose's paintings
are leaning against the side-
table, another hangs near
the fireplace.

Left] The entrance
verandah at Park House,
linking the studio to the
house.

Park House, the garden
pond and small canal.

filipes, planted with water-lilies, with *Iris ochroleuca* and *I. pseudacorus* at the edges, to
cool down the view.

The paved area outside the studio door, which gave access to the main part of the
garden, was also filled with clumps of good foliage – thalictrum, Solomon's seal,
alstroemeria, as always heracleum – and masses of irises. Most of Primrose's iris
treasures were seedlings given to her by Cedric Morris – she painted them, as he did,
in the delicious variety of their colours. They tried a green and amber border with
hostas, hellebores and amber plume poppies beneath a vigorous *Fatsia japonica*, and
horse chestnut and ailanthus to keep low, fine foliage, all mixed with heracleum,
Virginia creeper and Russian vine.

Though Park House had originally been given some old roses, Lanning introduced
more – removing the Hybrid Teas which he felt were too demanding of its poor soil.
He brought in musks, polyanthas, rugosas, his very favourite Bourbon 'Madame
Pierre Oger', and also 'La Reine Victoria' with perfectly shaped pink cup flowers, the
raspberry-smelling 'Madame Isaac Pereire', and the much younger, new in 1950,

44

'Celeste' with clear pink flowers and grey-blue foliage. Among the roses and the irises they scattered oenotheras, nicotianas, night-scented stocks and hollyhocks.

Another small addition that he made was to install a fountain in the canal across the lawn, for the purely practical reason that it would spray water and increase the damp area for plants. Thus he grew a bed of *Primula denticulata*, variegated mints, more rheums, kingcups and meadowsweet, with water hawthorn, water hyacinths and purple pickerel weed encouraged at the water's edge.

Lanning was blissfully happy in his 'workshop' garden. He came to understand thoroughly the habits of plants in town, and this would make him so successful later in creating green jungles in the centre of London. As I write this in the mid-eighties, it is hard to realize that our new-found concern for town gardens as a home for wild flowers and wildlife was being promoted over thirty years ago by an American who could see that English cities could have gardens of this kind.

But Lanning learned so much from Primrose. He learned to see better than ever before, with an artist's eye for details. Though he could not paint or draw, he watched her and he came to understand the painter's point of view. He wrote in *Country Life* of flowers that we tend to take for granted: '... if the common primrose were rare, it would rank among the most beautiful of all primulas, including the rare ones ... it would have received an Award of Garden Merit ... be cherished and cosseted.'[1] He remarked the dramatic sweep-back of the perianth petals of *Narcissus cyclamineus* (which reminded him of a shooting star), the beauty of poise and form of *Helleborus orientalis*, the Lenten rose, and the pink petals 'as delicate as the most fragile sea-shells' of his favourite 'Madame Pierre Oger'.

His artistic tastes were further developed. In 'The Delight of Foliage'[2] he paid tribute to Margery Fish and East Lambrook Manor, especially for a stunning illustration of angelica (*Angelica archangelica*), which was no angel in many gardeners' eyes, constrained within a hedge of *Lonicera nitida*. Gertrude Jekyll would have thoroughly approved of his praises of her stand-bys: bergenias, hostas, *Veratrum nigrum* and royal ferns. He also mentioned a little evergreen native of Japan which American gardeners had taken to their hearts, *Pachysandra terminalis*, one of many exotic strangers he was to turn into household names here.

He had tremendous fun with 'green flowers' – a green chrysanthemum, green hydrangeas, a green rose (*R. chinensis viridiflora*), *Daphne laureola*, *Garrya elliptica* and *Helleborus corsicus*, referring to them all as rather interesting acquaintances that he would like his readers to meet .... 'Who knows, in time there may be a daffodil with a pure green trumpet.'[3]

Lanning had his loyalties which he brought into the conversation whenever he could, and the green auriculas from Dr Thornton's *Temple of Flora* were brought in here. One of his earliest tasks for the RHS *Journal* had been to visit an exhibition, introduced by Wilfred Blunt, of books belonging to the Society of Herbalists at Londonderry House in July 1952. He had been fascinated to see Alfred Parsons's watercolours for Ellen Willmott's *The Genus Rosa* in close company with Redouté's *Roses*; he had been impressed with the wonderful *Flora Graeca* (1806–13) by Sibthorpe and Smith, with paintings by Ferdinand Bauer, and he had fallen in love with the plates in *The Temple of Flora*. He became a modest collector of botanical

The garden of Park House, photographed at the peak of its fame by Cecil Beaton.

books,[4] and his greatest 'prize' was a folio copy of *The Temple of Flora*, Part III of Robert Thornton's *Sexual Systems of Carolus Von Linnaeus, the Picturesque Botanical Plates*, originally published between 1797 and 1807. He had them framed (perhaps he should not have done!) and they became the constant companions of his life; his favourites were Philip Reinagle's tulips, the white lily, the auriculas, the hyacinths, and the carnations striped like Regency ladies' ball gowns.[5] The plates took their places on the green striped walls of his study at Park House. He delighted to share this particular passion with Primrose, with endless discussions on the complicated processes of engraving, aquatint, mezzotint, finished off with watercolour, that produced them.[6] Primrose painted her own version of the white lily.

Primrose was not all that robust, and liked to avoid the worst of the English winter;

during the fifties and early sixties they usually drove south, to France, Spain or Portugal, sometimes crossing to Madeira. Lanning revelled in these drives, especially through the Dordogne and over the Pyrenees, discovering flower pictures that remained in his mind. With longing he writes of Madeira:

> ... flowers are everywhere. Agapanthus and blue hydrangeas line the roads that ascend the mountains. Wild asphodel, gladioli and watsonias strew the fields in spring. In winter there are poinsettias flaming, dazzling and tall as the houses. Curtains of bougainvillea of vivid magenta, crimson, terra-cotta and apricot and cascades of scented wisterias, jasmine and sky-blue plumbago clothe the walls of the houses. In spring, after the winter rains, arums shoot up along the streams and lavadas, mimosas with their tousled yellow plumes stand out against the clear blue sky and camellias abound.[7]

Echiums, orchids, strelitzias and magnolias in such a bewildering array amazed and delighted them, and they spent happy hours in the gardens of Quinta do Palheiro.

On these winter holidays Lanning found time to write. In 1954 he began his book inspired by Park House's garden and dedicated to Primrose, *Successful Town Gardening*.[8] 'Town gardening' was an attractive but little-considered ideal of the fifties; Lanning felt that false security dwelt in many would-be town gardeners' minds – they felt that because the area was small, even though it might be just a rubble-strewn yard, it was only the odd weekend's work to get it straight, fill it with flowers, and keep it in effortless perfection for ever afterwards. His book tackles the subject by making friends with these deluded mortals, and the sunniness of Lanning's personality and his optimism immediately appear. These qualities set him well apart from the basic pessimism of professional gardeners of the old school.

There were problems, he admitted: lack of space, sun and air; the atmospheric

Hellebores, lamium, hostas and bergenias, crowded in the typical careless rapture of Primrose's and Lanning's garden.

pollution that was still at that time producing pea-soup fogs; the rubbish; the difficulties of adequate watering as well as adequate drainage; and the cats. Lanning loved cats – living with Primrose's giant *Rubus* he had little choice in the matter – but he despaired over their ability to invade the garden from every direction and use it as a battle or courting ground. But he also conveyed the challenge of making a good garden in town: the joy of cheating the all-pervasive tarmac with a little of nature's luxury, the chance of upstaging some country gardeners by growing tender rarities against a warm wall. Every word convinced his reader of *success*; Lanning's title was a winning one, but truly representative of the way he wrote.

It is also obvious from *Successful Town Gardening* that, when so many professional designers were going overboard for function and trying to prove just how many activities could be squeezed into a small garden, Lanning's quiet American drawl advocated the importance of design. The decision had to be made at the outset: children and activities *or* peace and plants – there could not be room for both. Gently, at his reader's elbow, he talks of viewpoints, access, changes of level, hard surfaces, walls and fences ... and colours: 'flowers in strong rich colours like bright reds, scarlets, purples and yellows look best on lighter walls ... walls were better tinted pale yellow, soft grey, a dusky pink or pale orange'. There were the endless possibilities of treillage, floodlighting, pools, ornaments, trough gardens, raised beds – thus he built up enthusiasm and the desire to get started. He was mildly

Walpole House, Chiswick: the garden made by the Benson family and greatly admired by Lanning.

revolutionary, suggesting the elimination of all grass when it clearly has not a chance, and ingenious – surplus ammunition cases painted green and champagne crates, drilled and painted, make excellent plant containers.

Above all, *Successful Town Gardening* was practical, with easily found information on soils, plants, the pitfalls of nursery catalogues, and watering. Most of the illustrations were of Park House garden, taken by Harry Smith; the dust-jacket was a painting by Primrose. There were also pictures of the Benson family's garden at Walpole House, Chiswick – a kind of *alter ego* for Park House – which Lanning much admired.

It goes without saying that Park House was not the kind of garden with plant labels. At the end of his book Lanning added substantial plant lists, which showed how hard he worked to research the Park House familiars and their fellows for the nucleus of his plant repertory. The plant lists in *Successful Town Gardening* are a guide to the good plants of the later twentieth century in English town gardens – *Prunus subhirtella*, almond, gean, *Malus* 'Golden Hornet' and 'John Downie', his favourite camellias, ceanothus, hibiscus, hydrangeas, lilacs, viburnums; herbaceous plants that were 'good doers' – *Achillea* 'The Pearl', *Anchusa azurea*, *Anemone hupehensis* and *A. pulsatilla*, anthemis, Michaelmas daisies, *Campanula carpatica*, cerastiums, pinks, geums, hardy geraniums, hollyhocks (which excel themselves in London), irises galore, London pride of course, and violas. To his foliage loyalties he added alchemillas, artemisias, bocconias, dicentras, hemerocallis, nepetas, rue, sedums, sempervivum, stachys, thalictrums, thymes and vines. The list is not endless, but far too long to go on further. Most of these plants have become our favourites now, but Lanning was writing immediately after the war, and Vita Sackville-West was only just making her White Garden at Sissinghurst: they were both innovators, making their not dissimilar ways into a new gardening era.

Successful Town Gardening was read avidly by a healthily regenerating species, the mid-twentieth-century amateur gardener in towns, and it was a great success. The year of its publication, 1957, was the year Lanning left the RHS, determined to make it on his own as a garden consultant and writer. His friend Patrick Synge sent him on his way with the promise of a commission for a handbook in the series Penguin Books published for the Society, and Lanning's cheerful contribution appeared as *Hardy Herbaceous Plants* in 1960.

But his launching ground was really Park House. During the late fifties and early sixties the garden became even more beautiful and more celebrated. They opened for charity, and Lanning noted with great pride that 1,500 people crowded in on two afternoons in June 1964, leaving only three crumpled yellow tickets and one white glove on a seat! His love for Primrose and her home gave him the confidence to see what he could do; Primrose's artistry had shown him a way of gardening that drew gasps of admiration from everyone who saw it or read of it. But by no means everyone had that good taste and ability. Lanning did, and he could combine it with sound practical skills and knowledge; this combination was a firm foundation for success in what he wanted to do. He was on his way.

4

EARLY GARDENS

The fragmentary evidence that has survived from Lanning's earliest garden work only emphasizes the ephemeral nature of this craft. Living with Primrose at Park House, with a small income from investments to call his own, enabled him to make his way by personal contacts, some of which grew into long-standing commissions. But he was emphatically neither an empire builder nor a fortune hunter, and he was to manage his whole career with one secretary working from wherever was his home. Much of his advice was given over the telephone or while walking around the garden; it was never recorded, and often never charged for on an account, written or otherwise. He always believed that gardening was a continuing process, never just a quick plan or list and goodbye, and he was to find his way of working by regular visits to clients, who became friends and so part of the fabric of his life. But, for posterity, when houses and gardens change hands, friends die and files are thrown away, there is little left behind. Picking up the threads of his early career is difficult, and I am aware that much has gone beyond recall.

In 1957 when Lanning left the Royal Horticultural Society's sheltering wing to start on his own, he had their good wishes, the encouragement of many friends and the beginnings of a writing relationship with *Country Life* magazine. Two particular but very different kinds of people must have pride of place among these early helpers – Barbara Agar and Sir Eric Savill.

Sir Eric Savill is perhaps best known as the Queen's Gardener – in the elevated sense that David Green referred to Henry Wise as 'Gardener to Queen Anne'.[1] His official title was Deputy Surveyor of Windsor Park and Woods, and from 1958 he was Director of Forestry to the Crown Estate; he had been King George VI's amanuensis in the making of the Valley and Savill Gardens (which the King wished to bear his name), and he was a kindly and highly respected royal servant, a pillar of the English gardening world. He was a Council Member at the RHS, and Lanning's passion for rhododendrons, as well as the Windsor landscape, gave them much in common. Out of this friendship came Lanning's large and splendid book *The Gardens in the Royal Park at Windsor*, with photographs by J. E. Downward and Anthony Huxley, which was published in 1959 by Chatto & Windus. Norah Smallwood of Chatto was a close friend of Grania Normanby and soon became Lanning's friend.

He was in his element during the monthly, sometimes more frequent, visits to the rhododendron glades, the Kurume Punch Bowl, the Savill Garden and Fort Belvedere, where the former Prince of Wales (later the Duke of Windsor) had shown a very real interest in collecting rhododendrons before the war. The book gives an elegant description of the history of the Park, and of the enthusiasm of King

The Old Mill, Woodspeen: the curving terrace path by Philip Jebb, with Lanning's mid-sixties planting for Jean, Lady Ashcombe.

George VI and Queen Elizabeth for the making of the Valley and Savill Gardens. Lanning luxuriates in whole chapters on his beloved lilies, camellias and primulas, as well as hybrid and species rhododendrons. He collected stories from the world of the lords of the rhododendron, particularly Exbury: how, at Lionel de Rothschild's house parties at the height of the flowering season, each guest was kitted out with a sable brush, paper bags and labels, to make crossings of species that took their fancy. The ripened seeds were collected, dried, sown and pricked out by the gardeners, and in due course the guests received a pan of seedlings as a memento of their visit.[2] And how King George VI, while inspecting the wartime Admiralty establishment at Exbury that Lanning knew, had broken the decorous pace of an official walkabout to examine his favourite flowers in the woods.[3]

Lanning was a little unusual in the rhododendron world for his affection for and interest in both hybrid and species rhododendrons; his chapter on species describes how Mr and Mrs J.B. Stevenson's collection at Tower Court, Ascot, started in 1918, was bought by the King and moved to Windsor. Between 1951 and 1956 Sir Eric Savill and his staff had moved 2,000 large plants, with no major mishaps. Lanning's telling of this story conveys the fascination of such dynasties as *cinnabarinum*, *falconeri*, *lapponicum* and *anthopogon*, beings far beyond the status of mere plants. *The Gardens in the Royal Park at Windsor* is large and sumptuous, printed on high quality paper, and a model of respectful presentation of a royal achievement in gardening to the world in general. Lanning's ability to do this kind of thing so well was to stand him in good stead.

But in after years, he always said that he owed most to Barbara Agar. Barbie, as she was called, was the eldest daughter of Sir Edwin and Lady Emily Lutyens, he the 'greatest English architect since Sir Christopher Wren', and she a Lytton of Knebworth in Hertfordshire. Barbie had first been married to Captain Euan Wallace, but he had died in 1941. In 1945 she married Herbert Agar, an American historian, who was in London as special assistant to the Ambassador, Lewis Douglas, at the time when Lanning was also in Grosvenor Square. The Agars lived in a house called Beechwood at Duncton on the Sussex Downs; Patrick and Peggy Synge, who had a retreat at nearby Fittleworth, knew them and told Lanning about Barbie's garden. She was an enthusiastic gardener; she had been making the garden at Beechwood since the war, and had enlisted the help of the legendary Norah Lindsay.[4] There was more than a little of Mrs Lindsay's genius for luxuriance and *laissez-faire* in this description, by Lanning, of a border at Beechwood:

> Lavender, rosemary, santolina, euphorbia and blue rue give character in winter. Clumps of tulips and irises in clear blues, whites and lemon yellows are grouped with lupins, delphiniums and pink oriental poppies. Then come daylilies and big clumps of vivid blue agapanthus, snowy romneyas, blue salvias with yellow achilleas and fragrant Spanish brooms. *Regale* lilies . . . madonna lilies . . . groups of floribunda roses . . . favourite old roses such as 'Fantin Latour' and 'Celestial' give lasting pleasure.[5]

Lanning wanted to learn about the elusive Mrs Lindsay's gardening from Barbie; they shared an interest in cottage gardens (after all, Barbie had grown up in the world of Gertrude Jekyll, her father's beloved Aunt Bumps), and she had some good ideas of

Bagnor Manor: a corner of
the swimming pool
glimpsed through Lanning's
planting massed by the
approach path from the
house.

Left] Sir Eric Savill (left)
with Hope Findlay, both
Lanning's long-standing
friends.

her own. Lanning took his taste for old roses and shrubs planted singly or in groups in grass from Beechwood.

He first went to stay at Beechwood in August 1957, and for the next twenty years he went back regularly, often twice a year. At first he and Barbie planned to write a book on cottage gardens together and they collected a large selection of photographs, but this was never published. Instead, she produced garden clients for him.

Barbie's life had been tragic. When she married Euan Wallace she inherited two stepsons from his first marriage, and then had two sons of her own. Two were killed in the war and one died soon afterwards. The heir to the Wallace fortune was her youngest son, Billy, who had bought Bagnor Manor on the River Lambourne near Newbury. The house was being remodelled by a Newbury architect, John Griffin, and Lanning started working there in 1960, in the early stages of the scheme.

For an American, and a plantsman, Lanning had an uncanny aptitude for the eighteenth-century English art of assessing the genius of a place. Up until now he had had no particular means of acquiring this (it certainly was not taught at Kew or Edinburgh) except by looking at Stourhead, Blenheim, Stowe and Studley Royal. He had seen all these places, but as yet his impressions of the eighteenth-century landscape style had appeared little in his recorded views of England. Unhesitatingly, though, he assessed Bagnor Manor:

> The problems were essentially threefold ... an increase in scale compatible with much wider vistas and the more generous proportions of the enlarged house ... the fact that so little of the river and the fish pond were visible from the house ... [and the need for] simplification by the elimination of walls, borders and detail.[6]

The wider vistas, and the view of the water, were obtained by re-grading: increasing the length of the gradient of the river banks and bringing it right back across the lawn to the terrace edge. The fish pond was planted with large clumps of yellow water irises, and the rest of the view was left clear, a green vista with water and sky, framed with long borders of flowers in which roses and silver foliage were predominant. Lanning thought that such borders were best viewed along their length, as part of the vista.

He and John Griffin made and planted the generous terraces at Bagnor. He felt strongly that paved spaces, steps and paths were too easily made small and mean – much better that they were large and generous so that equally generous plantings of *Juniperus horizontalis*, lavenders, rock roses, choisyas, even euphorbias and Jerusalem sage, could soften their outlines.

The swimming pool, in 'a natural green and not vivid Mediterranean blue', is fitted into the shelter of the old farm buildings. Like the terraces, its success was due to Lanning's and John Griffin's good working relationship. The pool is convenient and yet secluded, and it does not interfere with the serene vistas of the river, which are the essence of this garden.

Right from the outset Lanning's gardens were contagious, and in any given set of friends he found himself in demand. H.J. (Jack) and Drue Heinz knew Billy Wallace, and they had an English house, Binfield Lodge, farther east in Berkshire. For them Lanning made another elegant terrace, but more interestingly this was the first of his

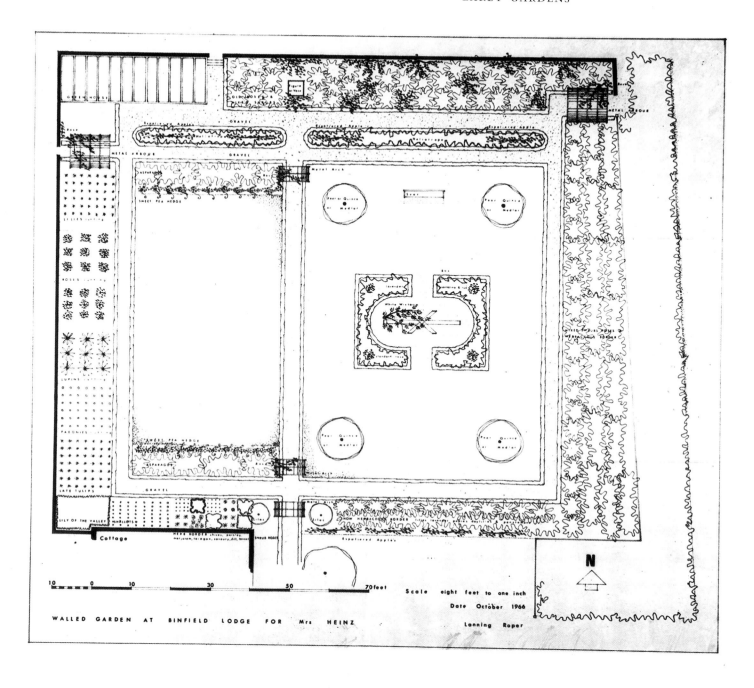

variations on the *jardin potager* theme. The plan, dated 1966, for the walled garden at Binfield shows how cleverly it is divided into unequal 'halves'. The larger 'half' is lawn and sitting area, with a herb parterre in the centre. In the smaller 'half' there are cutting plots for roses, lilies, lupins and peonies, asparagus beds and a vegetable plot for salads. In the true *jardin potager* tradition, every enclosure is edged with box and nearly all the trees are productive – apples, pears, quinces and medlars, with a flowery surrounding of shrubs. Most of the planting was planned for the Heinzes' Royal Ascot house party in June.

Binfield Lodge: the *jardin potager* and lawn as designed by Lanning in 1966.

The arbour in the centre of the lawn at Binfield Lodge, covered with white wisteria and surrounded by a close planting of lavenders, santolina and rue.

Right] The Old Mill, Woodspeen: the terrace with white Versailles tubs.

Near Bagnor, and also on the River Lambourne, Lanning gardened at The Old Mill at Woodspeen for Jean, Lady Ashcombe, during 1964 and 1965. The house was a pretty ramble of pink brick and provided a delicious backdrop, with a white trellis arbour inspired by a white clapboarded window bay that reminded Lanning of home. Again he removed the clutter to achieve a sweep of lawn that allowed a view up and down the river, but near the house the detail intensified. A new brick terrace with a curving path, designed by Philip Jebb, provided a setting for luxuriant and softening plants – stachys, the rose 'Little White Pet', bergenias, lavenders, salvias, potentillas and alchemillas. A row of immaculate white plant boxes, of a classic design that was to become Lanning's favourite, completed the picture.

The Old Mill, Woodspeen: the path curving away from the house, and the river.

It was undoubtedly Barbie Agar who introduced Lanning to the architect Claud Phillimore in Chichester, who ran a practice in country house building long after it was generally thought that English country house building had ceased.[7] Lanning did two jobs with Phillimore and Jenkins in the early sixties: there was a remarkable serpentine wall, a feature not seen in England for many years, at Ribblesdale Park at Ascot for J.R.Hindley; and some flower borders for the Dower House at Arundel for the Duke and Duchess of Norfolk.

The Dower House border plans have survived and are reproduced here. They represent a kind of planting that mid-twentieth-century taste loved, and at which Lanning could excel when most landscape architects were struggling to adjust to such a sophisticated mix of old and new virtues. Miss Jekyll's long sweeps or drifts have become shoulder-to-shoulder clumps of crisply complementary shapes and textures: her by now rather predictable graduations through the colour spectrum have been livened by Norah Lindsay into dashes of brilliance in a more sombre surround. Lanning's 'Red Dandy' roses, set among silver foliage with blues and fluffy whites, characterize his answer to the demands of swish sixties taste.

Ribblesdale Park: the serpentine wall was suggested by Lanning as a decorative feature for this garden which was formerly part of Buckhurst Park.

The Dower House, Arundel, Sussex: planting plans by Lanning for three borders illustrate an ebullience of planting and a superb mix of the best shrubs and herbaceous plants available in the early sixties.

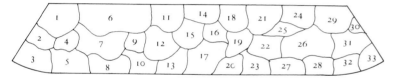

LARGE BORDER

1 *Mahonia beali*
2 *Hebe darwiniana*
3 *Rosmarinus prostratus*
4 Galtonia
5 Hoheria
6 Cistus 'Elma'
7 Rose 'Joy Bells'
8 Helianthemum 'Bengal Rose'
9 Physostegia 'Vivid'
10 *Verbena venosa*
11 *Senecio greyi*
12 *Robinia kelseyi*
13 Rose 'Penelope'
14 Potentilla 'Katherine Dykes'
15 Lavender 'Hidcote Blue'
16 Stachys lanata
17 *Gypsophila paniculata* 'Bristol Fairy'
18 Artemisia 'Silver Queen'
19 Tulips
20 *Rosa rubrifolia*
21 *Clematis montana*
22 *Elaeagnus ebbingei*
23 Rose 'Red Dandy'
24 *Ruta graveolens* 'Jackman's Blue'
25 *Campanula carpatica* 'Harvest Moon'
26 *Limonium latifolium*
27 *Lychnis coronaria*
28 *Buddleia fallowiana* 'Alba'
29 *Anchusa* 'Opal'
30 Rose 'Nevada'
31 Thalictrum
32 Scabious 'Clive Greaves'
33 *Zauschneria californica*
34 Lavender 'Nana Alba'
35 *Potentilla arbuscula*
36 *Senecio elaeagnifolius*
37 *Abutilon vitifolium* 'Album'
38 Ceanothus 'Ceres'
39 Anemone 'Margarete'
40 Gypsophila 'Flamingo'
41 *Salvia superba* 'Lubeck'
42 Potentilla
43 *Sedum spectabile*
44 *Geranium endressii*
45 Rose 'Lady Sonia'
46 Achillea 'Coronation Gold'
47 *Cytisus battandieri*
48 *Phlomis chrysophylla*
49 *Liatris spicata* 'Cobalt'
50 *Anaphalis triplinervis*
51 Bergenia
52 Tulips
53 *Caryopteris clandonensis*
54 Romneya
55 *Tamarix pentandra* 'Rubra'
56 Rose 'Cerise Bouquet'
57 Rose 'Kassel'
58 *Senecio greyi*
59 Rose 'Sarah van Fleet'
60 *Yucca filamentosa*
61 Lavender
62 *Hebe vernicosa*
63 Pinks
64 Rose 'Florence Mary Morse'

LION TERRACE BORDER

1 *Choisya ternata*
2 *Rosmarinus officinalis*
3 *Phlomis fruticosa*
4 Rose
5 Lavender 'Hidcote Purple'
6 *Rosa rugosa* 'Roseraie de l'Hay'
7 Rose 'Joybells'
8 Heuchera 'Red Spangles'
9 *Gypsophila paniculata*
10 Wallflower 'Heliotrope'
11 Romneya
12 *Acanthus spinosus*
13 Teucrium
14 *Cytisus praecox*
15 Romneya
16 *Galtonia candicans*
17 Rose 'Red Dandy'
18 Escallonia 'Donard Brilliance'
19 Fuschia 'Mrs Popple'
20 Dianthus
21 *Indigofera gerardiana*
22 *Ceratostigma willmottianum*
23 Bergenia 'Sunshade'
24 *Myrtus communis*
25 Agapanthus
26 *Potentilla arbuscula*
27 Lavender 'Hidcote Pink'
28 *Sedum spectabile*
29 *Rosa rugosa* 'Blanc Double de Coubert'
30 Lathyrus 'White Pearl'
31 *Rosa rugosa*
32 Dianthus
33 *Santolina incana*

SOUTH-WEST BORDER

34 Lonicera 'Serotina'
35 *Viburnum tinus*
36 Juniperus 'Repanda'
37 Tulip 'Tobacco'
38 *Veronica gracillima* 'Bowles Var.'
39 *Dictamnus albus*
40 Bergenia 'Sunshade'
41 Rose 'The New Dawn'
42 *Ceratostigma willmottianum*
43 Rose 'Red Dandy'
44 Potentilla 'Mount Everest'
45 *Convolvulus cneorum*
46 Hyacinth 'Heliotrope'
47 *Spiraea alpina*
48 *Rosa rugosa* 'Frau Dagmar Hastrup'
49 Fuchsia 'Mrs Popple'
50 Campanula 'Jewel'
51 *Liriope muscari*
52 Santolina
53 Rose 'Albéric Barbier'
54 *Phillyrea augustifolia*
55 Penstemon 'Garnet'
56 Thyme 'Silver Queen'
57 *Geranium cinereum subcaulescens*
58 Crinum 'Album'
59 Rose 'Vera Dutton'
60 Dianthus
61 Escallonia 'Donard Brilliance'
62 Tulips
63 *Anchusa caesptosa*
64 *Lonicera americana*
65 *Cistus lusitanicus* 'Decumbens'
66 Lavender 'Backhouse Purple'
67 *Coronilla valentina*
68 Tulips 'Tobacco'
69 *Sedum spectabile* 'Autumn Joy'
70 *Bergenia stracheyi*
71 *Veronica subalpina*
72 Penstemon 'Evelyn'
73 Pinks 'Doris'
74 Rose 'Red Favourite'
75 *Ceanothus dentatus*
76 Rosemary 'Corsican Blue'
77 Lavender

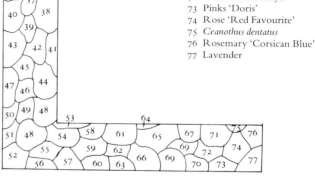

The paved terrace at
10 Holland Park, with beds
filled with 'Iceberg' roses.

Much of Lanning's early work was actually carried out by the contractors William Wood & Son of Taplow in Buckinghamshire, the Harrods of the landscape business. It seemed to be a mutually beneficial relationship, a product of his friendship with Denis Wood, with Lanning usually supplying the client and Wood's drawing the plans to his specifications and then submitting estimates for the work. Wood's worked on one of Lanning's favourite town gardens of these early days, 10 Holland Park, for Lord and Lady Blakenham. The Blakenhams' country home, Cottage Farm at Little Blakenham in Suffolk, was one of Lanning's favourite gardens, though he denied any official role in its planting or planning, which was mostly the work of John Blakenham.

10 Holland Park was Lanning's, though, with an assistant he employed at that time, Ian Mylles. Wood's estimate for the work, dated 27 November 1962, is a rare and interesting survivor from these early years. Thorn and cherry trees, existing flower beds and pavings were to be removed, and the garden remade to Lanning's design. The terrace beds were to be dug and manured, the lawn borders dug and manured,

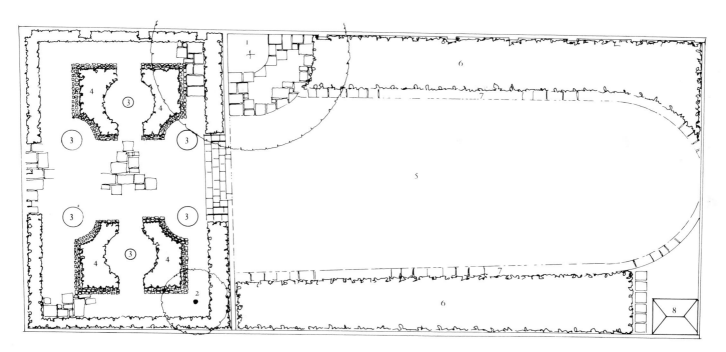

Above] 10 Holland Park, London: plan of the garden designed by Lanning Roper, from a drawing by Ian Mylles for William Wood & Son. Mylles was one of a number of assistants whom Lanning employed to draw up his designs.

The full width terrace, paved with random regular York paving, faces due south, and is partially shaded by an existing cherry tree(1) and a small thorn(2). Terracotta pots(3) and four rose beds(4) edged with granite setts ornament the terrace; four wide steps lead up to the lawn(5). The lawn is flanked by long flower and shrub borders(6) which are edged with a curved mowing strip(7). The cedar garden shed is at (8).

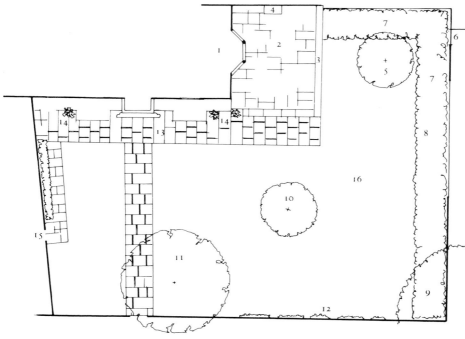

1 Swan Walk, London: plan of the garden designed by Lanning Roper, adapted from a drawing by W. T. M. Williams for William Wood & Son.

1 House
2 York paving terrace
3 Wall 16ins high with stone coping for seat
4 Base for statue
5 Robinia 'Frisia'
6 Trellis view panel
7 Shrub border
8 Base for sculpture
9 Shade planting beneath neighbouring lime tree
10 Existing pear tree pruned
11 Existing sycamore
12 Wall shrubs
13 Coursed York paving path
14 Flower tubs
15 Gate to service yard
16 Lawn

Bruern Abbey,
Oxfordshire: planting plans
for mixed borders designed
by Lanning Roper, taken
from a drawing by
W. T. M. Williams for
William Wood & Son.

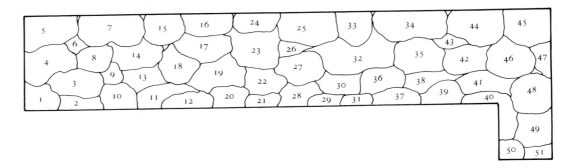

1 Phlomis chrysopylla
2 Cotoneaster congestus
3 Acanthus spinosus
4 Rose 'Roseraie de l'Hay'
5 Cytisus albus
6 Anchusa 'Opal'
7 Rose 'Nevada'
8 Iris 'Shelford Giant'
9 Gypsophila paniculata
10 Alchemilla mollis
11 Stachys lanata
12 Rosmarinus prostratus
13 Anaphalis triplinervis
14 Achillea 'Coronation Gold'
15 Mahonia japonica
16 Crambe cordifolia
17 Romneya trichocalyx

18 Eryngium tripartitum
19 Potentilla 'Katherine Dykes'
20 Lavender 'Hidcote'
21 Helianthemum 'Wisley Primrose'
22 Salvia verbascifolia
23 Rosa pomifera 'Woolley-Dod'
24 Verbascum 'Broussa'
25 Hippophae rhamnoides
26 Anchusa 'Opal'
27 Ceanothus 'Gloire de Versailles'
28 Ruta graveolens 'Jackman's Blue'
29 Festuca glauca
30 Sedum spectabile
31 Cytisus kewensis
32 Rose 'Blanc Double de Coubert'
33 Abutilon vitifolium 'Album'
34 Tamarix pentandra

35 Senecio greyi
36 Euphorbia epithymoides
37 Santolina incana compacta
38 White iris
39 Bergenia cordifolia
40 Rose 'Raubritter'
41 Anaphalis triplinervis
42 Eryngium violetta
43 Galtonia
44 Rhus 'Notcutt's Variety'
45 Rosa rubrifolia
46 Phormium tenax
47 Phygelius capensis
48 Euphorbia wulfenii
49 Yucca gloriosa
50 Veronica 'Pagei'
51 Cotoneaster congestus

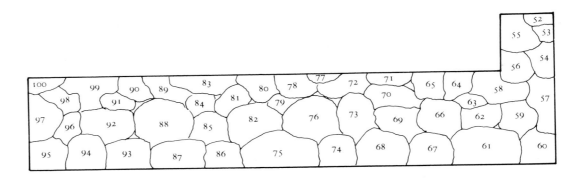

52 Cotoneaster prostratus
53 Clematis macropetala
54 Yucca gloriosa
55 Phlomis chrysophylla
56 Helleborus corsicus
57 Paeonia ludlowii
58 Potentilla arbuscula
59 Osmarea burkwoodii
60 Mahonia japonica
61 Rose 'Nevada'
62 Rosmarinus officinalis
63 Lilium regale
64 Stachys lanata
65 Ruta graveolens 'Jackman's Blue'
66 Romneya trichocalyx
67 Escallonia 'Donard Gem'
68 Rose 'Frühlingsgold'

69 Achillea 'Coronation Gold'
70 Artemesia furshiana
71 Helianthemum 'Wisley Primrose'
72 Acanthus mollis
73 Rhus 'Notcutt's Variety'
74 Bocconia cordata
75 Rose 'Blanc Double de Coubert'
76 Buddleia 'Lochinch'
77 Cytisus kewensis
78 Lavender 'Hidcote Pink'
79 Galtonia
80 Euphorbia (species)
81 White iris
82 Caryopteris clandonensis
83 Rose 'Raubritter'
84 Daphne burkwoodii
85 Rubus 'Tridel'

86 Verbascum 'Broussa'
87 Elaeagnus ebbingei
88 Rosa rubrifolia
89 Bergenia ligulata
90 Golden marjoram
91 Senecio maritima
92 Fuchsia 'Riccartonii'
93 Cytisus praecox
94 Rose 'Nevada'
95 Fatsia japonica
96 Eryngium planum
97 Senecio greyi
98 Potentilla 'Vilmoriniana'
99 Berberis stenophylla 'Irwinii'
100 Juniperus horizontalis

with additional peat, hoof and horn meal, bonemeal and a mulch of coarse peat provided after planting. Mowing strips were to be laid in old London paving, paving laid under the *Prunus*, existing grass to be raked and dressed, and turf laid where necessary. All this and a cedar garden shed (£49) came to a total of £716.

The result was a lush town garden which Lanning wrote about when it was fully matured.[8] The four small beds of the terrace were filled with 'Iceberg' roses, 'a *tour de force* both in early summer and again in autumn', with wild strawberries at their feet and creeping through the surrounding paving. The walls that bound the terrace were completely covered with camellias, *Syringa velutina* and *S. microphylla*, roses, clematis, jasmines and honeysuckles. Rose 'New Dawn', a Wichuraiana rambler with silvery-pink flowers, climbed over the arch that led through to the lawn area, a cool and serene vista of grass with its sweep broken only by a standard wisteria. The lawn borders were packed with shrubs and roses – golden privet, purple berberis, rhus, Japanese maples, hollies, philadelphus, kolkwitzias – with daylilies, hostas, irises and sedums at their feet.

William Wood & Son also worked with Lanning at 1 Swan Walk in Chelsea, for the Hon. Michael Astor. This was another simple and elegant town garden, with shrub borders that are illustrated here as part of the slim evidence available of Lanning's earliest planting schemes. Double mixed borders were also planned for Michael Astor's Bruern Abbey in Oxfordshire – and Lanning's plans for these are also illustrated here. The ultra-elegant town garden at 96 Cheyne Walk in Chelsea, designed by Lanning for Gerald Hochschild, was also carried out by Wood's. John Fowler[9] was working in the house at the time and probably discussed the garden with Lanning; the pleached limes which still survive on the road frontage may have been Fowler's suggestion.

Back in his favourite tract of Berkshire, Lanning called The Old Vicarage at Bucklebury for Sir Robert and Lady Sainsbury 'one of my most interesting assignments'. The garden was to be a setting for the Sainsburys' two magnificent sculptures by Henry Moore; I like to think Lanning may have met Sir Robert over the orchid stand at Chelsea Flower Show, but wherever the meeting took place, it was the beginning of what may be called the Sainsbury connection, a mix of friendship and patronage from a family that became one of the most important links in Lanning's career.

The Bucklebury correspondence begins in 1962 and continues for fifteen years – a wonderful mixture, the fabric of twentieth-century garden-making replete with problems of staff, trouble with Latin names of plants, the importance of a new greenhouse for the Sainsburys' orchid collection, all these vying with the hectic life in Stamford Street running the nation's grocery business. This usually left far too little time for gardening and made Sir Robert feel 'he was a hard taskmaster'. Through all this Lanning was developing his working practice. He made an annual visit to the garden, walking around, apparently taking few notes, but producing a prompt and detailed report, a firm critique on the state of things with suggestions for future action: 'The garden is in good shape and has not suffered unduly from the lack of a second gardener . . . a lot of roses are in need of spraying . . . for rust.' Equally typical is a note from Sir Robert dated 5 July 1965 – 'I notice I have not had an account from

Opposite above] Bagnor Manor: the lawn after re-grading so that this view of the restored fish pond and the River Lambourne could be enjoyed from the house.

Opposite below] Bagnor Manor: Lanning's own picture of one of his earliest and prettiest borders, the mix of pink and creamy roses, silvery spires and spreading clumps that became one of his signatures.

you since December 1963.' The account was soon submitted and immediately paid. The Sainsburys, like many others to come, were anxious to have Lanning as their friend and looked forward to his visits; at least Lanning's arrival meant a relaxing day's gardening for them. But they insisted that they should pick his brains only on a professional basis, and this endearing mix of private and professional relationships became the stuff of his life.

What he actually did at Bucklebury was to create settings for the marvellous Henry Moores: for a monumental seated female figure he swept clear a generous space, creating a gentle slope and a ha-ha, so that she could recline in a wide green grove, with fields and pastures beyond her. The figure was on a turntable, so she could change her view at will. The second and smaller sculpture was placed opposite the front door of The Old Vicarage, in a setting of flowering trees and shrubs against a dark yew hedge. A carpet of daffodils surrounded its plinth in springtime.

While working his way in as a garden consultant, Lanning continued writing for the RHS *Journal*, for *Country Life* and, more lightheartedly and occasionally, for glossy magazines. His articles for the *Journal*, about one a year, give an idea of the kind of people he was meeting: Mark Fenwick at Abbotswood, Stow-on-the-Wold (where the house and formal garden were predominantly Sir Edwin Lutyens's design and Mark Fenwick had made a spectacular hillside rock garden), Lord and Lady Rosse at Birr Castle in the heart of Eire, and Brigadier Heber Percy at Hodnet Hall in Shropshire, a lake landscape with drifts of rhododendrons, primulas, astilbes, lupins and roses. From his annual trips home he wrote about American gardens: the wonderful Dumbarton Oaks in Washington, Longwood in Pennsylvania, and the Charleston gardens – Middleton, the Nathaniel Russell house and the Cypress Garden.

In *Country Life* he continued to philosophize, with provocation. 'A Plea for the Unmown Lawn'[10] and 'Can a Garden be too Tidy?'[11] were fairly shocking notions in a gardening world that had not yet been reminded of the word 'ecological'. He approached both notions in a positive and optimistic way, knowing that the problems of upkeep were a cause of real despair to so many garden owners in post-war Britain. Much better to face up to this, making sure that available resources were concentrated on formal and architectural parts of a garden which by their nature must be tidy with neat lawns. Outlying parts of a design could be allowed to become meadows and wild gardens. Lanning firmly believed that beautiful gardens could still be made and kept in a world of diminishing resources by getting these priorities right, and all his advice was given to this end. I suspect that he had become aware of designers such as Russell Page and Peter Coats, who were bitterly disappointed and felt threatened when clients talked of 'streamlining', but for the essentially practical Lanning this was all part of the challenge.

Though he entered the invaluable world of *Country Life*, his philosophizing was a kind of apprenticeship. The really important articles in each week's issue were those describing the houses and gardens visited by Christopher Hussey, Arthur Oswald, the young Mark Girouard and Arthur Hellyer (with planting ideas from Peter Hunt and Michael Haworth-Booth). Lanning kept a hoard of these articles from 1960 and 1961

as models of the house style. One of his earliest articles in this mainstream, a descriptive visit to the garden that Mr and Mrs Michael Hornby had made at Pusey House, near Faringdon in Berkshire,[12] shows how well and quickly he had learned. He takes his readers on a long and leisurely stroll around – from the terrace that Geoffrey Jellicoe had made, along the curving long border to Lady Emily's Garden, back across the lawn to the temple of the Four Virtues and along the waterside to the white Chinese Chippendale bridge. He supplies the historical background and the colour that is missing from even superb black-and-white photographs. It was typical of everything that Lanning did that quietly, so quietly that it seemed effortless, he joined the ranks of the *Country Life* stylists, and became a habitué of the country house and garden world that John Cornforth has recently captured so aptly in *The Inspiration of the Past*, his book about John Fowler and his influence on country house tastes.[13]

Lanning had met John Fowler while they were both working at 96 Cheyne Walk, but it would be surprising if they had not encountered each other elsewhere. One of Lanning's oldest gardening friends was Peggy Munster, Countess Paul Munster, the former Peggy Ward, who had worked with Sybil Colefax and John Fowler before the war.[14] He was a frequent weekender at her home, Bampton Manor in the Cotswolds, where she gardened brilliantly, proving that a fine taste in interiors and in gardens is much the same thing. It was Lanning's opinion, often expressed, that Bampton in the 1950s and 60s was 'the perfect English garden'; he returned there over and over again to buy plants for his clients. He also must have met John Fowler at Ramsbury Manor in the mid-50s, when they both worked there for Lord Wilton, and possibly at Daylesford, where Lanning was a guest giving advice to Lord Rothermere. At this time Lanning also frequented Lyegrove, the lovely garden made by the Countess of Westmorland in the Cotswolds, and it seems likely that he also first met Mrs Nancy Lancaster, his vivacious and talented countrywoman, for whom John Fowler was working and who made gardens at Kelmarsh Hall and then at Haseley Court in Oxfordshire. This was the world that required Lanning as consultant gardener. The substantial outcome was in 1958, when Lord Wilton sold Ramsbury to Lord Rootes and found himself a house at Milton Lilbourne and a row of cottages called Hillbarn Farm at Great Bedwyn. The latter was converted into Hillbarn House by the Newbury architect John Griffin, and, with William Wood & Son, Lanning started on one of his most important and enduring garden schemes. It seems fair to say that he was no longer merely on his way – he had arrived.

The seal seemed to be set upon Lanning's arrival as a force in English gardening with his appointment as gardening correspondent to *The Sunday Times*, which he took up on 7 January 1962. His inaugural piece was an introduction to Park House's garden – 'I have always a great curiosity about other people's gardens and therefore it is logical to suppose that the converse is true,' he wrote. He followed up with weekly articles on his now favourite themes – scented plants for winter, good foliage, hyacinths, herbs, planting in the shade, gardening on chalk (after a visit to Highdown at Worthing), Prim's geraniums, fuchsias, rhododendrons (of course) and good bedding plants. On 20 May he did the first of what became annual Chelsea Flower Show pieces, written

The Countess of Westmorland's garden at Lyegrove in the Cotswolds, one of Lanning's earliest haunts.

Binfield Lodge, Berkshire
Above] The box-edged borders of the *potager* filled with orange, purple and gold.
Right] A close-up of the wall border.
Opposite] The ordered elegance of the terrace front. All three photographs come from the Lanning Roper Collection.

Queen Elizabeth the Queen
Mother and Princess
Margaret in one of the
exhibition gardens at the
Chelsea Flower Show,
1954. Lanning was proud to
number himself among the
Queen Mother's gardening
friends.

with his prior knowledge of the best things to look out for, and usually published on the Sunday before the show opened; in 1962 his highlights were miniature roses, lilacs, strawberries and auriculas. From now on Chelsea week was the key to Lanning's year; it was his place for meeting old friends and making new contacts, a time for endless tall gardening stories, dreams and after-show dinner parties, which he never missed. After the show week he would sit down quietly, work out just what he had committed himself to, and plan his working schedule to start the following autumn.

Three weeks after Chelsea 1962, Lanning recorded the death of Vita Sackville-West at Sissinghurst Castle; she actually died there on 2 June. He had been a frequent visitor to the garden during her last years, and had encountered her in garden conversations and on some of her visits to Vincent Square. He adored and admired the garden, especially the herb garden, which he thought the most lovely ever made, and he probably understood better than most just how the ingenious geometry of Harold Nicolson's devising found a perfect foil in Vita's flowers. There is another point as well: for fourteen years Vita had monopolized the Sunday gardening reading public with her famous column in *The Observer*, to which thousands turned before they bothered to read anything else. Lanning was only asked to do his piece in *The Sunday Times* after Vita had given up; at first he did try to assume her mantle (which he was quite capable of doing), but he was really much more practical and technically skilled than she, and his hopeful, informative and businesslike pieces came to be appreciated by a younger and rather more hurried generation of Sunday gardeners. On occasions, though, and always when he had been to Italy – often to stay with Freya Stark at Montoria – he turned in a piece that would have delighted Vita:

I have never been more aware of white flowers than I have over the last two weeks in Italy. White wisterias and creamy-white double Banksian roses cascade over roofs, loggias and trees; massed plantings of white spiraeas bloom so freely that there is no hint of green and huge false acacias scent the air and carpet with fallen flowers not only the country lanes and grassy meadows, but also the city pavements and the dark waters of the canals of Venice. Huge white peonies, tall white irises, clove-scented pinks and spicy stocks grace many a dooryard, and stately white arums enjoy the rich moist loam of boggy ditches. Curtains of the humble Snow in Summer, with its silvery-grey foliage momentarily marked with sheaves of pure white flowers, cover the walls and slopes. White ox-eye daisies with scarlet poppies star the fields.[15]

He went on to the fragrances of Roman hyacinths, Madonna lilies, summer jasmines and tuberoses, and then lights on philadelphus; at that point his practicality reasserted itself, and the rest of the article is devoted to recommendations of the philadelphus hybrids 'Belle Etoile', 'Beauclerk' and 'Sybille' and how to prune them.

Lanning in the early sixties.

The Old Vicarage,
Bucklebury
Above] Garden border for
Sir Robert and Lady
Sainsbury.
Right] A delicious mix of
Viburnum plicatum 'Lanarth',
blue hostas and London
pride.
Opposite] Henry Moore's
'Seated Woman', for which
Lanning arranged the
garden setting.

5

IRELAND

T HE LOVE OF GARDENS and gardening was shared with at least one of Lanning's Harvard classmates, Henry McIlhenny. Out of their friendship came a celebrated garden, that of Glenveagh Castle in County Donegal, now the property of the Irish Government and in the care of the Forest and Wildlife Service. From Glenveagh Lanning ventured over the whole of Ireland: to him it was a plantsman's paradise and he revelled in the gardens – Mount Usher and Powerscourt, the Glasnevin Botanic Garden and Malahide Castle, Rowallane and Mount Stewart in the North, Fota in Cork Harbour and Ilnacullin in Bantry Bay, Derreen and Rossdohan in Kerry and Birr Castle in the remote centre of the island.

Remembering how uncertain Lanning had been after his graduation, how it had seemed impossible that he could earn a living doing the thing he loved, there seems a striking contrast in the apparent inevitability that marked Henry McIlhenny's life from that time. The McIlhennys had gone to America from Donegal, and had made a fortune out of Philadelphia steel. Even while he was still at Harvard, Henry had been encouraged to buy nineteenth-century paintings, especially French Impressionists, and after postgraduate studies he became curator of decorative arts at Philadelphia Museum of Art, a post that suited him for twenty-nine years. During that same graduation summer he had heard of Glenveagh and the possibility of renting it for the following summer. It was then owned by Mrs Kingsley Porter, whose husband, the Harvard art historian and expert on Celtic art, had disappeared without trace on an expedition from their cottage on Inish Bofin, one of the Tory Islands off the north Donegal coast. The McIlhennys rented the castle for the summer of 1934 and Henry fell in love with it; he eventually bought it in 1937. Lanning saw it for the first time on one of his pre-war holiday trips to Europe.

Glenveagh is not an overly large castle, nor is it ancient. It is surrounded by the forested glens of a vast deerstalking estate, once the land of the Earls of Leitrim at nearby Mulroy. In the middle of the nineteenth century the land was bought by a colourful rogue, Black John Adair, who built the castle on the level foothold beside the lough. To it he brought his American wife, who was as loved by the tenantry as he was hated, and she began to make the garden on what level land there was, and planted rhododendrons on the rocky slopes. In 1981, when it was known that Henry McIlhenny would be handing Glenveagh over to the Irish Government, Lanning arranged for John Cornforth to visit the castle and have it photographed; the two articles he wrote, which appeared in *Country Life* on 3 and 10 June 1982, tell the rest of Glenveagh's history, and the photographs capture it as Lanning knew it for over forty years.

Glenveagh: the castle viewed from the lough. The limit of level space for gardening can be imagined.

75

Henry McIlhenny had decorated the interior, says John Cornforth, as 'an American challenge to Balmoral'. Stags were omnipresent – stags' heads on the walls, chandeliers and tables of stags' horn, stag motifs on towels, and large Landseers, of stags, on the walls of the main rooms. There was a tartan walled room – the music room – but there the similarity to the cluttered Victorian Balmoral ended, for the rooms of Glenveagh were elegantly furnished with Irish Georgian furniture and silver, with other and more generally appealing paintings, by Richard Ansdell, James Collinson and J.W. Horsley, on the walls. All was arranged with the certain eye of an expert who loves his beautiful things.

Lanning made his first working visit to Glenveagh in July 1959. He went back almost every year, usually in high summer, but sometimes twice, in spring and autumn. During most of his visits he worked hard, planting new arrivals, moving plants around, and taking considered walks around the garden, with Henry McIlhenny or alone, to decide on future plans. Out of the walkabouts came his detailed reports, which followed every visit and were the working basis for the gardeners until he came again.

The castle faces west across Lough Veagh. To the north is the Pleasure Ground, and to the south the Italian Garden, both relatively level. Behind the castle is the Walled Garden, made by cutting into the slope and fairly level. The rest of the garden is made up of walks winding up the tree- and shrub-clad slopes, at one point up a dramatic flight of sixty-seven steps to a viewing terrace. The rain can be interminable at Glenveagh (70–80 inches a year), the gales rage down the glen and whip the black waters on to the rocks, the soil is painfully thin and the deer are ever ready for invasion if their chance comes. But one glimmer of the sun transforms it into a magician's castle of silver, set among flowers; the mildness allows tree ferns, palms, tender fragrant rhododendrons, cordylines, echiums, mimosas and drimys to grow far from their native haunts. For Lanning it was a gardener's paradise.

From the outset there were two basic aims for Glenveagh's garden – to grow as many of the exotic rarities as possible, and to have masses of colour and abundant flowers and vegetables for the streams of guests who would enjoy the hospitality of one whom his friends quickly called 'the monarch of the glen'.

The Pleasure Ground with its large and level green lawn surprised visitors to the rocky outpost. It was still surrounded by some of Mrs Adair's rhododendrons, *R. arboreum* and the yellow flowered *R. falconeri*. To these were added tree ferns, palms, cordylines, with gunneras, rodgersias and hostas in damp areas beside streams that trickled down from the mountain. In front of these exotics Lanning planted drifts of colour – azaleas, Japanese maples, astilbes, candelabra primulas, agapanthus, meconopsis and lilies. Lilies were to become the flower of Glenveagh. Here in the Pleasure Ground there were clumps and drifts of white *martagons* and *regale*, yellow, apricot and pink *Lilium testaceum*, and *L. auratum platyphyllum* which especially loved Glenveagh – Lanning recorded it growing ten feet high, with thirty-six flowers on a single stem. *L. speciosum* was grown in pots for the house, and in the Pleasure Ground the crosses of *auratum* and *speciosum*, 'Imperial Silver', 'Imperial Crimson' and 'American Eagle', and the trumpet strains, 'Green Dragon' and 'Black Dragon', 'Destiny' and 'Enchantment', were planted in profusion.

Opposite] Glenveagh Castle garden: the sixty-seven steps which climb to the high-level viewing terrace.

Lilies became the flower of Glenveagh: Lanning planted them in masses for Henry McIlhenny, and they were amazed how high the lilies grew – sometimes to ten feet. This photograph was taken by Lanning in the View Garden walk.

The gothick conservatory at
Glenveagh.

Glenveagh Castle:
plan of the garden.

1 High terrace
2 Deer fence
3 Sixty-seven steps
4 Viewpoints
5 Rose garden
6 Walled Garden
7 Belgian Walk
8 Path to nursery garden
9 Pleasure Ground
10 Entrance road
11 Landing stage
12 Lough Veagh
13 Tower
14 Castle
15 Terrace
16 Italian Garden
17 Swiss Walk
18 Road to the glen
19 View Garden
20 Thorn circle, or Pixie Ring

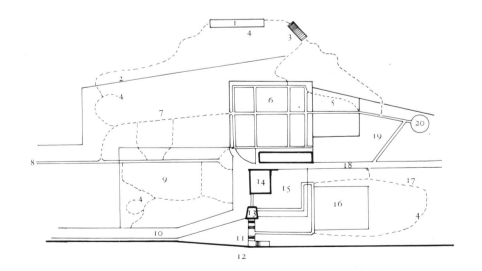

In complete contrast the other level area, the Italian Garden, was a plain green rectangle surrounded by greens, a green *giardino segreto* as a setting for statues of Roman emperors and sphinxes. The late-flowering blue *Rhododendron augustinii* and white pillars of eucryphias were the only other colours seen here.

From the Italian Garden a path climbs the slope through the View Garden. It is an upward-curving grass path, flanked with *Lilium auratum* growing shoulder high, to a vase on a tall plinth backed by swaying pines. Turning right at the vase, the green walk continues to an immaculate circle of clipped thorn, sometimes called the Pixie Ring, which with trees frames a view of the lough and the distant mountains. The ground is carpeted with ivies, pachysandra, drifts of white heather and green glaciers of *Cotoneaster horizontalis*.

In strong contrast again, the Walled Garden is busy with colour and ornament. It is the most sheltered and inviting place for sitting out and for growing abundant herbs, vegetables and flowers. The paths are edged with flowers in Lanning's favourite *jardin potager* tradition – penstemons, campanulas, asters, delphiniums, phlox, sidalceas, verbascums, anchusas, achilleas, hardy geraniums, lupins, poppies, artemisias, hemerocallis, with masses of peonies, dahlias and roses for cutting. In 1959 it was decided to build a gothick conservatory to overlook the Walled Gardens, and by

Glenveagh: the white 'Venus and Cupid' by B. F. Spence amongst the plants of the conservatory [*above*] and 'Bacchus' outside in the View Garden [*left*].

Lanning's visit in the spring of 1960 this was in place. It was designed by Philippe Jullian and painted battleship grey: it houses pale yellow acacias, blue plumbago, passion flowers, strelitzias and daturas, and a beautiful white 'Venus and Cupid' by B.F. Spence. From the summerhouse the view across the flowers, cheek by jowl with neat rows of peas, courgettes, lettuces, artichokes and spinach, is to the planted hillside. The energetic can climb the upward paths, through a green rocky glen full of ferns and mosses, passing drifts of primulas, fuchsias, hydrangeas, pernettyas, fothergillas, mimosas, New Zealand flax, and masses of the fragrant rhododendrons, especially *R. ciliatum* and *R. cinnabarinum* and *concatenans* hybrids. The very energetic will achieve the flight of sixty-seven steps to the viewing terrace looking out over the castle, the garden and the lough to the Derryveagh Mountains.

Opposite] Borders in the Walled Garden at Glenveagh as planted by Lanning: penstemons, campanulas, asters, delphiniums, phlox, sidalceas, verbascums, anchusas, achilleas, hardy geraniums, lupins, poppies, artemisias . . . with masses of peonies, dahlias and roses for cutting.

The Italian Garden at Glenveagh seen through the window of the library.

Glenveagh: the terrace
dressed for spring.

Gardening at Glenveagh was one of the most rewarding of Lanning's jobs: in Henry McIlhenny he had a client who would spend lavishly on exciting flowers and shrubs, as well as a friend whose tastes he admired and largely shared. They had few altercations over matters of taste in the garden. Lanning arranged his visits so that he could plant new arrivals and supervise trimmings, prunings and movings of resident plants. He was content to have Henry to himself, or with his agent Julian Burkitt or the head gardener, and sometimes clearly stated he wanted no one; the sign 'artist at work' went up and he was left to work and think. He was amused when he happened to coincide with one of Henry's effervescent house parties, but Lanning really preferred to socialize where there was no work to be done.

Glenveagh and its plants, along with the exasperations of travelling, each other's health, the weather in Ireland, London, Philadelphia or Honolulu, friends in common, the Glyndebourne *La Bohème* or *Don Giovanni* at the Metropolitan, all these were the substance of their constant correspondence. When Henry was in London they would lunch at the Connaught or Wilton's, and over the years Lanning managed to pierce the highly organized schedule that Henry set himself to take him to Abbots Ripton to meet Lord and Lady de Ramsey, to the Hornbys at Pusey House and to Peggy Munster at Bampton. Chelsea Flower Show was a regular buying spree, and after it the orders for Glenveagh flew out – tulips by the hundred, lilies of course, more dahlias for cutting, peonies galore, lists of tender trees from Harold Hillier and for more rhododendrons and other shrubs from Cornish nurseries and from Jim Russell at Sunningdale. A fair proportion of RHS exhibitors during the seventies must be represented at Glenveagh, and occasionally it was necessary to go farther afield, to Duncan & Davies in New Zealand for the phormium 'Dazzler', libertias, clianthus, cyatheas and *Cordylines kirkii*, *stricta* and *indivisa*. Sometimes there were panics, as when the health of the lilies in the View Garden walk was suspect, and Lanning either issued a prescription or managed to inspect for himself. And sometimes even their well-ordered communications broke down. A letter from Henry, 29 May 1975 – 'I have been trying to label the new plants that you planted this Spring and I simply cannot find *Rh. formosum* or 'Blue Ribbon'. Can you possibly remember where you stuck them. Also, I can't find ten hydrangea 'Ayesha', three *Cordyline purpurea* and three pittosporum 'Sunburst', all from South Down Nurseries, Redruth. Of course, I may come across them . . . .'

One of Lanning's own photographs of a corner of Glenveagh which gives the feel of how lavishly exotic and exciting plants were crowded in.

Glenveagh: the top of the flight of sixty-seven steps.

The Walled Garden at Glenveagh in early spring, with the new lilies sprouting.

Lanning had another dear friend whom he usually saw when he went to Glenveagh, Dorothy Jobling-Purser. He had started gardening for her at Marble Hill, Port na Blagh, near Letterkenny, in 1971. He completely reorganized the surroundings of this lovely small Georgian villa, which had a marvellous view out over Sheep's Haven Bay. On the front, which had the view, he made a broad gravel forecourt, with a second, sheltered lower terrace for enjoying the view. Banks of pink rugosas, 'Frau Dagmar Hastrup', berberis 'Rose Glow', rosemary, lavender, *Viburnum davidii* and horizontal junipers sheltered the sitting area. Lanning also made a rock garden on a natural outcrop, keeping sacred Donegal thorns, and with the architect Caroline Dickson he arranged a modern terrace and garden room within the walled garden so as not to disrupt the period feel of the house.

In 1979 Mrs Jobling-Purser found herself a small modern house in Bunclody, County Wexford, where she could be back near her many Dublin friends and her family. Lanning produced her favourite plants again for borders; he planted stream banks and shrubs around the lawn and encouraged her towards a small and compact kitchen garden. In May 1981 the Royal Irish Horticultural Society descended to see what had been achieved in two years, and the visit was a great success. Dorothy Jobling-Purser proved a staunch ally for Lanning during many hectic working trips to Ireland; she could be relied upon to meet him at the airport, and for a quiet refuge when he needed one. Her letters were alway welcome – written in a large and generous hand on blue paper, they were always what he called a good read, full of family news and of doings in and around Glenveagh and Dublin; these letters came to comfort him right up until the end of his life.

The garden at Marble Hill where Lanning worked with Dorothy Jobling-Purser in the mid-seventies.

Castlecoole: an old photograph showing the elements of landscape gardening – the sweeps of green and clumps of trees – which Lanning worked to restore.

In September 1967 Lord Antrim, then Chairman of the National Trust, asked Lanning if he would help with the restoration of Templewater at Castle Ward near Downpatrick in County Down. The following year came a request from Lord Clanwilliam, then Chairman of the Northern Ireland Committee of the National Trust, to assist at Castlecoole, Enniskillen, in County Fermanagh. For the next ten years Lanning ran these two jobs in tandem, often combining his visits with trips to Glenveagh or Dublin.

At Castlecoole, built in restrained Grecian style in 1789 for the 1st Earl of Belmore under the supervision of James Wyatt, Lanning found himself cast in a 'Capability' Brown role which was wholly satisfying. The landscape around the lovely house had degenerated, and he had to re-create sweeps of green, plant new clumps of trees, open vistas and align a ha-ha.

86

Castle Ward, the mixed Palladian and Strawberry Hill gothick house of slightly earlier date, 1765, for Lord Bangor, was set in 600 acres of parklands and woods beside Strangford Lough. Lanning accepted this job with alacrity, but was a little perturbed when the Trust almost immediately decided to use the long canal in front of the house as a wildfowl lake, with the intention of turning Castle Ward into another Slimbridge. Lanning, who visited Slimbridge and the Askews' Bentley Wildfowl Collection in Sussex, was worried that birds *en masse* and the green serenity of an eighteenth-century landscape were incompatible; he became slightly more worried when it was decided that the old walled garden should be devoted to bird-rearing pens.

He was, however, always a creative conservationist, and despite some squabbles with the wildfowl interests, he proceeded to work towards the best general results. There were massive replantings of trees – maples, chestnuts, birch, limes, beech, ash and willows, as well as a few rarities that he felt were in keeping with the original landscaping of the house. These included *Zelkova serrata*, *Leucothoë catesbaei* (*fontanesiana*) (1793), *Nothofagus antarctica* (1830), *Nyssa sylvatica* (1750), and the tulip tree, *Liriodendron tulipifera*, known in the seventeenth century. In the walled garden he surrounded the bird pens with a bird's banquet – shrub roses with hips, sorbus, prunus, privet, elaeagnus, cotoneasters and honeysuckles, with hollies and sea buckthorn as human deterrents.

The success of the replanting of the Templewater and the restoration of its temple by the architect Robert McKinstry was recognized in early 1972 with a Civic Trust Award. One of the interesting outcomes was an inquiry from Michael Downing, lecturer in landscape design at Newcastle University, for a summary of the conservation philosophy that Lanning had applied to Castle Ward. Lanning's reply throws interesting light upon both his work in Northern Ireland and his other work for the National Trust, which is covered in a later chapter:

> The story here is a fairly simple one in the fact that the Templewater existed and had not been altered in shape over the years. Obviously, the planting in the park had suffered from both time and gales off the sea. The problem involved the restoration of the Temple itself, the dredging of the long canal, replanting. This was done in the spirit of the eighteenth century but we had to consider the amenities of the public and also the fact that the area is now a bird sanctuary.
>
> The selection of trees was limited to plants that would be sympathetic and in character with the eighteenth century. We have avoided the inclusion of modern exotic flowering trees and there has always been a question as to whether or not we ought to have removed some cordylines at the head of the canal. They have been left, as they create a foreground, but obviously they were not introduced until a much later date.
>
> Old photographs, prints and drawings of which there are a number were useful as guidance.
>
> Our aim, however, was not to be strictly purist and with such a big landscape it would be impossible to put it back exactly as it was . . . in a project such as this the landscape must evolve naturally and not become too much of a set piece.
>
> In Williamsburg in the United States and a lot of the Southern plantations, a great deal has been done and restoration has been carried out along archaeological lines . . . everything has been done in a most accurate way, but here the aim was a completely different one.

Castle Ward, the
Templewater
Opposite] The temple was
restored by Robert
McKinstry and Lanning
replanted the lake surround
for the National Trust.
Left] View from the temple
of the lake after replanting,
with Strangford Lough
beyond. The project was
given a Civic Trust Award
in 1972.

In this case, as we were dealing with a large landscape, we worked directly on the
ground and not on a plan. We were using unskilled labour, a lot of it on unemployment
relief, and it was far easier to direct operations by indicating contours, and by putting in the
actual stakes and markers for individual groups of trees, island plantings etc. It is obviously
an enormous saving in cost and where it is adapting an existing landscape it is far easier than
doing a tremendously detailed and expensive survey, showing every tree and then
blocking in new planting.[1]

Another dimension was added to Lanning's work in Ireland in October 1973, when
he was asked to consider the proposals for the surroundings of the New Arts Building
at Trinity College, Dublin, being built by Ahrends, Burton & Koralek. The area in
question was on the east side of College Park, where the Arts Building was sited, on
Nassau Street, between the Old and New Libraries and the Provost's House. A new
court, to be called Fellows Square, would be created, which he proposed should be
simply treated with a central lawn surrounded by broad paths of stone or a
sympathetic hard surface. There should be a group of trees off centre in the lawn, and

Trinity College, Dublin
Above] The New Arts Building and Fellows Square from the terrace of the New Library. Lanning was landscape consultant for this development from 1973. *Right*] Lanning subsequently became consultant to the college and revamped many of the spaces between the older buildings, such as this one which is known as Botany Bay.

evergreen shrubs in bold masses used to relate the buildings, old and new, to the new space. This sound formula, of serene green spaces with good trees, of trees and shrubs framing the buildings and relating them to vistas and to each other, was carried through in the following five years. Lanning became landscape consultant to Trinity College, working closely with the agent, Lieutenant-Colonel John Walsh, and Captain John Martin, the General Services Officer, and he helped with several more of Trinity's landscape problems. He eventually retired officially in May 1982.

Almost ten years at Trinity College, quite demanding years, fitted into the weave of Lanning's Irish working life. He was able to save Trinity money by buying herbaceous plants from Dorothy Jobling-Purser's garden at Marble Hill and by a good working relationship with Philip Wood at Lord Hamilton's Baronscourt Nursery at Newtonstewart in County Tyrone. Plants from Baronscourt also went to the Castlemartin Stud, County Kildare, where Lanning gardened from 1977 for Dr Tony O'Reilly, the legendary Irish rugby international who was then in charge of Heinz-Erin and is now managing director of the whole Heinz empire. It was wholly appropriate that the plants for Dr O'Reilly's garden knew no boundary, for he, as founder of the Ireland Fund, holds the cause of peace close to his heart. Lanning came to enjoy the company of Tony and Susan O'Reilly and of their lively young family, which included triplets, and seeing them relax from their jet-setting life in a garden he had largely made for that purpose gave him another kind of satisfaction.

His work in Ireland also illustrates so well the working friendship that became the very staff of life to him. Lanning was that rare creature, in the twentieth century at least, who loved and understood both land and landscape and possessed an instinctive regard for the welfare of both. Other sympathies – for art, for opera, perhaps even for flowers – were additions to this basic trait that made him a delightful companion or amusing dinner party guest. But his basic sympathy drew him into natural affection for like minds, for those who also worked in what we call the land-based professions. On almost every job there were, to put it simply, two Lannings – the Lanning of the dazzling smile and easy conversation who was happy to take tea on the terrace in the afternoon sun; and the purposeful, weatherproofed Lanning, striding out in the teeth of a gale to inspect the young trees or assess the view. He could adjust them at will, but he never failed to appreciate the friendships that his second self collected. Julian Burkitt, Henry McIlhenny's agent at Glenveagh, was a staunch working ally, and so were John Lewis-Crosby and David Good, the Secretary and Assistant Secretary of the National Trust's Northern Ireland Committee, with whom Lanning worked through difficult times on Castle Ward and Castlecoole. Lanning's chief desire was always to get on with the job in hand. I cannot resist the rather amusing illustration from his letter of 30 September 1969, when, having been informed that his visit to Castle Ward would coincide with a deputation of the Trust's arbiters of taste, Robin Fedden, James Lees-Milne, John Fowler and George Oakes, he felt 'intimidated', wanted to get quietly on with his work with David Good and avoid getting involved: 'Pop me into a pub if it isn't convenient for me to stay with you' was his chosen solution!

6

AMERICAN ALLEGIANCES

AN APPRECIATION of Georgian architecture and the English landscape style, a taste for impeccable tweeds and picnics at Glyndebourne, are not exclusively English characteristics – rather the contrary. Lanning never pretended to be an Englishman, and he always remained a loyal American citizen. I think he found in England, in the English way and pace of life, an America that – except for a privileged few – had ceased to exist. He had seen that America through his mother's memories of Boston and Concord, and certainly it was alive at Harvard in the early thirties. Newport before the war must still have resembled Van Wyck Brooks's 'American Eden' – ('so like the Isle of Wight') – and the Newport and Long Island gardens that he loved so much were the last survivors of that America of Henry Thoreau, Emily Dickinson and Henry James. It also survived in his friendship with Henry McIlhenny; for Christmas 1978 Lanning had sent to Glenveagh a copy of Duff Hart-Davis's book, *Monarchs of the Glen*, and in return he received an Edith Wharton omnibus. Lanning's instinct for where other remnants of this world were to be found guided the American dimension of his life, and was certainly to be reflected in his gardens.

Even after he had married Primrose and settled at Park House he returned home regularly to visit his parents, first at their apartment in Gramercy Park in New York and then back in their last home, which he found for them, in Engle Street, Englewood, New Jersey. His mother died in 1961 and his father in 1966; Lanning planted trees in their memory in Gramercy Park. After that his home was where work took him; he stayed at the Harvard Club in New York, and was often invited to Henry McIlhenny's home in Rittenhouse Square in Philadelphia. From 1973 onwards he renewed his acquaintance with the art and architecture of Chicago, as he made trips to the famous Mies van der Rohe Farnsworth House at Plano, Illinois, which was bought by an English friend, Peter Palumbo.

Lanning's family base after his parents' death was in Washington DC, at the pretty Georgetown house of his brother Crosby and his wife Laura. 1973 was a year of celebration, for Laura Wood Roper published the result of thirty years' work, her definitive biography of Frederick Law Olmsted, America's great pioneer landscape architect. 'A splendid and worthy biography', said the *New York Times Book Review*; 'a fascinating picture of American civilization a century ago', added *Newsweek*. Laura Wood Roper had met Olmsted's son, Frederick Law Olmsted Jr, and his wife, Sarah Sharples Olmsted, in the forties, and they had given her access to the massive collection of F.L.O.'s papers for her book. In her Foreword[1] she summarizes her subject: '... during his own long day (1822–1903) [he] was recognized as a prophet

Dartington Hall from across the Azalea Dell. This part of the garden was originally conceived by Beatrix Farrand before the Second World War; it was her only English garden and symbolizes an Anglo-American allegiance in gardening that Lanning was to continue.

The Pebble Garden at Dumbarton Oaks: made by Mildred Woods Bliss as her last project in the great Washington garden, it has now become Dumbarton Oaks's most photographed feature. Lanning found in Mrs Bliss and her garden the tangible connection with the America of Beatrix Farrand and Edith Wharton that he loved.

by a few and held in simple gratitude by multitudes. At his death, he was praised from one end of the nation to the other. Within a quarter of a century he was half-forgotten ... and his great landscape works were let lapse toward ruin ....' The powerful presence of Olmsted was alway 'there' on Lanning's frequent visits to Georgetown, and part of the warm friendship he shared with his sister-in-law. Ironically, Laura Wood Roper recalls, the Olmsted association played a part in Lanning's decision not to live and work in America after the war. Frederick Law Olmsted Jr, to whom she introduced Lanning, was so disillusioned about the lack of regard for his father's works, and the then low standing of the profession that he inspired, that he would not have recommended it. (Happily, because of the publication of the *Olmsted Papers* under the editorship of Dr Charles C. McLaughlin, as well as Laura Wood Roper's biography and the work of a steady band of Olmstedians, scholars and enthusiasts, F.L.O. is now widely revered and his work appreciated.)

The great inspiration of Olmsted was not lost on Lanning, but it probably made him feel more than ever that he was born out of his time: his romantic self might bemoan the fact that it was no longer possible for one man to improve the surroundings of thousands of his fellow citizens or save great wildernesses for all time: his practical self, and he was extremely practical in a large part of his New England soul, would get on and make the best of what it was open to him to do.

Just around the corner from Crosby and Laura Roper's home on O Street, on the corner of Q and 29th, was 'The Shack' – the name Mrs Mildred Woods Bliss gave to the elegant house that she came down to after giving Dumbarton Oaks to Harvard University in 1940. Lanning knew Mrs Bliss in the last years of her life (she died in 1969), and he paid court, as everyone who was interested in gardens did, to this real link with the Jamesian world. The diplomat Robert Woods Bliss and his wife had bought Dumbarton Oaks in 1920, with the intention of making it into a country home in the city and a repository for their collections of pre-Colombian and Byzantine art. This was achieved over the following twenty years. The garden, an amalgam of French, Italian and English inspirations and the ingenious use of a hillside site, came out of a partnership between Mrs Bliss and her landscape architect Beatrix Farrand. Beatrix Farrand was Edith Wharton's niece, and she had learned much of art and architecture and Italian gardens under the tuition of her aunt.

Lanning visited Dumbarton Oaks time and time again. (He eventually wrote about it in *Country Life*.[2]) Because it has been so carefully maintained according to its designers' intentions, this great garden brilliantly illustrates both Mrs Farrand's skills and the taste of the rich and cultured Americans, like Mrs Bliss, who were her clients. Beatrix Farrand is called the Gertrude Jekyll of America, but in fact her sense of architectural detail was far greater than Miss Jekyll's, so perhaps she could more correctly be called a Lutyens/Jekyll hybrid in garden terms. She gave Dumbarton Oaks Italianate terraces and garden rooms furnished with classical vases and fountains, formal pools and balustrades and distinctive arbours and pergolas of wood derived from designs by du Cerceau. It also has winding paths and groves in the best English landscape tradition. And yet, I think, no English or Italian gardener would ever think of Dumbarton Oaks as anything but American. Mrs Farrand was able to fulfil her clients' cultural yearnings and yet give them something of their very own: Dumbarton Oaks, like all her gardens, has 'a subtle softness of line and an unobtrusive symmetry. No surface completely flat, no object balanced another of exactly equal weight and position'.[3] It has romance and poetry and the stuff of dreams: 'No other garden in this country,' wrote Eleanor McPeck, the American designer and former Dumbarton Oaks Garden Fellow, 'has the power to evoke on so many levels, other passages, other moments in time. It is the chambered nautilus of gardens, suggesting at every turn deeper levels of meaning and experience.'[4] And to English eyes it has an American polish and verve; whole hills of crab and cherry blossom, a bank of kalmias, 'a river of gold' forsythia lapping the silvery boles of tulip poplars, and the most statuesque of American silver beeches occupying a terrace all to itself, like a giant candelabra upon an inlaid table. (This elegant adoration of an American tree is also a feature of the Phipps garden at Old Westbury on Long Island.) And the rose garden terrace at Dumbarton Oaks – 'the ball-room' among the garden rooms – bursts with a colonial pride, reminiscent of Williamsburg parterres with added republican assurance, exact mounds, twists and walls of box laced with pink and creamy roses.

Cherry Hill, Wentworth: the garden was replanted by Lanning for, and with, John Hay Whitney while he was American Ambassador in England from 1956 to 1961.
Above] The pool and rose garden.
Opposite] Rhododendron and azalea glades.

With eleven others, including Olmsted's two sons, Beatrix Farrand had been a founder member of the American Society of Landscape Architects in 1899. She had practised from 1891 until 1949, at times running three offices and fulfilling some 170 commissions. She survived the Depression, when she lost many of her rich garden clients, because she was able to work on public landscapes for academic buildings and parks. She worked extensively on the campuses of Yale and Princeton Universities. Out of this work she developed her use of ground cover plantings, carpets of Baltic ivy or *Vinca minor*, with massings of evergreen shrubs and low growing conifers as companions to campus pathways, with jasmines and vines softening and colouring gables and walls. She mastered the 'desire line' for a paved walkway, the judicious relationships between these powerful academic piles and their serene lawns set with beautiful trees. Thus Beatrix Farrand passed down a great deal of both her garden and her landscape experience to the generation of young landscape architects that burgeoned in America in the fifties and sixties. Their early work was much in evidence in the America that Lanning returned to, whereas it had hardly been re-learned in Engand at all.

96

Apart from details of design, Lanning shouldered an important piece of Farrand philosophy. She believed 'more than most landscape architects'[5] in a continuity of supervision – in intervening, reminding, rethinking a garden design over a long period of time so that the change inherent in plant life was taken into account. This was exactly the reason for Lanning's chosen way of working. Ironically, both Beatrix Farrand's success at Dumbarton Oaks and Robert and Mildred Woods Bliss's bequests to Harvard University contributed greatly to the strengths of the landscape school, the school that Lanning did not attend.

Beatrix Farrand came to England in the thirties to work for her friend Dorothy Whitney Elmhirst at Dartington Hall in Devon. Dorothy was not only a Whitney, she was the widow of Willard Straight, for whom Mrs Farrand had worked on Long Island; when she married Leonard Elmhirst she came with him to England to start their Dartington venture. There would have been a nice justice if Lanning had worked at Dartington, but he did not; instead he visited it and wrote a long article, 'The Making of a Great Garden'.[6] But he was very much in sympathy with Americans gardening in England. He helped John Hay 'Jock' Whitney and his wife Betsey Roosevelt make a garden at Cherry Hill, Wentworth, in Surrey, their little retreat by the golf course from the Ambassador's grander home in Regent's Park. (John Hay Whitney was American Ambassador in London from 1956–61.)

Claverton Manor, the American Museum in England: part of the re-creation of George Washington's garden at Mount Vernon in which Lanning was always interested.

In 1965 Lanning advised Willard and Dorothy Straight's son, Whitney Straight (Jock Whitney's cousin), on the planting that would screen the passage of the M4 motorway through his parkland at The Aviary, Southall, in Middlesex. The Aviary became a happy garden for Lanning, and he worked there until 1979. The screening was successful and the beauty of the place belies its location so close to the motorway. The Aviary's garden has a lake, with banks massed with Japanese irises, primulas, hostas, rodgersias and ferns. From the Regency house the lake is viewed in a favourite way, across grass framed with flower borders, with the colours yellow, blue, white and silver predominating. The paved rose garden is planted with pink, pale apricot and white roses in generous helpings, and there are borders with a now recognizable Roper touch – masses of his beloved clear pink rugosa rose 'Frau Dagmar Hastrup', with groups of the modern showy pink little 'Ballerina' and the polyantha 'The Fairy', growing rather lower with crowds of tiny pink globe flowers – these set with blue cranesbills, rue, asperula, white lilies and pink and white peonies.

Lanning gave much of the credit for The Aviary's lovely garden to his client and friend, 'the gardener', Lady Daphne Straight. In the last years of his life he helped her with a small garden in Aubrey Road, Notting Hill Gate. Whitney Straight had been brought up at Dartington;[7] The Aviary was a very different garden but it had one honoured presence in common – a symbol of childlike things, the sculptured donkey by Willi Soukup. In Aubrey Road one of Lanning's chief tasks was to arrange a new setting for the donkey.

The sculptured donkey by Willi Soukup in the garden at The Aviary, Southall.

Ivy-leaved geraniums and marguerites – one of Lanning's favourite mixes for pots – here at Claverton Manor, but exactly as he specified for Mrs John Hay Whitney's garden in Beekman Place, New York.

In England Lanning was always advocating good American planting ideas, as well as the recognition of plants and ideas that were American. *Kalmia latifolia*, the American mountain laurel, *Magnolia virginiana*, the sweet bay, and the swamp honeysuckle (confusingly, *Rhododendron viscosum*) were all his favourites, and he must take some credit for the new-found popularity and desirability (not to say availability) of *Carpenteria californica*, *Romneya coulteri*, the white bottlebrushes of *Fothergilla monticola* and the grey-blue catkins of *Garrya elliptica*.[8] He wrote of American wild flowers – recommending cypripediums, the bloodroot (*Sanguinaria canadensis*) and the Virginian bluebell (*Mertensia virginica*).[9] He was always ready to sing the praises of an American's love of autumn colours in leaves and berries (this was a qualification he demanded from so many of his favourite plants, notably 'Frau Dagmar Hastrup'), of their restorations of parterres and *potagers* in Williamsburg and Monticello, of good American herb gardens, such as that in the Bonnefont Cloister at the Cloisters Museum in New York, and of the American love of mass plantings, whether of dogwoods in the wild or the billowing azaleas of Middleton Place on the banks of the Ashley River in South Carolina.

During the late sixties and the seventies Lanning's American trips took on a frenetic tempo; he liked them to be highly organized and pinned to definite engagements and visits – a lecture at the Pennsylvania Horticultural Society or the New York Botanic Garden, visits to Charleston to write about 'ante-bellum' gardens for *Country Life*, to see a San Francisco park or the PepsiCo headquarters in New York for the same purpose. Always, always, the times between were filled with looking at pictures at the Frick or Phillips Collections, at the National Gallery or the Metropolitan Museum; he was overjoyed to renew his acquaintance with the Impressionists at Chicago's Art Institute, but he was fascinated by an Alexander Calder exhibition there too, and he revelled in repeated visits with Laura Wood Roper to the Hirshhorn, where Monet Bonnard and Braque melt into Miró, Modigliani, Epstein and Moore. Slowly, America moved him from his natural affection for nineteenth-century art into his own time, a process started in England with Sir Robert Sainsbury's Henry Moore figures and Lanning's meetings with Peter Palumbo.

An article usually meant at least two visits, for he was very careful to get his details correct. He greatly admired the PepsiCo gardens at Purchase, New York, where the works of Moore, David Wynne, Giacometti, Henry Laurens and others are set among carpets of ivy, junipers and grasses, in courts of flowers and water gardens.[10] Even so, it was with trepidation that he set out to see how mere plants could cope with the monumentality of I.M.Pei's new East Wing for the National Gallery in Washington. He saw the building newly opened, and then returned after two years for his article on the gardens, to see what a collaboration between Mrs Paul Mellon and Don Kiley of Kiley, Tynedale & Walker – 'and obviously Mr Pei had definite ideas about the presentation of his building' – had produced. Restraint in selection of species, an adoption of the grand scale, the use of large specimen trees transplanted and uniformity of purpose had produced something that American landscape skills could be proud of, he concluded. Regimental magnolias in beds outlined in box and stone, long, deep evergreen borders, curving beds of *Prunus yedoensis*, the Yoshino cherry, that is the mark of Washington in spring, and avenues of willow oak and seas of cotoneasters all contributed to changing landscape pictures. In this modern picturesque setting the East Wing stands free, 'like an enormous piece of sculpture'.

Between these assignments Lanning was always giving gardening advice to his friends; he could not help it, but much was done on an informal basis and no record remains. He stayed with the John Hay Whitneys at their Long Island house and discussed their garden, and he helped Mrs Whitney with her small New York garden in Beekman Place. A visit from Lanning is well described by George Cecil of Biltmore Dairy Farms in Asheville, North Carolina:

> When my wife and I were planning to build and landscape our new house in 1978, I wrote Lanning and asked if he would be able to help us . . . he came down to visit us a few months thereafter . . . . He was in great form and we spent all of one day, a good part of the night, and the following morning, walking through the woods planning in the most general terms where and how the garden would fit in with the house, which was then barely coming out of the ground. We planned the location of walls, flower beds and the swimming pool . . . . [11]

In this way Lanning inspired and 'organized' his gardening friends, setting them on the right track; he had only time for one brief visit back to Biltmore, where Mrs Cecil had successfully carried on with her own good gardening in the framework of Lanning's design.

Ananouri, at Highland Falls, New York, the house designed by Lanning's former pupil Alexander Perry Morgan Jr, for which Lanning began to do the garden in 1976.

Rather more paper evidence survives for a garden at Highland Falls, New York, for Constantine and Anne Sidamon-Eristoff, whom Lanning advised from 1976. Their house had been built by Alexander Perry Morgan Jr, of architects Holt, Morgan & Schwartz at Princeton, who was one of the boys Lanning had tutored in his schoolmastering days. In Anne Sidamon-Eristoff he found a client with very firm ideas of her own and an ability to express them:

> The house which Perry has built for us and in which we have lived for the past ten years is a modern house, not a copy of any traditional architectural style, nor an eclectic mishmash ... it is the creation of a widely cultivated mind (with influences from wide sources) ... including perhaps quiet cloisters; stone towers of medieval fortresses; the wooden floor of a Japanese palace; skylights which date back to ancient Rome; masonry and roof-pitches which owe something to Frank Lloyd Wright. None of this is obvious, and all the influences together produce only ... a resonance, a sense that the present is not mindless, heedless and self-satisfied .... [12]

The garden was to be conceived on the same basis: Italian classicism and French formality were rejected as inappropriate to the wild Hudson highlands; Anne Sidamon-Eristoff felt at home with English landscape ideas, but did not want to fall for that 'siren temptation' the herbaceous border – and she had been fascinated by gardens in Japan: 'In short, I would like a garden ... which is not a copy of any garden style, nor a collection of passing thoughts picked up all over the world, but a garden which really fits into its natural setting.'

Lanning's reply is contained in a report dated 23 July 1976:

Ananouri: Anne Sidamon-Eristoff felt that her house possessed 'a resonance, a sense that the present is not mindless ....' Lanning found it a wonderful place to make a garden.

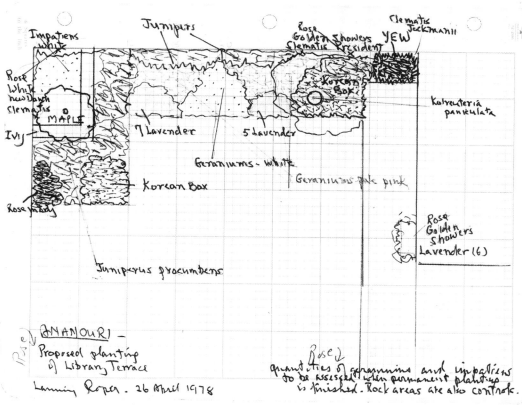

Impatiens white

Rose
White
newDawn
clematis

Ivy

Rosemary

Juniperus

Juniperus procumbens

Korean Box

7 Lavender

Geraniums - white

5 lavender

Geraniums pale pink

MAPLE

Rose
Golden Showers
Clematis President

Clematis
Jackmanii

YEW

Korean
Box

Koelreuteria
paniculata

Rose
Golden
Showers
Lavender (6)

ANANOURI -
Proposed planting
of Library Terrace

Lanning Roper - 26 April 1978

Rose]
quantities of geraniums and impatiens
to be assessed when permanent planting
is finished. Rock areas are also controls.

Above] Ananouri, the
Library Terrace.
Left] Lanning's sketch plan
for the planting of the
terrace, which he gave to
Anne Sidamon-Eristoff.

... Your analysis of the lines along which the garden should be developed is sound. Both the position of the house and the house itself require a very special simple treatment. I agree wholeheartedly with your statement, 'In short, I would like a garden at Ananouri which is not a copy of any garden style, nor a collection of passing thoughts picked up all over the world, but a garden which really fits into its natural setting.'

The two big outcrops of rock, one to the north of the drive and the other to the west of the avenue of maples, and the mound created at the end of the property beyond the cutting garden are important clues to the garden.

Perry's house is remarkable. I found a sense of space and peacefulness that I have seldom experienced, yet in some strange way I felt curiously part of it and it of me. The garden should be an extension of the house in mood and feeling. It should be less enclosed to the west with a feeling of space, and at the same time of intimacy to counterbalance the vastness of the river views.

There should be far more play of light and shadow on the lawns and a feeling for the natural contour of the land. Emphasize the subtle contrast of the level, well kept, smooth-mown lawns with wilder rough-cut, undulating areas merging with trees and natural woodland on the fringes. There should be vistas but within this frame concealed areas for special purposes that come as a surprise. Mystery is an essential to a garden.

At the moment the grounds lack cohesion. The vegetable garden, the cutting garden, the duck pond path and the orchard path to the pool bear little relation to the house and to each other. I would like to try to link all these elements and give to each its own individual character, with even a post and rail paddock for the horses, if the grazing area can be defined.

The avenue which bisects the south end of the property is problematical as it starts for no apparent reason and ends in an area to be hidden and forgotten. Screening at the far end with hemlocks as agreed, and removal of poor specimens, and the freeing of the big maple at the corner of the paddock will help, but we must give careful thought to the treatment of the whole area. The avenue is now a remnant of a past scheme and nothing to do with the present one.

Seasonal aspects of landscape are all important. Near the house there should be evergreen planting for year-around effect, and obviously it is essential for the screening of the intrusion of buildings on boundaries and other undesirable features. However, the native trees are essentially deciduous. Autumn colour, the pattern of bare branches against the winter sky, and the haze of tender green in spring are essential to the river valley. Native shrubs, wild flowers and ferns are to be encouraged where they seem natural, and bulbs naturalized in key places. Although rhododendrons should be used with restraint, they can be very effective. ... [13]

From these generalities, as he called them, Lanning turned to specific solutions. The rock outcrops were revealed, one with lawn flowing around it, the other by adjusting its related maples; vistas were created by the clearance of cluttering and unsightly trees and shrubs – but, he warned, leave trees in the foreground and middle distance, don't over-clear, do some and then live with it for a while. The upper terrace was 'excellent' – narrow borders against the wall could be planted with ferns and spring bulbs, or variegated euonymus, or a low hedge of silver ivy – or bedded, with polyanthus, tulips, forget-me-nots and English daisies, followed by white impatiens or blue ageratum or white geraniums in summer, with dwarf yellow chrysanthemums for autumn. A second terrace was to be organized into a garden room with new paving, furnished with yews and junipers, with lavenders, stachys or santolina in

Two photographs which illustrate the achievement of Ananouri:
Above] Ground levels and planting were carefully organized to control the views of the Hudson River.
Below] The house was clothed, and its terraces enclosed and planted, to a comforting human scale.

Ananouri: like any good judge of form, Lanning could spot potential.

sunny areas; an existing pear tree was to be underplanted with pachysandras or periwinkles, and all these ideas could be augmented with flowers as desired.

A mown grass path was cut around the garden to unite the disparate directions of the duck pond, swimming pool and kitchen gardens; the whole garden was protected by trees, whose winter bare branches could now be seen clear against the cold sky. At eye level evergreens were used for shelter, security and for outlining the views from the garden – Lanning added groups of *Rhododendron yakushimanum* which would stand the wind and cold of the Hudson heights, with massings of old shrub roses.

In August 1980 Anne Sidamon-Eristoff wrote of the 'deep and almost astonished gratitude' with which she and her family were enjoying the increasing beauty of their garden. Lanning made several more visits, but they were never enough – he often wished he could just pop out and see the garden in the way he did his English gardens – 'I do so love to see my children grow,' he wrote. This was an ideal working relationship as far as mutual respect was concerned, and Lanning got on very well with Henry Feil, the landscape gardener who actually did the work he recommended in his reports and letters. But it was gardening over too great a distance, and even in such a sympathetic and supportive situation it was just too difficult for him to keep in touch with weather conditions, or the availability of plants, or often simply to be there at the most useful time. Lanning became so busy that too often he had politely to send his regrets. I have described this garden fully because it shows just what wonders can be achieved by intuition. But this transmuted empathy, which was so important to the way he worked, was not enough with an ocean in between, and he knew it; this was why, though he could never refuse help to his friends, he never wished nor wanted to be a transatlantic gardener.

For a while, though, the warmth and enthusiasms of home did beckon him back in the late sixties, when he probably felt he had skills enough to make a living on either side of the Atlantic. There were tempting offers, one from the New York Botanic Garden, and he briefly considered the possibility of being a consultant to the famous White Flower Farm at Litchfield, Connecticut. The reason that America beckoned once again was that Lanning and Primrose had parted. They had sold Park House in the summer of 1964 and moved to a flat in Trebeck Street, off Curzon Street. While this must have lessened the burden on their busy lives, it was of course Park House that had brought them together, and it was Park House and its garden that they had in common. The wisdom of hindsight, of which I am dubious, does indicate that they may have been rather too alike in other aspects – they were both absolute perfectionists and experts in the kitchen, in their tastes in furnishing and flowers, and in their work. While Primrose wanted time to paint and travel and to spend time with her artist friends, Lanning's success was embroiling him in a rigorous work schedule which he had to plan farther and farther ahead. The week of the Chelsea Flower Show brought him a deadline for his annual piece for *The Sunday Times*, and an endless round of encounters and meals out with the foregathered horticultural world and his friends and clients. From then he would plan his working schedule: gardening and plant inspection visits, which had to be slotted in with writing deadlines, weekends, often working ones, around England – Glyndebourne, the Sussex Festival, Wexford Festival were all musts (but perhaps not quite so important to Primrose); then it was travelling in the autumn – always America, Ireland, France – away to the sun after Christmas for Primrose's health, back to a hectic spring of gardening and writing before another Chelsea again.

And so the years raced away. Lanning and Primrose parted in the autumn of 1964 and were finally divorced in September 1968. There was no one else involved on either side. Lanning was heartbroken. His much loved and most applauded book, *The Sunday Times Gardening Book*,[14] was published the same year, and its success must have come with bitter-sweetness. It is the most wonderful gardening book, perhaps the one gardening book a late-twentieth-century gardener needs. There is no need for me to say anything about it here except to exhort my reader to go out and find a copy, though I suspect that most will already possess it. The first pictures are of the Park House garden, the frontispiece is of Primrose's pelargoniums in their riotous reds, and Lanning begins with a fond and familiar description of the garden in which he once lived. He has titled his chapter 'Down to Earth'.

The Aviary, Southall
Above] Flowers in cream
and gold, leaves in silver
and green – some of
Lanning's favourite colour
combinations.
Below] The serenity of the
garden is retained by the
screening of the motorway
which passes beyond the
distant hedge.

Cherry Hill, Wentworth:
two views of the small
colourful garden which
Lanning planted for the
Whitneys, one of his earliest
commissions in the late
fifties.

7

GEORGIAN GARDENER

I N THE AUTUMN OF 1964 Primrose went to live in a little pink-washed hillside villa at Claviers, near Grasse, which was to be her real home for the rest of her life. The flat in Trebeck Street was hers, bought out of the proceeds from the sale of Park House, so Lanning left it; bereft of Primrose, he resorted to hard work and the kindnesses of his friends, especially Barbie Agar, Oswald and Grania Normanby, Pat and Dione Gibson and Christopher and Betty Hussey. In November 1964 he decided to take the lease of a garden flat at 29 Clarendon Gardens, a short street of stucco terraces within a stone's throw of the Grand Union Canal in Little Venice. Number 29a was his home and office for the rest of his life. From now on, except for a very few relaxations with old friends that he allowed himself, work and life were all one.

By virtue of *not* being a flamboyant designer, of not being able to express himself imaginatively in graphic terms, perhaps even because he no longer had Primrose to do that for him, Lanning made an ideal conservator of gardens. He had three qualities that fitted him for this task – his innate ability to see a landscape in the way that eighteenth- or nineteenth-century 'improvers' had seen it, the skill to produce flowery settings that could withstand the low-maintenance resources of our times, and the self-effacement that is necessary to perpetuate someone else's taste and ideas. These qualities meant that he was in demand by the National Trust as a garden consultant, and by private owners who wanted their gardens to look well but could no longer afford, or find, enough gardeners to do this.

In dealing with an historic garden, Lanning's self-effacement was suffused with a sympathy for the gardener who was gone. While he admired the National Trust's Gardens Committee, and earnestly hoped that gardens would go on being conserved in the way that houses were, he was only too aware of the supreme difficulty of keeping a highly personal garden:

> A committee, with the best will in the world, cannot replace the highly personal, day-to-day interest and individual taste of the owner. In some cases gardens are so personal and so poetic in their conception that their spirit dies with the owner .... A garden is a picture painted with flowers and foliage. Each year and each season there is a slightly different picture, but when the painter is gone the picture may easily alter increasingly with the years until it becomes a bad reproduction.[1]

Being so aware, he was obviously the best person to try this difficult task. He was writing at the time when Sissinghurst came into the ownership of the National Trust; I remember Nigel Nicolson saying recently that he wished Lanning could have had that garden under his care, but he was already busy with Chartwell and Scotney

Two views of The Hunting Lodge garden made by John Fowler for himself. Lanning often expressed his admiration for John Fowler's sense of style and enchanting designs for details such as these.

Castle when the wish was expressed, so it was impossible. Lanning, however, would have had a lot of sympathy with Vita Sackville-West's gardening.

In providing the kind of gardens that historic houses needed, Lanning's taste matched that of a new generation of owners, who, as John Cornforth writes in *The Inspiration of the Past*, wanted to revive their houses, bring them to life again and find new roles for them. In garden terms this almost always meant 'streamlining', but this was closely akin to the achievements inside the houses, where the newly restored decorations had to be maintained by a skeleton staff and a few electric labour-saving machines. Lanning was the garden equivalent of John Fowler, and greatly admired Fowler's talent for gardens, especially his own garden at The Hunting Lodge, Odiham, Hampshire – a wonderfully controlled creation of pleachings and pavilions that was as elegant as any indoor room, and yet had more light and gaiety. When John Fowler died in 1977, Lanning added the following paragraph to John Cornforth's obituary in *The Times*:

> His sense of scale and proportion of paths, avenues, terraces, borders and lawns was unerring, and his masterful use of pleached limes and hedges, especially those of beech and hornbeam to define outdoor rooms and vistas, has created charming settings for various country houses. He will also be remembered for his enchanting but highly controlled designs for gates, seats, arbours and plant containers.[2]

One evening towards the end of September 1968 Mrs Nancy Lancaster telephoned Lanning with an SOS about the state of some of the box trees in the famous garden of chessmen at Haseley Court. He quickly involved the RHS Laboratory at Wisley and Longwood Gardens in Pennsylvania for verdicts on the dying box, which were diagnosed as suffering from eelworm infection and/or waterlogging. With the box trees duly fed, medicated and recovering, Lanning went to Haseley to discuss the garden. Mrs Lancaster was planning to move out of Haseley Court into the much smaller Coach House, but she wanted to retain control of the garden. Lanning's schemes were for four south-facing borders along the south front of the house and its gothick-enriched wing, which looked across the chessmen to the Oxfordshire fields. He kept good things – groups of yuccas, bergenias, bocconias, hypericums, yellow roses on poles ('Golden Showers' and 'Golden Glow'), kniphofias, rue, alchemillas and Japanese anemones. He added berberis 'Rose Glow', artemisia 'Lambrook Silver', clumps of sedum 'Autumn Joy', the potentillas 'Katherine Dykes' with primrose yellow flowers and 'Elizabeth' with large canary-yellow flowers, and *Ilex crenata* 'Golden Gem', cushions of tiny-leaved hollies. His sketch plans are reproduced here to show how this overhaul was carried out to produce good borders of golds and yellows, with touches of purple and grey. It was a happy compliment to Mrs Lancaster's home state that *Rosa virginiana* was fitted in here, with its leaves turning from purple to gold; it had a companion in the unusual modern shrub rose 'Elmshorn', with crinkly foliage and late pink flowers. *Virginiana* and 'Elmshorn' among the silvers and purples would have given Mrs Lancaster a warm splash of autumn colour to remind her of home. Even from this brief example of working together, and from their few but affectionate letters, it seems that Lanning and Nancy Lancaster had more in common than just being American: they certainly shared what

The garden at Chartwell. Lanning's great achievement as consultant to the National Trust, now in charge of Sir Winston Churchill's former garden, was to coax the garden into its new role of coping with thousands of pairs of visitors' feet. He planned the layout of the new York stone pavings so carefully, and planted the borders so generously, that the garden retains its feeling of an English country refuge.

Haseley Court,
Oxfordshire: the Chess
Garden where Lanning
came to the rescue of some
ailing box trees.

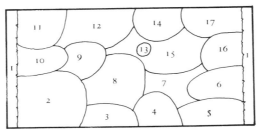

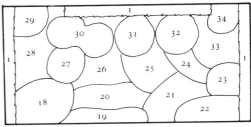

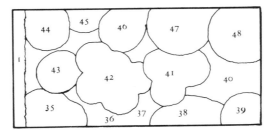

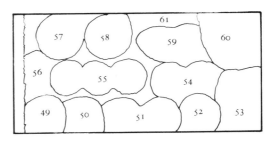

Haseley Court: four small
borders, in golds, creams
and greens, planted by
Lanning Roper on the
south front of the house
between existing yew
'buttresses' (marked 1 on
the plans).

2 Yucca (existing)
3 *Alchemilla mollis*
4 *Berberis thunbergii* 'Atropurpurea'
  with Helianthemum 'Wisley
  Primrose' underneath
5 Bergenia (existing)
6 Kniphofia (existing)
7 Artemisia 'Lambrook Silver'
8 *Rosa rubrifolia*
9 *Euonymus japonicus* 'Ovatus Aureus'
10 *Philadelphus coronarius* 'Aureus'
11 Berberis 'Rose Glow'
12 *Rosa moyesii* 'Geranium'
13 Rose 'Golden Showers' trained on
  a pole
14 *Elaeagnus pungens* 'Maculata'
15 Sambucus 'Plumosa Aurea'

16 *Lonicera nitida* 'Baggesen's Gold'
17 Bocconia (existing)
18 Lavender (existing)
19 Helianthemum 'Ben Nevis'
20 Sedum 'Autumn Joy'
21 *Ilex crenata* 'Golden Gem'
22 *Ruta graveolens* 'Jackman's Blue'
23 Rose 'Golden Showers'
24 Crocosmia (existing)
25 Potentilla 'Elizabeth'
26 *Lonicera nitida* 'Baggesen's Gold'
27 Potentilla 'Katherine Dykes'
28 *Antholyza paniculata* (existing)
29 Sambucus 'Plumosa Aurea'
30 *Elaeagnus pungens* 'Maculata'
31 Robinia 'Frisia' (bushy)
32 *Buddleia fallowiana* 'Alba'

33 Sambucus 'Plumosa Aurea'
34 Rose 'Souvenir de Claudius
  Denoyel' (existing)
35 Bergenia (existing)
36 Helianthemum 'Fire Brand'
37 Berberis 'Atropurpurea Nana'
  (existing)
38 Potentilla 'Elizabeth'
39 *Anemone japonica* (existing)
40 Hypericum (existing)
41 *Rosa virginiana plena*
42 Rose 'Elmshorn'
43 Artemisia 'Lambrook Silver'
44 Bergenia 'Rose Glow'
45 Clematis (existing)
46 *Rosa highdownensis*
47 Bocconia (existing)

48 Yew (existing)
49 *Ruta graveolens* 'Jackman's Blue'
50 *Alchemilla mollis* (existing)
51 Potentilla 'Elizabeth'
52 *Anaphalis triplinervis*
53 *Berberis thunbergii* 'Atropurpurea
  Nana'
54 Sedum 'Autumn Joy'
55 Potentilla 'Katherine Dykes'
56 Hypericum (existing)
57 Amelanchier (existing)
58 *Elaeagnus pungens* 'Maculata'
59 Aconitum (existing)
60 Golden privet
61 Clematis (unspecified)

John Cornforth calls her 'American desire for perfection'[3] – but a perfection that was natural and witty rather than leaden and dead.

Mrs Lancaster 'breathed' her lively Virginian spirit into three great English houses: Ditchley, Kelmarsh and Haseley Court. Kelmarsh did not enter Lanning's life, but Ditchley did. From 1973 to 1976 he was a member of a small group of advisers, called the Arts Advisory Committee to the Ditchley Foundation, at the behest of the Director, Sir Michael Stewart, who like Lanning was a friend of Freya Stark. Ditchley's setting had been made in the thirties by Geoffrey Jellicoe for Ronald and Nancy (as she then was) Tree. He had created a long north terrace with a grand view over the park, and the famous east garden with parterres flanked by pleached limes, the vista closed with a semi-circular pool and a curtain of water. In the intervening years much of the elaboration of the parterres had gone (indeed, a stone-edged layout had been restored to Wrest Park, whence it had come), but the formality of the structure has been immaculately maintained. Lanning's work was purely for renovation and repairs to ailing trees and shrubs, clearing and reinforcing vistas, and he recommended a survey of the important park trees for a future management plan.

In August 1972 Lanning went to Mottisfont in Hampshire to see the house Mrs Gilbert Russell was moving into, having given Mottisfont Abbey to the National Trust. He designed the whole garden for Mrs Russell, and Hillier's of Winchester carried out the contract, starting work in October 1972. The house, by Bournemouth architect John King, was entirely new, and sat virtually in the middle of a square plot. There was a row of limes on the road boundary to the east, and cottages to the south; the house looked west, over a hedge to the adjoining farmland. Lanning was optimistic: 'The house sits well as there is a lot of light on all sides with a low horizon.' His basic plan was for a large gravel forecourt from the limes to the house on the east; the house needed firmly anchoring and clothing, with bold groups of box, skimmia, *Mahonia japonica*, prostrate junipers, osmanthus, osmarea, *Senecio greyi*, lavenders and santolinas on the north side and curving round to link on to the west front, where there was a long, bare terrace. He proposed a loose and flowing border along this terrace front of the house, with fragrance and colour – lavenders, rosemary, santolinas, rock roses; hedges were to screen the working end of the house and a small sitting area. The vistas from the terrace and the main rooms should be to a feature – a Lutyens or white Chinese Chippendale seat, on a paving set with thymes and campanulas, flanked with pyramids or balls of box. This, together with the rustic folly and gothick pavilion that Mrs Russell considered, were rather nice features for a lady who had had Rex Whistler to paint the delights of her gothick drawing-room, but never materialized. The large lawn to the north of the house was to be broken with island beds, the plans of which are reproduced here as they are unusual planting schemes in Lanning's repertory. By April 1974 Mrs Russell was ready to settle her final account, and she and Lanning remained the best of friends.

Other early consultations on the surroundings of important houses included three in 1970. For Crewe House in Curzon Street he recommended birches underplanted with ivy and *Vinca minor*, with masses of *Senecio greyi* and *Elaeagnus pungens maculata* alternating along a border. The window-boxes for this most elegant house 'would be improved' with an evergreen (*Hebe subalpina*), with polyanthus, forget-me-nots or

Overleaf] Woolbeding House, West Sussex
Left] The terrace border for which Lanning's planting plan is reproduced on page 130.
Right] The Fountain Garden.

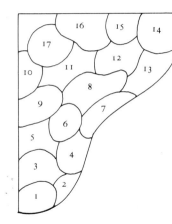

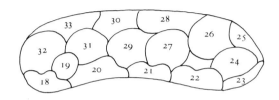

North End House,
Mottisfont, Hampshire:
planting plans for the
garden adapted from
Lanning Roper's rough
sketches, 1972.

SOUTH-WEST FACING
SHRUB BORDER

1 Euonymus 'Silver Queen'
2 *Helleborus corsicus*
3 *Cytisus praecox*
4 Hypericum 'Hidcote'
5 *Kerria japonica* 'Variegata'
6 *Cytisus praecox* 'Allgold'
7 *Mahonia aquifolium* 'Atropurpurea'
8 *Hydrangea paniculata* 'Praecox'
9 *Philadelphus delavayi calvescens*
10 *Philadelphus coronarius* 'Aureus'
11 *Viburnum tinus* 'Eve Price'
12 *Elaeagnus pungens* 'Maculata'
13 *Hypericum moserianum*
14 Mahonia 'Charity'
15 *Viburnum bodnantense* 'Dawn'
16 *Philadelphus coronarius* 'Aureus'
17 Robinia 'Frisia'

SMALL SOUTH-EAST ISLAND BED

18 *Senecio monroi*
19 *Genista cinerea*
20 Potentilla 'Mount Everest'
21 Caryopteris 'Heavenly Blue'
22 *Lavandula vera*
23 *Ruta graveolens* 'Jackman's Blue'
24 *Phlomis fruticosa*
25 *Cytisus kewensis*
26 *Cotinus coggygria* 'Foliis Purpureis'
27 *Viburnum henryi*
28 *Ceratostigma willmottianum*
29 *Rosa moyesii* 'Geranium', with
   Alchemilla mollis underneath
30 *Philadelphus coronarius* 'Variegatus'
31 *Kolkwitzia amabilis*
32 *Rosa rugosa* 'Roseraie de l'Hay'
33 *Santolina incana nana*

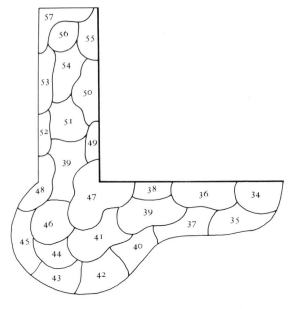

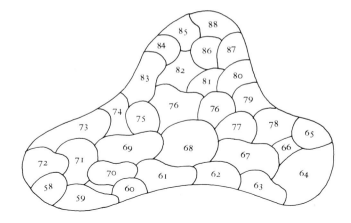

HOUSE BORDER FACING
NORTH-EAST

34 *Mahonia japonica*
35 *Skimmia rubella*
36 *Elaeagnus pungens* 'Maculata'
37 *Sarcococca ruscifolia*
38 *Jasminum nudiflorum*
39 *Viburnum tinus* 'Eve Price'
40 *Hosta fortunei* 'Albopicta'
41 *Elaeagnus ebbingei*
42 *Hypericum moserianum*
43 *Juniperus tamariscifolia*
44 *Viburnum plicatum* 'Lanarth'

45 *Cotoneaster horizontalis*
46 *Hydrangea villosa*
47 Hydrangea 'Lanarth White'
48 *Viburnum davidii*
49 *Parthenocissus henryana*
50 *Hydrangea petiolaris*
51 Symphoricarpos 'Variegatus'
52 *Hedera helix* 'Goldheart'
53 *Viburnum davidii*
54 *Skimmia japonica* 'Fragrans'
55 Lonicera (late flowering Dutch)
56 *Daphne odora* 'Marginata'
57 *Juniperus* 'Pfitzeriana Glauca'

LARGE ISLAND BED

58 *Daphne burkwoodii*
59 *Ruta graveolens* 'Jackman's Blue'
60 *Hebe albicans*
61 *Fuchsia magellanica* 'Variegata'
62 *Hebe subalpina*
63 *Senecio greyi*
64 Potentilla 'Elizabeth'
65 *Phlomis fruticosa*
66 *Genista aetnensis*
67 Ceanothus 'Indigo'
68 *Photinia serrulata*
69 *Rosa rubrifolia*
70 Berberis 'Rose Glow'
71 *Acer hersii*
72 *Berberis buxifolia*

73 *Spiraea arguta*
74 Genista 'Lydia'
75 *Berberis thunbergii* 'Atropurpurea'
76 Escallonia 'Donard Seedling'
77 *Spartium junceum*
78 Rose 'Blanc Double de Coubert'
79 *Euphorbia wulfenii*
80 Viburnum 'Park Farm Hybrid'
81 Cytisus 'Minstead'
82 *Viburnum hillieri* 'Winton'
83 *Weigela florida* 'Foliis Purpureis'
84 Philadelphus 'Sybille'
85 Berberis 'Rose Glow'
86 *Cupressus glabra* 'Pyramidalis'
87 *Spiraea thunbergii*
88 Hebe albicans 'Marjorie'

pansies, followed by nasturtiums or fibrous-rooted small-flowered begonias (*not* large and tuberous-rooted!). For the black and white extravaganza of Little Moreton Hall at Congleton, Cheshire, he recommended simplification and masses of good foliage, royal ferns and gunneras around the moated building. Different again was classical Ickworth in Suffolk, the property of the National Trust but still very much the concern of the Earl of Euston. Ickworth, said Lanning, had 'enormous scale and the garden should be essentially lawn, trees and park'.[4] His recommendations were also fairly grand: cutting vistas, re-curving hedge lines to match the curves of the house, establishing flowing lines of grass, livening up the existing flower borders, simplifying, removing misshapen trees – and nice ideas for the orangery: 'Try introducing blue *Plumbago capensis* and big groups of geraniums. Pots of *Ipomoea* "Heavenly Blue" . . . pots of *Humea fragrans* . . . and silver-leaved *Buddleia* "Lochinch" grown as a pot plant will flower all summer.'

Of course, the greater the garden, the more the conserving arts are tested. This applies especially when the garden is not very large, not, at least, a matter of far-flung vistas and vast terraces. The house and garden at Folly Farm, Sulhamstead, in Berkshire is one of the most complex achievements of the partnership between Sir Edwin Lutyens and Gertrude Jekyll. The house, which is really an extended Georgian farmhouse, was built in two stages, in 1906 and 1912, and it was not until the second addition was completed that the garden assumed its final form – a series of complex rooms, closely related in scale and atmosphere to different parts of the house. Lutyens was very fond of Folly Farm. It was the only one of his houses in which he lived for any length of time – he spent most of the summer of 1916 there, and Miss Jekyll was inveigled away from her Surrey home for a visit. The house has been very lucky in its owners, who have all looked after it well, though of course garden régimes have had to change. Hugh and Emi-Lu Astor came to Folly Farm in 1951, and in 1971 they called Lanning in to advise on the simplification of the garden. Though it was known that Miss Jekyll's drawings, including some for Folly Farm's garden, were in the library of the School of Landscape Design at Berkeley, California (bequeathed there by Beatrix Farrand, who had rescued them from England), the drawings had not at that time been examined. So Lanning had only the old *Country Life* photographs of the garden for evidence, along with his own knowledge of Miss Jekyll's taste. He firmly believed that the garden must also reflect some of the tastes of the present owners, and it was to this end that most of the discussions took place.

The courts between the old farmhouse, the barn and Lutyens's 1906 building are of small scale, with narrow brick herringbone paths with stone edgings and small borders. The entrance court was divided into four box-edged grass squares (which may once have held flowers), and Miss Jekyll's main intention had been to clothe the walls with jasmines, clematis, laurustinus, the perfumed rambler 'Aimée Vibert', 'The Garland' and 'Dorothy Perkins' roses, cistus and hardy fuchsias. Small beds in the barn court and the wall borders were planted with roses, nepetas, irises, poppies, columbines, and campanulas in delicate colours, and Miss Jekyll's edgings of bergenias and *Stachys lanata* were almost certainly present. Lanning (without this information) clothed the walls with roses, clematis, honeysuckles, rosemary and lavender in clumps, interspersed with irises, wallflowers and stocks for seasonal

patches of colour. The rose beds were softened with lavender, and sprouted forget-me-nots and tulips in spring. He made the wall planting of the entrance court more architectural.

On the canal front of the Dutch house extension he advised against putting back the beds of irises that had originally flanked the water, as they would be impractical; the water was to be cleaned and left clear for reflections, though a few groups of water-lilies would have been thoroughly approved of by Miss Jekyll. The grass sweeps that replaced the iris beds were broken at a point beyond the half-way mark by a pair of *jardinières* and seats, and the vista closed, as was intended, in a wisteria-swathed raised balustrade.

In the next axial room, set on the gabled front of Lutyens's 1912 extension, the wide, loose borders that Lanning planted would have pleased Miss Jekyll:

> Yuccas, acanthus, bergenias, irises, *Stachys lanata*, santolinas, lavender and nepetas, all beloved by Gertrude Jekyll . . . all grouped with delphiniums, phloxes, achilleas, heleniums and michaelmas daisies. Recently shrubs such as buddleias, ceanothus and shrub roses have been introduced to cut down labour and give scale.[5]

The borders were brought to the paving to eliminate an awkward band of grass; they show, though, that Jekyll abundance is possible with careful planning.

In the sunken rose garden, Lanning replaced the small seats on each of the four platforms with those of Lutyens's design made by Robin Eden. Lanning thought that the lavender on the central island wasn't happy because it was too damp, and replaced it with *Senecio greyi*. The yew walls of this room had grown to enormous size (they have since been cut back), and as part of the setting for a happy family life I have no doubt that this was a rather sombre feature, which the Astors wanted enlivened with bright roses. The Edwardian 'golden afternoon', however, had a taste for subtle, dusky colours – Christopher Hussey wrote of the pink and cream and carmine petals that carpeted and scented the brick paths in Arthur Gilbey's time between the wars – and Lanning was anxious to revert to these. They had a long-running discussion in which Lanning's historicist approach came into conflict with the Astors' more modern taste. Lanning's letter of 11 July 1977 shows well how he approached the situation:

> Dear Hugh,
>
> Emi-Lu called this morning, asking about roses for the four centre beds around the pool in the Rose Garden. It is a difficult choice. 'Paddy McGredy' is good because it is compact and low and it has an attractive flower. For some reason I've not had terribly good luck with it in several gardens but it may have been because the position was too dry. 'Tony Jacklin' I've not used as it has only recently come on the market. It again has a good habit but it is rather a strong coral pink. I don't know it well enough to give definite advice. I'm very taken by 'Anne Aberconway', which is an apricot yellow and would go well with 'Peace' which is in the top bed. It's a good doer. My one reservation is whether or not it would grow too tall. I don't think so, but you could check with Mattock. Of the Hybrid Teas, 'Blessings' would be a possibility, 'Grandpa Dickson' (pale yellow), 'Prima Ballerina' is very striking, a good doer and very clean; 'Pink Favourite' is similar but again a clean rose with very well formed flowers.
>
> If the upper beds are going to be replanted, keeping 'Peace' as Emi-Lu suggested, you would have to choose companions which would tie in with the pink in the centre.

Scotney Castle: the ruined castle seen from the bastion. Lanning was consultant in charge of this great picturesque garden from 1970 until his death.

121

Folly Farm, Sulhamstead, Berkshire: plan of the layout showing how Sir Edwin Lutyens and Gertrude Jekyll had imposed a strong axial formality on the design of house and garden. The original farmhouse(1) and the 1906 extension by Lutyens(2) allowed the creation of the entrance court(3) and barn courts(4). The barn is (5). The 1912 extension, the west wing(6), has the flower parterre(7) on its southern axis, and the covered corridor which connects the two stages of building enclosed the Tank Court(8). A long formal canal(9) and the Lime Walk(10) form two more parallel garden areas. The walled kitchen garden(11) closes the main axis across the lawn(12), and the sunken rose garden(13) with yew walls, complex paving patterns and rose beds on differing levels is one of the most famous of the garden rooms that Lutyens and Miss Jekyll made.

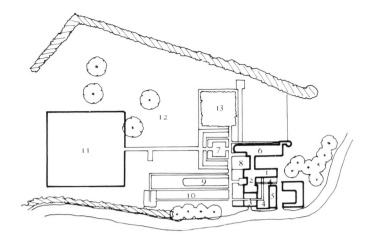

Right] The flower borders beside the parterre. *Opposite*] The vista from the walled kitchen garden. These borders at Folly Farm were photographed while Lanning was in charge of the planting of the garden between 1971 and 1977.

I am very keen for a loose informal effect on two roses, 'The Fairy' and 'Little White Pet'. These are spreading...; [The Fairy'] flowers a bit later than the Hybrid Teas and helps to spread the season. With it you could plant a charming white rose with clusters of fragrant flowers called 'Little White Pet'. I notice that Mattock doesn't list it, but again it has a rather looser informal habit which might be suitable. They do list 'Yvonne Rabier' .... You could have two beds of white and two of pink. Because of their habit I like them, but they certainly are not going to please you, if you want larger flowered Hybrid Teas or floribundas.

I hope that these comments will be of help and not merely confuse. The choice of roses is definitely a matter of taste and you will both have to make the final decision.

Mattock's are a reliable firm and they will give you sound advice as to ease of cultivation, habit and cleanliness. The last is a very important factor in a large rose garden.

Yours ever,
Lanning

Tatton Park, Cheshire
Above] The long terrace border.
Right] One of the L-shaped borders, photographed for an article Lanning wrote about the garden and bearing the stamp of his work as consultant for the garden.

Shortly after this he relinquished Folly Farm because of pressure of work, but Vernon Russell-Smith has stepped most successfully into his shoes, and, at the time of writing, the rose problem has been resolved.

There was immense variety in Lanning's work in historic gardens over the years. In his earliest days with William Wood & Son of Taplow, Lanning made a formal garden at Daylesford for Lord Rothermere; Wood's also worked for him in 1964 making the garden for The Aviary at Waddesdon Manor near Aylesbury. This garden for the National Trust, a masterpiece of understatement in a highly architectural setting, was of granite setts framing box-edged borders filled with white roses.

Another early job for the National Trust was at Tatton Park in Cheshire, where he soothed a fractious management problem and gave advice on long borders of careful colour groupings; the harmonies of pinks, mauves, blues and pale yellows 'with lots of fragrant heliotropes, lilies, nicotianas, lavenders and rosemary', and a series of separately coloured gardens — one in reds, purples and silvers, another in pinks, mauves, whites and greys, and a third in yellows, creams and blues — are his.

Waddesdon Manor: The Aviary garden which Lanning restored for the National Trust.

In complete contrast was the occasional advice he gave to Lord Saye and Sele at Broughton Castle, moated and Tudor, in Oxfordshire. Lanning's opening remark was: 'Treat area simply and play up the beauty of the buildings, walls and landscape. Elimination is as important as planting.' He felt useful giving long-term advice that would set a garden on the right track for ten years. In the last working year of his life, 1982, he did this for Richard Carew Pole at Antony House in Cornwall and for the National Trust and Lord Fairhaven at Anglesey Abbey near Cambridge. The latter was an especially interesting example as Lanning had written, at the 1st Lord Fairhaven's request, a splendidly illustrated monograph, *The Gardens of Anglesey Abbey*, published in 1964.[6] The book was a great help in the garden's management, but the Trust's regional director, Merlin Waterson, had problems, as he explained to Lanning in a letter of 15 June 1982: 'As I am sure you know, the first Lord Fairhaven made a rather unusual stipulation. There is a Memorandum of Wishes which states "I particularly enjoin the National Trust to keep the Abbey, inside and out, and the gardens arranged as they are at the date of my death." In theory this is very straightforward . . . . But of course, no garden ever stands still and at Anglesey Abbey the natural evolution has been interrupted by the ravages of Dutch Elm Disease.' Lanning, Merlin Waterson and John Sales, the Trust's gardens' adviser, visited Anglesey on 11 October 1982; Lanning was actually very ill, but no detail escaped him and he returned a long report, too long to be described in detail, but full of vision and phraseology about correcting the 'lack of harmony' here, sweeping curves there, planting, clipping or removing for the good of vistas or enclosures, all the fine detailing that is essential to the atmosphere of this immaculate garden. Throughout the visit he had discussed and come to agreement with John Sales, and their combined reports, as Merlin Waterson wrote to Lanning, did 'set out our long-term objectives in a very clear way'.[7]

On a lighter note and in happier times, he planted a border at Parham House in West Sussex, a place of both Elizabethan and eighteenth-century garden glories. A surviving plan has been reproduced here for its understatement – simply hydrangeas, romneya and buddleia with hebes, artemisias, hypericum and genista, all in violet-blues, silver and gold. The Parham border, done in 1975, came about because of Lanning's long gardening friendship with Patrick and Dione Gibson, for whom he

Parham House, West Sussex: planting plan for a long border, 1975.

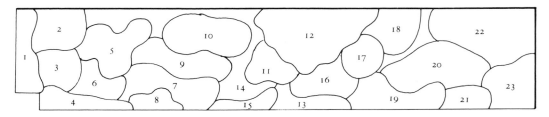

1 *Ruta graveolens* 'Jackman's Blue'	9 Ceanothus 'Henri Desfosse'	17 *Hydrangea villosa*
2 Eucryphia 'Nymansay'	10 *Spartium junceum*	18 Buddleia 'Dartmouth'
3 *Rosa rugosa* 'Alba'	11 *Romneya coulteri*	19 *Hebe albicans*
4 *Stachys lanata* 'Silver Carpet'	12 Bay tree (existing)	20 Hydrangea 'Bluebird'
5 Buddleia 'Lochinch'	13 *Ceratostigma plumbaginoides*	21 Sedum 'Autumn Joy'
6 *Inula hookerii*	14 *Achillea taygetea*	22 *Genista cinerea*
7 Artemisia 'Lambrook Silver'	15 *Salvia × superba* 'East Friesland'	23 *Romneya coulteri*
8 Hebe 'Midsummer Beauty'	16 Hypericum 'Hidcote'	

Chartwell: Lanning's
planting complements both
the house [*above*] and Sir
Winston Churchill's famous
hand-built wall [*left*].

127

gardened at Penns in the Rocks near Groombridge from 1967. At Penns he gave just a gentle progression of advice and support, working happily in the garden when he was a weekend guest; he enjoyed it especially, both because he was with friends and because he was perpetuating the garden made by the poet Dorothy Wellesley (later Duchess of Wellington), with some help from her friend Vita Sackville-West – where W. B. Yeats had walked and talked and Rex Whistler had decorated the house.

It was the long-term commissions that he found most rewarding, and I have saved until the end of this chapter three which, in their vastly different ways, meant a great deal to him. He felt honoured that he, a foreigner, was asked, at the request of Sir Winston Churchill's daughter Mary (Lady Soames), to care for the garden at Chartwell when it came into the ownership of the National Trust. Loyalty made him determined to help with the upkeep of the gardens of Scotney Castle after Christopher Hussey died in 1970, and from 1974 he created a garden in a most beautiful setting at Woolbeding House in West Sussex.

Lanning began work at Chartwell after a meeting with Lady Soames in 1966. It was the year that '145,000 visitors had seen the garden between early June and the end of October ... [and] there was little grass left on the paths or in places where the crowds converged to look at the magnificent views over the Kent countryside'.[8] That was his decorous way of putting it for *Country Life*, though his private opinion was probably more aptly expressed by the architect Philip Jebb – that the garden looked like a point-to-point course, after the meeting.

In Sir Winston's time it had been a quiet country garden – nothing spectacular – a lovely sequence of grass paths and flower borders and lawns and lawn terraces that overlooked the string of lakes and the Weald. It was a flowery refuge from politics, as well as the repository for his famed bricklaying: in the late 1920s he had built the wall surrounding the three-acre kitchen garden, and he also worked on the swimming pool and the lake dams. The difficulty was to preserve this idea of a refuge *and* make the fragile garden work as a place of pilgrimage for thousands of pairs of feet. The solution was obviously to provide a lot of hard surfaces, but they must not be too evident and subtle changes in the planting would be necessary to disguise the more spacious scale that the garden had to assume. Lanning won the admiration of many for the way he worked at these problems. Philip Jebb was working on the house at the time: 'I remember how impressed I was when ... he had to lay what seemed like acres of York stone paving and somehow did it without altering the character of the garden at all.' Arland Kingston, the National Trust's regional director with Chartwell in his domain, is full of admiration for how Lanning rescued the garden from its fate. The walls that Sir Winston built are complemented with masses of dusky roses and delphinium spires; the now wide paved paths have a planting of bergenias, *Stachys lanata* and lavenders that softens their impact but does not impair their purpose. In other sensitive places tricks have been employed, for example the orchard path that is hard-based but masked with rolled chippings, and the grass that is reinforced with paviours. Just as visitors do not go to Chartwell to see the architecture of the house, neither do they go for the design of the garden – but to keep such a garden exuding health and dignity and functioning as a suitable setting for the Churchillian legends has taken a great deal of ingenuity and skill.

Woolbeding House
Left] One of Lanning's
long borders which flank
the vista to the entrance
front.
Below] In the Fountain
Garden.

Nothing could be in greater contrast to Chartwell's crowds than the quiet of Woolbeding House in West Sussex, one of the many properties that it is more practicable for the Trust to keep in the care of an understanding tenant. The small, demure and rather French-looking house sits in a miniature park beside the Little Rother and a tiny Saxon church. The house's most striking feature is its Ionic-columned front, which faces directly up a broad vista to the road. This vista – an 'impeccable formal approach' says Ian Nairn's *Buildings of England* – is now framed by two of Lanning's most luxuriant flower borders: masses of white and blush roses, white potentillas, lilies, lavenders, alchemillas, mallows, pink and blue cranesbills, irises, gypsophilas and astrantias.

Terrace border plan for
Woolbeding, 1975.

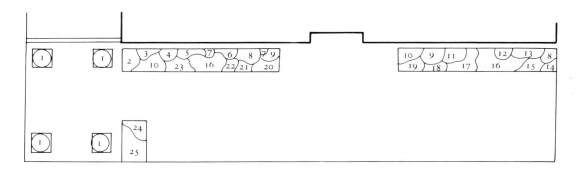

1 Box bush	10 Rosemary	19 *Santolina incana*
2 *Senecio greyi*	11 Hebe 'Midsummer Beauty'	20 Lavender
3 Ceanothus 'Delight'	12 *Cistus corbariensis*	21 *Calamintha nepetiodes*
4 *Euphorbia wulfenii*	13 *Perovskia atriplicifolia*	22 Iberis 'Snowflake'
5 Potentilla 'Mount Everest'	14 *Teucrium chamaedrys*	23 *Ruta graveolens* 'Jackman's Blue'
6 *Cistus corbariensis*	15 *Ruta graveolens*	24 Helianthemum 'Wisley Primrose'
7 Climbing rose	16 Rose 'The Fairy'	25 *Senecio greyi*
8 *Phlomis fruticosa*	17 Potentilla 'Elizabeth'	
9 *Choisya ternata*	18 *Sedum spectabile*	

On the south side of the vista a series of garden rooms have been created around an orangery built to the design of Philip Jebb in 1974. The orangery and its pool occupy a highly formal room, with related ports of call for vegetables, herbs and cutting flowers, but the 'best' room of all is devoted to the great treasure of Woolbeding, a fountain with a boy standing on dolphins, variously attributed to Cellini or (the more appropriately named) Rustici, and bought in Italy in the eighteenth century by Viscount Montague. The original statue is now in a museum but a cast copy adorns the Fountain Garden, a small walled and hedged enclosure with paved paths around L-shaped beds crammed with spring flowers, peonies, tree peonies, lilies and roses.

Lanning worked intensively at Woolbeding from 1974 until 1977, the period of construction and planting when he paid as many as six working visits a year. After that he kept an eye on things until 1980, and since then the garden has been developed – as he intended – with subtle changes of the picture every year.

By yet another contrast, Scotney Castle brought Lanning into direct contact with landscape history. Scotney's romantic landscape was created by Edward Hussey in the 1840s, with advice from William Sawrey Gilpin, the nephew of the Very Reverend Gilpin whose adventures with a Claude glass and sketches of Lake District landscapes had inspired the taste for the wild and picturesque at the end of the eighteenth century. Their materials had been the wooded site, with a deliberately ruined castle and its surrounding moat. Edward Hussey's mother had decided that the castle was unhealthy and rejected it for a new house, the present castle, which the architect Anthony Salvin built between 1837 and 1841. Scotney was, as Lanning observed in a draft for the National Trust guide, one of the last English landscapes made in the tradition of William Kent, and its romantic naturalness would also have pleased William Robinson and Gertrude Jekyll.

Lanning had become friends with Christopher and Betty Hussey at about the time they inherited the castle in 1952; Lanning later wrote: 'So completely did

Opposite] Scotney Castle: the old ruined castle seen across the moat.

[Christopher] understand the history of Scotney and so deeply did he love it that at times I found it hard to realize that it was Edward Hussey and not Christopher himself who planned the siting of the new house and garden . . . .'9 During the sixties Lanning and Christopher became gardening friends, working at Scotney together; it is not difficult to imagine how Lanning, with his predilection for interesting landscapes, found both Scotney and Christopher and Betty Hussey's devotion to it fascinating. When Christopher died in his seventy-first year, in 1970, Lanning naturally felt that he had learned enough of his intentions to be able to give useful advice both to help his widow, who would continue to live there, and Scotney's new owners, the National Trust.

The reports from an average of four visits a year between September 1970 and the autumn of 1982 are a mass of keenly observed details and attentions to small things that make up the continuing management of a designed landscape. Because he was not there to give daily instructions in the traditional squirarchical managing way, Lanning gathered his observations on many visits, for weekends or lunch, and included them in his reports so that they could be communicated to the National Trust and the gardeners. Through all he writes shines his belief in using his expertise for Scotney and for Betty Hussey, for someone else's benefit rather than his own. One day these reports should be analysed in detail for they would form an object lesson – or half an object lesson with the Scotney landscape itself – for a subject now so much in demand, the skilful management of historic parks and gardens.

Here it is only possible to take one small example from Scotney and follow it through the years. I have chosen the old castle itself, which is the most definable and interesting image. It is approached across a bridge, once the drawbridge, via a ruined gateway, into a romantic court of herb and flower beds, with a Tudor range of buildings, largely intact, on the right and south, and the seventeenth-century classical style ruin immediately ahead. Through the arch the roofless hall forms one of the most romantic of sets, exactly right for *Romeo and Juliet*, and beyond it the lawn spreads to the moat again, on the east side.

In September 1970 Lanning decided that the herb beds needed to be remade gradually; the first one was to be cleared and prepared for new planting, saving fennel seedlings, alchemillas, thymes and any other good plants. Early the following spring two more beds could be cleared, and all the time there was clipping, tying of wall plants, and removing of weeds and too rampant ivy to be done. The herb beds were duly replanted but were of course unimpressive for summer visitors, so *Stachys lanata*, heliotropes and scented pelargoniums were added. In the other main planting area, the rose border against the south wall (to the left) facing the herb beds, unsightly roses were replaced with groups of five of 'The Fairy' and 'Ballerina', with stachys, purple sage, catmint, and pink and white lavenders. For a year, i.e. till the spring of 1972, the gardeners' routine was adequate, with a few reminders about weedkiller on weeds sprouting from walls, cutting back the dogwood by the lake bank, and training roses higher up the walls. During 1971 two small stone seats arrived at Mrs Hussey's request, because she felt that many people would like to sit looking at the herb garden and the moat. These were duly paved in, with subtle extensions to the paving in other areas – a continuing matter – as the wear became evident.

In the summer of 1972 it was decided to make a border for shade-loving things — hostas, hellebores, alchemillas, skimmias, Solomon's seal and sarcococcas — inside the ruined hall; ferns, Japanese anemones and white valerian were added. In the autumn of 1972 the verdict on the replanted herb beds was 'good', and tulips, yellow and white, and wallflowers were to be added for the spring. 1973 was a year of tiny adjustments — the rose 'Lavender Lassie' over the ruined doorway, more hostas, euphorbias and Japanese anemones (from Great Dixter) in the shady borders, mignonettes in the herb borders, and death to a sycamore seedling that had dared to root in a window opening. The plant beds were 'balanced' during 1974, and in early 1975 one of the shady borders inside the ruin was cleaned out and replanted, along with some serious tree work all over the castle island. In October 1975 the lilac purple tulips entered the yellow and white colour scheme, and the following year more yellow and white tulips with blue hyssop for the herb beds arrived, along with

Scotney Castle, the herb beds within the courtyard of the old castle.

Pulmonaria saccharata 'Margery Fish' in the shady borders. There was a great deal of attention to the white Japanese anemones inside the ruined hall, for they have such a peculiar elegance and etherealness in the summer dusk among the stones; but there was also the desire to provide evening fragrance – daphnes, roses, kalmias, viburnums all found their way around the ruined walls.

The spring of 1977 was the date of the arrival, supervised by the artist, of Henry Moore's draped female figure, to be set on its special site in a glade opposite the old castle ruin. This was to be a memorial to Christopher and the Hussey family, and Lanning played a large part in carefully adjusting the setting, of which Henry Moore approved.

The following year he ruefully noted that too much of the gardeners' time was to be spent on preparations for the Scotney theatricals, which did not allow the much-needed rejuvenation of the rose border in the old castle. This was eventually done the following year (annuals – mallows, salvias, nicotianas – held the fort through the summer of 1980) and replanted after discussions – 'low planting along the front with lavender, sage, rue, *Sedum spectabile* etc., then group roses, using large shrub roses, hybrid musks, rugosas, species ... so that we can keep the scale large'.[10] The roses became whites, pinks, mauves and purples, 'with early yellows to flower with the blue irises' – he recommended inclusion of 'Alba Maxima', 'Celestial', 'Fantin Latour', 'Ville de Bruxelles', 'Queen of Denmark', 'Nevada', 'Blanc Double de Coubert', 'Constance Spry', 'Wolley Dod', 'Fritz Nobis', 'Ispahan', 'Madame Hardy', 'Tour de Malakoff', 'Madame Isaac Pereire', climbers 'New Dawn' and 'Blushing Lucy' and hybrid musks 'Penelope' and 'Felicia'.[11]

This border was Lanning's last big effort at Scotney. As he became aware of how ill he was, a new determination crept into his instructions, and he worked harder than ever. He would be out early, with secateurs and other pruners, and afterwards he would say what he had done for future reference: 'On the big lawn I pruned up the base of the liriodendron planted by the Queen Mother. At the back I started to cut away the *Hypericum* "Hidcote" ... and I left big clippings ... the rest of it should be cut back ....'[12] And on this same visit, in July of 1982, of the rose border in the old castle court – it 'is extremely good. I like the blue convolvulus with the ageratum; it's a pretty combination. The roses seem to be taking off rather slowly. It's important they are not swamped by vigorous annuals ... we planted a lot of rose "New Dawn" at the back .... Another year should see a really good display of roses.'

On 1 September 1982: 'Next season we must give supports to the rose "New Dawn" to get a big mass of colour which will go on until frost ... the white and purple violas in the kitchen garden would be ideal in the shady borders (in the old castle) to give continuous colour. We'll have to have a war on the ferns as they are taking over in various places ....'

Of course, it was not always like working in paradise. There were disagreements and disputations, the lawns were a disgrace, the gardeners not up to the mark, the plants failed – and most serious of all, he was once made aware that perhaps he was treating Scotney as a rather too private passion, making decisions on his own, cutting and clipping at weekends when the gardeners weren't around and making them feel unimportant and unconsulted. But Lanning, once made aware, smoothed all these

things over in his inimitable way, and he and the head gardener, Mick Martin, became the best of friends.

Lanning was concerned with Scotney's every landscape need for twelve years. It became his 'second home', and perhaps must rank with Park House's garden as expressing the other side of his landscape nature, the side that wished it had been born in the eighteenth century. He knew that he was lucky to find such work to do in the twentieth. His friendship with Betty Hussey was of the strongest and safest kind, exactly what he needed and desired. He indulged her with *Lilium giganteum*, treasures of blue meconopsis, carefully tended, and special trees which he bought as presents because he felt they would adorn Scotney. When he knew he was dying, he privately resolved that anything he could leave would be given towards Scotney's upkeep. He would have been pleased to have known, though I think he never did, that with advice from Dame Sylvia Crowe an extra piece of land would be taken into Scotney's garden and planted as a little landscape garden in his memory in the place he loved most. But that is to anticipate the end of his story.

Scotney Castle, the ruined hall of the old castle. Of all Lanning's English gardens, it was Scotney he came to love most.

135

8

SETTINGS FOR MODERN BUILDINGS

ARDEN SETTINGS FOR MODERN BUILDINGS was the title of an article Lanning wrote for *Country Life Annual* in 1960. He was concerned with housing – blocks of flats and modern houses with strident verticals and repeated horizontals and lots of glass for reflections or viewing. The lifestyles of those living in these buildings demanded easy upkeep and minimum labour, yet they wanted planted settings for the buildings that looked good and interesting the whole year round. Very different from romantic gardens. Lanning quoted a Frank Lloyd Wright house in California, with enormous overhanging eaves, where the interest was in how the architect had related his building to a splendid existing tree and actually built around another; he illustrated glass walled rooms that needed to look out onto the texture and dappling of foliage and a serene courtyard planted with evergreens; he illustrated, via a steelworker's cottage of mid-fifties Pennsylvania, how 'landscaping' of a permanent evergreen planting was part of the original plan and layout in modern American developments on all levels. Plants for these modern settings had to be selected with the same care and purpose as a piece of sculpture; trees with interesting stems and branches were to be chosen – thus the popularity of the peeling-bark maples and contorted hazels, as well as the magnolia and robinia. There was a 'suppression' of grass in favour of durable paving, but this demanded softening with periwinkle or *Pachysandra terminalis* as ground cover, and generous clumps of horizontal juniper or the oval, ridged leaves of *Viburnum davidii*.

When he actually wrote the article, in 1960, Lanning probably hoped that the chance to carry out these well-understood theories would come his way fairly often. In fact, he was only to do the planting for one modern house, and that was one of the masterpieces of modern architecture, the house that Mies van der Rohe built for Dr Farnsworth at Plano, Illinois, which comes later in this chapter. In most of his work with modern buildings Lanning had to contend with another dominating element, that of scale, for his garden settings would be made with modernism as 'the establishment style' of governments, institutions and corporations. The phrase comes from his adored and admired Ada Louise Huxtable, architecture critic of the *New York Times*, whom he read avidly; he would have been glad that he was too old to equate with post-modernism, which she called 'Jeweler's Mechanical'.[1]

Modern architecture pleased Lanning's taste for simplicity and pure form; he was exhilarated by towering walls of glass or stone, like Mr Pei's East Wing to the National Gallery in spacious Washington. But in the closely packed business centres of downtown New York or the City of London, he was far more concerned for the people who worked there in large modern buildings and who needed somewhere

A corner of the Farnsworth House, Plano, Illinois, designed by Mies van der Rohe.

green and cool to take a breath, or who needed the sight of a familiar tree to remind them that there was still a green and pleasant land beyond the concrete jungle. His particular enthusiasm was for the vest-pocket park movement in America, and a little patch called Paley Park, just forty-two by one hundred feet of park near the corner of Fifth Avenue on East 53rd Street in New York.

Paley Park was made in 1967 by William S. Paley, chairman of CBS, as a privately financed pilot project which he hoped would set a good example. It was probably brought to Lanning's notice by Mrs Huxtable, who described it as a model of 'excellent design',[2] achieving seclusion and comfort through self-containment. This was the achievement of the landscape architects, Zion & Breen Associates of New York, and its details are described by William S. Paley, its maker:

St Pancras churchyard, as it was after the outcome of the story told on these pages of how Lanning hoped it would become a lavish and exciting 'vest-pocket' city park.

Its ceiling is a natural canopy, formed by the lacy foliage of seventeen full-grown locust trees set at twelve foot intervals, and its high walls are covered with ivy. Its floor is mahogany granite squares and the steps and walk are Laurentian pink granite blocks. Its backdrop is a high waterwall providing motion and sound and muffling the roar of the traffic ... during the day the sun breaks through the Park's sheltered canopy to form irregular patterns of light and shade. At night, the Park is imaginatively lighted.[3]

The ideal of Paley Park – that an individual could make such a statement, or that a company could design a scheme or set back part of its office building to provide a piece of green space – was shared between Lanning and his friend Peter Palumbo. Palumbo, for whom Lanning gardened at his country home Buckhurst Park, Ascot, from 1966, was an avowed modernist with a great admiration for the work of Mies van der Rohe, and he had considerable interest in the City of London through his construction firm, F.G. Minter. Since 1958 he had been working towards a complete redevelopment scheme for a site between Poultry, the Mansion House and the east end of Queen Victoria Street in the City, which involved building a Mies van der Rohe tower block and creating a new open space to be called Mansion House Square. In conjunction with this large development he wanted to provide smaller green spaces, for which former city churchyards seemed ideal sites. It was intended that the Paley Park inspiration should be used for a highly formal garden in the former St Pancras churchyard in Pancras Lane, off Bucklersbury between Queen Victoria Street and Queen Street. In a report of 8 July 1975,[4] Lanning stated how this should be done, with a cascade or water wall at one end, and a split-level sitting area under trees and incorporating a kiosk for serving teas and cold drinks. Another small space, the site of St Benet's Sherehog, burned down in the Great Fire of 1666, also in Pancras Lane, would be simply treated but would add to the effect.

The design for St Pancras churchyard was drawn and costed by the architect Donald Armstrong Smith; estimated costs presented in March 1977 were considerable, including £26,000 for mechanical and electrical services, £6,500 for the granite for the water wall, £3,000 for furniture, £1,400 for metal gates and balustrades and £1,000 for planting. There were many smaller items, and the allowance for Ibstock bricks and paviours at around £100 per thousand would run into thousands of pounds.

Lanning's planting recommendations were for robinias or gleditsias. A consultation with Harold Hillier about the 'locusts' of Paley Park resulted in the opinion that they were *Robinia holdtii*, a cross between *R. luxurians* and *R. pseudoacacia*, which they thought would do well in the City. There were to be ivies, skimmias, laurustinus and mahonias, 'so that the garden looks well clothed in winter', with a minimum of good seasonal planting for colour, including the use of plants in pots.

However, problems then arose of which New Yorkers were blissfully unaware! The Bukerels and the Sherehogs had been prominent City families in the eleventh and twelfth centuries and had left their mark. The St Pancras ground had been deconsecrated and burial remains removed, but excavations for surrounding developments in the 1960s had revealed the remains of a medieval church on the site. While the GLC Historic Buildings Committee considered whether to schedule the remains or not, the City Corporation, delighted at the prospect of being presented with a garden, debated whether or not it could afford to maintain it. In the summer of 1977 the City decided that it would maintain the garden, and, as it was beginning to appear that the footings for the cascade wall could avoid or span the medieval remains, it was decided to proceed. But in January 1978 Peter Palumbo was informed that the medieval remains beneath the east end of the site (the place for the proposed cascade wall) were to be scheduled, adding another burden to the escalating costs of the project. Then the City, struck by a crisis of poverty which even denied the Lord Mayor new window-boxes for the Mansion House, wondered whether the costs of upkeep could be shared? They tried to assess these costs, but Lanning found it difficult. He wrote on 19 May 1978:

> If we do seasonal planting with bulbs, annuals, chrysanthemums etc. in pots in order to give colour, there would be the expense of the plants and the labour of planting. The actual maintenance of the rest of the garden should be fairly low, although the plants will need careful feeding, watering, pruning and grooming, as the garden must be immaculately kept, and the position surrounded as it is on three sides by buildings is not going to make it easy.[5]

By the time this information had wended its way to the Finance Committee they had gone off for the long recess.

With more and more doubts setting in and the dream withering away, on 11 September 1978 Peter Palumbo reported to Lanning that his board of directors felt that the scheme had to be abandoned. Salt was applied by the manager of the Girard Bank, one of the modern glass and concrete buildings overlooking the site, who wrote to Peter Palumbo on 26 September 1978 to complain that the original tree had been removed, trenches had been dug and that the site looked like wasteland. He proposed that perhaps the Bank, in association with Mr Palumbo, could turn the plot into a pleasant garden and sitting area.

In early 1979 St Pancras garden was laid to rest, quietly gravelled over, and four *Robinia pseudacacia* and three gleditsia 'Sunburst' were planted, with care taken that the tree pits did not damage the archaeological remains. Lanning himself went and planted ivies to grow up some of the walls. St Benet's Sherehog was dominated by an enormous plane tree, and the surface around this was also gravelled; Lanning hoped that Virginia creeper and climbing hydrangeas could be encouraged on to the surrounding walls.

There was a much happier outcome in the churchyard of St Stephen's Walbrook, which is overlooked by Peter Palumbo's own London base and where he is one of the churchwardens. It is a very shady spot, but is now full of camellias, rhododendrons, azaleas, roses, hydrangeas and a spring cavalcade of snowdrops, *Iris histrioides*, crocuses, *Anemone blanda*, dwarf daffodils and blue and white hyacinths, followed by 'big blocks' of white and pink impatiens for summer. The furniture designer Charles Verey, to whom Lanning was now going for most of his garden furniture, provided a wavy-backed bench for the garden in the autumn of 1981, and named the design 'Walbrook'. The garden had been formally opened the previous spring, and Prebendary Chad Varah, founder of the Samaritans, whose headquarters is in St Stephen's Crypt, wrote to Lanning of his pleasure and gratitude for the garden. He also remarked how the Lord Mayor had enjoyed himself at the opening, and wondered it he might acquire a key so that he could retire quietly into the garden at weekends. Knowing, as we do, of the shaky nature of his window-boxes, it is nice to know that the First Citizen of London at least has some flowers to enjoy.

The saga of the city churchyards will come as no surprise to any reader familiar with the world of landscape architecture and with the continuing and painful battle to win spaces for people and plants in the plot-ratio-conscious city centres. Lanning would have regarded the outcome philosophically; the landscape setting for our lives is always the loser in such affairs, but he had known that when he made his choice for trees and flowers rather than bricks and mortar at Princeton so many years before. His disappointments would have been on behalf of Peter Palumbo, now a friend, and a close friend, for over fifteen years, whose father Lanning was well old enough to have been, and who relied on the support and soothing influence of Lanning's presence. But the city churchyards were only one of three facets of their friendship, and the other two loomed large. They worked together on the landscape setting for the Farnsworth House at Plano, Illinois, and on the scheme for Mansion House Square in London.

To understand why both these places became so important to Lanning, it is necessary to know something of the legend of the architect Mies van der Rohe. Fortunately, as I write this in the spring of 1986, the centennial of his birth, assessments of the legend are becoming like the proverbial buds in May. Mies is back, in articles, books, exhibitions and analyses, after seventeen years in the wilderness (and no wilderness is darker or more fraught with vicious serpents than the architectural wilderness), and it is possible to find out why, as Peter Palumbo has frequently asserted, 'Mies is like a god to me.'

He was born in 1886 in Aachen in Germany. He was talented and ambitious, but poor, a stonemason's son who learned reverence for materials before he left the stonemasons' yards for wilder shores. He was also single-minded, solitary and self-absorbed, and he carved his way through personal and professional relationships to the élite art circles of 1920s Berlin. He was made head of the Bauhaus in succession to Walter Gropius in 1930, and after skirmishes with the Nazis he left, having been invited to Chicago, before the outbreak of war. In thirty years of living, teaching and working in Chicago he changed from a handsome, stocky, hard-working man into the taciturn, slow, herculean legend – described by Ada Louise Huxtable as 'heavyset and crippled with arthritis .... His tastes in his advancing years were simple and sybaritic – a few expensive dark suits of excellent cut, preferably tailored by Knize, and an endless supply of martinis and Havana cigars.'[6] He died, from complications caused by the arthritis and alcohol, in 1969, aged eighty-three. And, of course, he was a genius who worked tirelessly and endlessly for perfection in a search 'for the most magnificent and compellingly beautiful clear-span space enclosed by the most elegant structural systems made possible by modern technology'; and he drew like an angel – 'No architect ever drew more beautifully.' He was the giant of the Modern Movement, and all his buildings were refined into perfect works of art. You buy a Mies as you would buy a Miró, a Ben Nicholson or an Alexander Calder.

Lanning first saw one of Mies's smallest and most exquisite works of art, the house completed in 1951 for Dr Edith Farnsworth in Fox River Drive, Plano, in cold and snowy February 1973. Mies had sited the small steel and glass house on steel *pilotis* above the flood plain of the Fox River, next to a giant black sugar maple. The maple leaned over the little house in a gesture of protection; its leaves and branches patterned and brushed the windows and shaded it from the intense summer heat. It is at this point that every architect needs a good landscape architect, and every landscape architect gets excited at the opportunity to extend a concept into the landscape. At the Farnsworth House it seemed that either twenty years had ruined the landscape setting, or Mies had settled on the sugar maple and left it at that. Most likely the latter, for Dr Farnsworth had continued to use the contractors' 'drive', which chose the line of least resistance straight to the house and deposited the cars right in front of it. Lanning's first task, through three feet of snow, was to peg out a new drive line that approached the house subtly and left the cars parked behind a line of existing trees. His client and friend is still amazed at Lanning's unerring judgement in finding and marking the right course through the snow, which was proved to be accurate when the graders arrived in the spring.

Peter Palumbo had made Lanning promise, even before he bought the house, that they would spend at least one week gardening together each spring and autumn to create the Farnsworth House landscape. Lanning kept his promise and came to look forward to the trips. They landed him in a world which was not his own, but for which he had a great admiration, where every aspect of living had been subjected to that refinement of pure form that is modernism, not only devoid of the clutter that we employ at every turn, but demanding self-control and a sympathy with nature – rather like spending a night on a bare mountain or on an ascetic retreat.

But of course for Lanning the great attraction was in completing a work of art for and with a sympathetic friend and client. What he did is best described in Peter Palumbo's own words:

> I saw the house very much like the temple at Paestum, rising like a jewel out of the informal setting of a rough cut meadow. Lanning felt the same. We debated the age-old question of whether great architecture should be exposed and distanced from its surroundings so as to be seen to maximum effect from afar; or whether it should render up its secrets gradually by a series of tantalizing glimpses .... Lanning, was, above all, pragmatic, believing that each case must be judged on its merits. The black sugar maple in such close proximity to the house told him all that he wanted to know of the architect's intentions. From then on, he decided to 'shrink' the large meadow surrounding the house by a policy of strategic tree planting with the species indigenous to the territory – honey locust, linden, ash, oak, maple, willow, hackberry, redbud, alder and river birch. Later on he was to add amelanchier, spirea, burning bush, red and yellow dogwood, euonymus, pachysandra, periwinkle – the latter underneath the house to take the eye from the line made by the edge of the grass and the black soil beyond; and drifts of snowdrops, chionodoxa, dwarf iris, mertensia, narcissi, daffodil, crocus, hosta and dwarf cyclamen.

It was in this context – of long-shared sympathy and friendship, of the Farnsworth House and Mies in the wilderness, of a belief in green oases in the City – that Lanning prepared for the launch of the Mansion House Square scheme in the summer of 1981. The scheme, as he knew, involved the demolition of a wedge of Victorian buildings between Poultry and Queen Victoria Street which would open up a rectangle of

space, slightly smaller than Trafalgar Square, fronted by Lutyens's Midland Bank in Poultry, the side of Dance's Mansion House and the front of Wren's St Stephen's Walbrook. Opposite the latter two, on the far side of the new square, would rise the eighteen floors of glass and steel of a tower designed by Mies van der Rohe. There would be a shopping development beneath the square. Lanning fully realized in the summer of 1981, from studying the model and the site, that the scale of the project would require bold planting and use of large trees. He thought the London plane would be a natural choice, with robinias, gleditsias, birch, and solid, sheltering shrubberies of camellias, osmareas, mahonias, skimmias, viburnums and some rhododendrons. Careful thought would be given to creating pleasing vistas, patterns of light and shade and pleasant places to sit, enhanced with colour from spring flowers and summer bedding. The views of this oasis from surrounding windows would be almost more important than the experience. He had been doing these things for long enough to be certain of his skill and knowledge.

But, of course, architects and architectural critics do not understand such things. Among the whirlwind of debate and protest that raged through the spring of 1982 about tower blocks, buildings by dead architects, the value of the Victorian wedge of buildings, wedges and circuses being the character of the City, Lutyens's intention that his Midland Bank should be seen obliquely, or not, the open space – which would be wind-swept, traffic-ridden and noisy – was often a target. Lanning's defence was expressed in a letter to *Country Life* which he sent on 29 March:

Model of the proposed Mansion House Square scheme: the Mies van der Rohe tower is on the left, Lutyens's Midland Bank straight ahead, and the side of the Mansion House and St Stephen's Walbrook are on the right. Lanning was convinced that the new square could be so constructed and planted as to make a welcome green oasis in the heart of the City.

Opposite above] Model of the Hambro Life Centre (now Allied Dunbar Centre) showing the layout of the external spaces and the interior courtyard, which is actually a roof garden on top of the underground car park. *Opposite below*] Lanning's garden in the courtyard, which contributed to the award of the *Financial Times*'s 'Architecture at Work' Commendation for the building in 1982.

... a landscaped open space was mooted for this area and a comparable proposal devised by Sir Christopher Wren ... and John Evelyn and Robert Hooke .... After the catastrophic bombings of the Second World War, a similar concept was endorsed by Dr C.H.H.Holden and Lord Holford ... the basic concept and even the smallest refinements for [this scheme's] execution have been considered over the years. No modern concrete wasteland this. The Mies building is of bronze with pale tinted glass to give a warm glow. The pavements, steps and the square itself are travertine and fine granite, worthy of so distinguished a building and the other important historical buildings surrounding the proposed square. Moreover there will be trees, flowers, seats and other features to attract the public .... [7]

Lanning's belief in the healing power of a patch of greenery, especially in a place where people spend long hours at office desks, his conviction that he could manipulate it successfully, carried him through that last summer of his life in staunch defence of the scheme. He lobbied his other friends, even people he did not know well but whom he thought would be useful; withstood *Private Eye*, *The Times* and architectural critics; he defended at every turn and supported Peter Palumbo. It would have been out of character for him to do less.

Whatever the faults or merits, the battle of Mansion House Square made a sad end to one aspect of Lanning's life. It must have been all the more puzzling to him after the triumph of the Hambro Life Centre in Swindon. He had heard in December 1977 from the architect Peter Carter (the job architect for the Mies building in Mansion House Square) that planning permission had been received for the Hambro Life headquarters, a building in the Miesian tradition by Carter and Yorke, Rosenberg & Mardall, and construction would start in April 1978. The building, three storeys of buff aluminium cladding and glass around a central court, needed planting around its junctions with surrounding streets, and a garden in the centre court, which was actually a roof garden on top of an underground car park. Through the autumn of 1980 and the spring of 1981 Lanning worked at the planting with John Stubberfield and Cotswold Estate Services, doing much of the actual planting, as was his habit, himself. The success of his scheme can be judged from the accompanying illustrations; the ivy 'lawns' show the building off to the outside world, the courtyard garden sets up a pattern of reflections and a kaleidoscope of colour that changes with every mood of the days and seasons, and both the reflections and the reality add endlessly to the variety of views from office windows. The hundreds who work at what is now called Allied Dunbar Centre delight in the garden; they stroll and sit in it and hold parties in it at evenings and weekends. The success of both the building and its garden was formally recognized by a Commendation in the *Financial Times*'s prestigious 'Architecture at Work' award in 1982; all the assessors commented upon the landscaped court, and Colin Amery, the *Financial Times*'s architectural correspondent who organized the award, summed up:

The commendation of the Hambro Life building represents the recognition of a successful British use of the kind of office architecture that is more common in the United States. Its characteristics are derived from the architecture of Mies van der Rohe, and consist of finely detailed and regular components producing a pleasing place of work that is classically disciplined and enhanced by a finely landscaped courtyard. [8]

Lanning doing what he loved best – planting the courtyard garden at the Hambro Life Centre.

A lot of friends came from this project. Hambro Life's administrative director, Joel Joffe, invited Lanning to his home at Liddington Manor, just outside Swindon. It presents a great contrast with the office building to come across this seventeenth-century stone manor house at the end of a green tunnel, in complete seclusion, contemplating its outgrown moat. Joel and Venetta Joffe fully appreciated the subtleties, the dimensions of delight, that Lanning had added to the office building courtyard, and became lost in admiration of how he adapted to the setting of their home. In the course of a long walk around the garden, six acres, during which he sustained a lively conversation on all kinds of topics, Lanning divined the essentials of grace: lift some branches here, remove overgrown yews there, keep that old stump and plant a rose to clamber over it, mow the grass to a point, leave it rough thereafter, plant an enlightening group of narcissi – the kind of minimalist gardening that repairs the ravages of time and an unsympathetic hand, but which so few people understand. He did the usual thing of suggesting shrubs and where to plant them, but it was this artistry of refinement that most impressed them. It is worth adding that two partners in Yorke, Rosenberg & Mardall, David Allford and Brian Henderson, joint architects for the Hambro Life Centre, asked for Lanning's help with their gardens too, though he became too ill to complete either task.

Maybe Lanning's sympathy for modern architecture came from something as intangible as a sniff of that exhilarating air of the thirties at Princeton. Near contemporaries like Sir Peter Shepheard and Sir Geoffrey Jellicoe also have that sympathy, and I can only suppose that it comes from closeness to the contagion, applied at a young enough age. It also has much to do with the great schism of architecture between those who believe they are rational and geometric in loyalty, and those who are irrational and organic. To the former the land or landscape is merely something on to which the architectural idea is to be imposed; *in extremis* this view tolerates the presence of trees and a garden as the bourgeois expression of popular taste, and the role of the landscape or garden designer as a menial who provides plants that don't die, at least not immediately. This attitude, inculcated into generations of post-war architects, has so infuriated the rising young profession of landscape architecture that a meeting of minds between the two is all too rare. Even the other kind of architect, the one who believes in a landscape setting as part of the concept of his building, perhaps even in the inspiration of nature and the landscape as Frank Lloyd Wright did, has found the bristling sensitivities of landscape architects sometimes hard to bear. It is into this general context of an undeclared war between a David and Goliath of professions that Lanning's relations with architects must be slotted. I think he would have faced up to a live Mies van der Rohe at the Farnsworth House with equanimity and enthusiasm. And a great deal of the success of the Hambro Life project (which would probably have been translated to Mansion House Square) lay in the fact that Lanning and the architect Peter Carter found themselves to be kindred spirits. When one learns that Peter Carter studied at the Mies school in Chicago and was taught there by Alfred Caldwell, the champion of the landscape architect Jens Jenson and of Frank Lloyd Wright, with a direct connection in tradition to Walt Whitman and Thoreau, then all becomes clear. Lanning was only too delighted to discover how the firmly held bonds of his distant past were aligning him

Farnsworth House, where Lanning fulfilled his promise to his friend Peter Palumbo and worked for at least one week a year on the setting, so that the little house 'should render up its secrets gradually by a series of tantalizing glimpses'.

to work with a much younger English architect in the 1970s. In return Peter Carter found a being rare in any architect's experience – an artist prepared to enter into the spirit of his building, extend its essence and enhance its presence by its setting – and with the skills and knowledge to carry through his ideas to fruition.

But in all these respects Lanning's most difficult challenge was as landscape consultant for the Sainsbury Centre for the Visual Arts at the University of East Anglia in Norwich. The site for the building had been settled between the architect Norman Foster and Sir Robert and Lady Sainsbury. Lanning's earliest involvement was to go, with the Sainsburys and Foster Associates' Birkin Haward, to Thomas Rochford & Sons to talk about internal planting, using hydroculture.

The setting for Norman Foster's dazzling silver chameleon of a building was a far less tangible matter. It is a building that excites wonder and surprise; even in hard-bitten architectural journalists it provoked rhapsodies – 'a gleaming machine-made precision object aspiring towards a society which can send men to the planets ... undoubtedly a masterpiece' – trumpeted the *Architects' Journal*[9] on the opening.

The Sainsbury Centre is, and with no lessening of the wonder, a steel-framed hangar, clad in aluminium or glass panels, with ultra-flexible internal structures and systems to accommodate the changing needs of teaching, relaxation in coffee rooms and common rooms, a gallery for temporary exhibitions and the permanent home of the collection of art that Sir Robert and Lady Sainsbury donated to the University. It is, as its critics said, a freight shed, but one transformed by beauty. Most of its critics and admirers seemed to agree that it had little 'landscape' at all, just because they could not see the flower beds ranged around its feet. For this is manipulation of the most subtle, unobtrusive kind; it expresses perfectly just why landscape design suffers from a lack of public appreciation, for, as Sylvia Crowe repeatedly says, the mark of a good landscape designer is simply that you don't see that there has been any design at all.

The building was on its site when, in June 1977, Foster Associates sent Lanning a revised contoured site plan which took account of some of the extra soil that had come from the excavation of the Broad, a large lake nearby, but they acknowledged that 'the final contour should be achieved by site direction to ensure the correct interpretation of your requirements'.[10] From that time Lanning conducted a delicate dialogue between the architects, the University and the contractors. With a sympathetic amanuensis in the University's landscape architect Rosamunde Reich, from Feilden & Mawson – and with the skill of an intuitive dozer driver, Cyril Loynes – the Sainsbury Centre was gradually melded into its setting, related to the Broad and surrounding contours, down to the nearest half an inch of levelling. There were of course endless little details – lines of footpaths, fire paths and their reinforcing, drip from the buildings, the clearance of undergrowth near the Anti-Magnetic Room to allow an existing oak to be seen in a clearing of short grass. The major levelling and topsoiling was finished towards the end of the summer in 1977. Most of the planting was planned, discussed with the Sainsburys and accomplished during 1978. The result, which recent photographs show best, is the right setting to complement and enhance a wonderful building. This chapter must end in pictures rather than words, for it holds one of the most important lessons of Lanning's career: with the right landscape artist the architect has nothing to fear and everything to win . . . .

Norman Foster's Sainsbury Centre for the Visual Arts on the campus of the University of East Anglia at Norwich. This aerial view shows the relation of the building to the Broad, the lake from which soil was excavated and spread on the adjoining open space. Lanning was responsible for the final contouring of the site.

Lanning cleared the surrounding clutter from existing trees so that their shapes and shadows were revealed, and they made graceful reflections in the building. On the left, where he felt the space between the Arts Centre and the road rather narrow, he decided it would be more effective if planted with trees; these trees provide a 'treetop' walk for the high-level ramp, and also break up the length of the silver wall for passers-by on this side. Conversely, the pure form of the building is kept 'clean' on the landcape side, and Lanning arranged for it to be revealed in many differing guises when approached from the surrounding parkland paths.

Left] The Sainsbury Centre
at night – the reflection of
the building in the water of
the Broad was the challenge
Lanning set himself when
he organized the grading of
the slopes.
Above] Here the building
reveals itself rising from a
meadow of wild flowers.

Opposite] The Sainsbury Centre from the service road. It was Lanning's intention that the surrounding landscape should reveal the building in many different ways; he was especially careful about the trees that would be reflected in the glass walls.

Left] The aerial walkway approaches the building through the tops of newly planted trees.

Left below] Henry Moore's 'Seated Woman' (brought from the Sainsburys' former garden at Bucklebury – see page 73) found herself in a less than elegant setting, marred by the safety rail surrounding the underground entrance. Lanning, notwithstanding a few official eyebrows rising, simply covered the offending railing with greenery.

9

FIVE GARDENS

A T THIS POINT in my book it is sad to have to write of a consciousness that the shadows are already drawing in. Lanning was seventy years old when he died, but as he was a late starter in his career, and as his energy and enthusiasm made him seem younger than his years, there comes an overwhelming feeling that he just did not have long enough. The sadness of his failing physical strength, which so infuriated him, has already become evident in his work with the National Trust and on the Mansion House Square project, discussed in the preceding chapters. When one realizes that almost all his work was crammed into less than two decades, it is easier to understand just how hard he worked, and how vital – in two senses – was his energy.

His most successful years can really be numbered as fifteen, from 1965 until 1980. During these years he did most of the work that has made up this book so far, but between the time spent travelling and the long sessions at home catching up on reports, plant orders and accounts, there was a persistent infill of days and weekends spent in English gardens. In varying ways he worked on over seventy moderately sized gardens during these fifteen years; they are essentially domestic, family gardens, with features that adapt to any 'ordinary' garden. They are the kind of gardens that the world thinks of as essentially English, now that the realism of landscaped parks has passed away, and I hope that Lanning will be given the credit for perpetuating this kind of garden into the difficult and intolerant late twentieth century. This chapter concentrates on five gardens in particular, as illustrations of so much of the mood and practice of Lanning's life and work. In all of them the sunny generosity and enthusiasm of his personality turned gardening consultancy into gardening friendship in the way he liked best. Apart from the different gardening opportunities, they illustrate the differences in individual tastes that he found so fascinating, and the contact with like-minded clients that he found so important. As he told an RHS audience on 24 September 1968:

> . . . some put great emphasis on colour, others are collectors of plants and care relatively little for design or juxtaposition of plants, for contrasts of foliage, textures, shapes and colours. Others think in terms of shape, proportion, the balance of masses and voids, silhouettes of trees, expanse, water and the careful placing of garden ornament.

For those fifteen years of frantic activity these considerations were the chief absorption of his life. These gardens, and the life within them, are the reality of his dream.

The first garden is that of Hillbarn House, in the village of Great Bedwyn, near

Hillbarn House: the green alley alongside Tania's border. The metal arches were originally designed by Lanning and John Griffin for this garden, but the design was used again and again in later gardens.

Right] One of Lanning's first plantings at Hillbarn House – the row of pleached limes which adds height to the old street wall.
Below] Hillbarn House: the orangery and swimming pool court are overlooked from this hornbeam tunnel on the higher level.

Pewsey in Wiltshire. Hillbarn is not a distinguished manor house, it is rather a jumble of comfortable cottages and outbuildings with a variation of roofs, made into a rambling L-shaped house by the architect John Griffin for Lord Wilton in 1958. The buildings are next to the village street, and the original garden of less than an acre rose up the slope behind them, demanding what Lanning called 'sound architectural treatment' to cope with the changes in level. This was resolved by building retaining walls around upper and lower courtyards within the arms of the house, which were paved and cobbled, with the walls softened with cascading greenery. The major part of the garden was the upper lawn, at first simply treated with new trees and shrubs to supplement some existing yews. John Griffin designed and built the small white painted gazebo on the upper lawn. Lanning's only other work at this time was to screen the front garden with a row of pleached limes to give height to an existing old wall; roses and irises were planted under the limes.

In 1962 Lord and Lady Bruntisfield bought the house, and were also able to acquire the cottage at the end of the front garden and the land behind it, doubling the size of the garden, with most of the new land on the high level, next to the upper lawn. Again the architect was John Griffin, with whom Lanning had formed an easy working relationship. Another walled court was made behind the front garden for the swimming pool, and the former outbuilding facing the court was turned into an orangery/pavilion. From the pool court steps led to the upper level, where the new land was laid out as a *potager*, with a tennis court, cold frame and nursery garden behind hornbeam screens. Hillbarn's personality is that of a hornbeam garden – the prominence of this plant brings harmony and order to a fairly busy design, and the greenery adds lushness and yet is eminently manageable. The screen of pleached hornbeams against the tennis court wire is particularly effective, and the walk immediately above the pool court has been trained into a tunnel, with windows cut to allow glimpses to the pool, and at one end a delicious hornbeam cottage, of which the idea was Lanning's and the structure was devised by John Griffin. Indeed, John Griffin's wire arches, originally designed with Lanning here at Hillbarn to carry the hornbeams and fruit trees, found their way into many other Lanning gardens, at home and in Switzerland, Ireland and America. John Griffin sent him the drawings in September 1970, and Lanning gave him some advice on his rose garden by way of thanks; they were to work on several projects together and always remained good friends.

Most of the framework planting of Hillbarn's enlarged garden, the *potager* and its borders, was carried out for the Bruntisfields between 1965 and 1971. A long mixed border beside the *potager*, with old roses, philadelphus, pink and white peonies, lilies and agapanthus, is still called Tania's border after Lady Bruntisfield.

In 1971 Hillbarn was bought by Alistair and Anne Buchanan, who were young and keen but not knowledgeable gardeners, and who thought they could not possibly afford Lanning as a consultant. (He was probably charging about £80 per day plus expenses at that time.) He went anyway, and by casual visits and advice he gently guided them into making the garden that is seen in most of these photographs, an essentially happy and productive garden for a growing family. They maintain it with one very good head gardener and some additional and wavering part-time help. The

Hall Place, West Meon,
Hampshire
Opposite] The River Walk.
Left] One of the pair of
raised borders which flank
the lawn on the west front
of the house.
Below] A border of creams,
mauves and blues against
the rose garden wall. The
wall is covered with
clematis and *Hydrangea
petiolaris*.

garden is an important part of their lives but does not dominate them. It was part of Lanning's particular skill, well expressed here, that he was able to accept other people's view of the part their garden should play in their lives, and adjust accordingly; he never wanted to overburden his clients. Hillbarn is, after all, a number of useful spaces connected by intriguing paths and hornbeam tunnels. The *potager*, where most of the labour is required for the vegetables, is close to the frame yard and working area making a compact and efficient daily operation. Both the pool on the low house level and the tennis court at the farthest and highest point of the garden can be used without interfering with, or being overlooked by, the garden work. Though in the *potager* borders Lanning's plantings of subtle pinks and mauves, or yellows, blues and silvers, have been carefully maintained as the contrast and complement to the busy *potager* beds, across the high lawn in the beds beside the gazebo Anne Buchanan has been able to do her own white planting to great effect. Hillbarn beautifully expresses how Lanning *gives* his garden back to its owners for their own use. In such a place he would not have dreamed of making harsh and impractical rules, he would rather impart ease and confidence to a new generation. This is one of the least tangible but, over the years, most impressive aspects of his working personality.

Hillbarn House
Opposite below] The metal arches newly planted with apples and pears.
Below] The box-edged beds in front of the gazebo on the upper lawn.

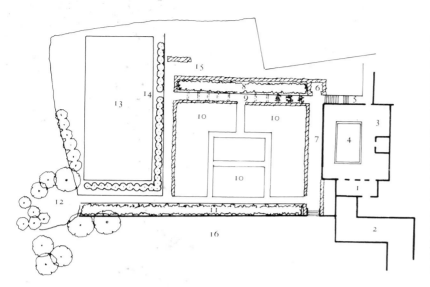

Hillbarn House: plan of the garden. The orangery(1) connects the house(2) to the swimming pool court(3), and the pool(4) is protected by surrounding walls. Steps(5) lead up to the higher level of the main garden, with its dominance by hornbeam hedges. The hornbeam summerhouse(6) faces down an alley(7) which overlooks the pool court from the higher level. Tania's border(8) is viewed from beneath trees trained on metal arches(9); the *potager* beds(10) are sheltered by hedges, and the south border(11) is a mixture of shrubs and herbaceous plants predominantly of mauves, pinks, purples, silver and gold. The glade(12) is carpeted with various kinds of ivy. The tennis court(13) is screened by pleached hornbeams, an aerial hedge(14), and the frame yard and working area (15) is also well screened. The upper lawn(16) is part of the original garden of the property, a stretch of grass ornamented with trees and shrubs, in contrast to the intensity of the *potager* area.

The second garden in this chapter is also a garden of the chalk country, but is otherwise in complete contrast to Hillbarn in every way. Hall Place, at West Meon in south-east Hampshire, has been the home of the Hon. Mrs Sonia Cubitt since before the war. She was a friend of Barbie Agar and so had known Lanning for several years before he started to work for her officially; the reports and correspondence on Hall Place date from 1973. Lanning also knew that Mrs Cubitt was an extremely knowledgeable and capable gardener, with a natural good taste and flair for the subject, as for most other facets of domestic art. Before she married her beloved Rolie Cubitt, son of Lord Ashcombe, she was Sonia Keppel, the younger daughter of Edward VII's last mistress, and the (long time unadored) sister of Violet Trefusis.

The story of their childhood has been amusingly told by Sonia Cubitt in *Edwardian Daughter*[1]; she tells of the nursery games with 'Kingy' and of even more exotic times when, after his death, Mrs Keppel took her children around the world. As she so disarmingly puts it at the beginning of her book, she was born a fortnight after the relief of Mafeking, which means that by 1973 she felt that her enthusiasm and confidence in her large garden needed occasional boosts. It was to become a gardening partnership in which Lanning revelled.[2] The surviving papers represent most of a very lively, nine-year-long conversation between two enthusiasts on the niceties of the management of one cherished garden.

Hall Place is a most lovely late-seventeenth-century brick house, full of historical associations – with Shakespeare's third Earl of Southampton, who might have lived in it, and Sir Christopher Wren, who might have had a hand in its brick façades. It sits beside the water meadows of the River Meon away from the village street, and these water meadows have been planted as a small park, with willows, poplars, alders, dogwoods, viburnums and maples; in spring there are drifts of daffodils, unusual in that they are planted carefully in groups of single varieties, in golden yellows, primrose or white.

The garden around the house, made by Sonia Cubitt since before the war, has, like the house, a quality of serenity and English expectancy, a happy logic that comes easy on the eye and feet. The water meadows with their daffodils lead to the north front. On the west façade, the west lawn stretches between raised borders and rose-covered walls as a garden room on the grand scale. On the south front, between the projecting wings of the house, is a paved and planted sitting terrace, with four smooth grass steps leading up to the south lawn, plain green, decorated with stately beech. From the west end of the terrace steps lead to a rose garden, made as a victory celebration in 1947; the east side of the terrace leads to the kitchen garden. The only garden building is a small brick orangery by Jeremy Benson (1955), which is tucked beneath willows and surrounded by roses.

Everywhere there are flowers, of the expected English kind: lavenders, roses, 'silver sprawlers', peonies, phlox, rock roses, campanulas, pots of scented-leaved geraniums and polyanthus, agapanthus, hardy fuchsias and purple berberis against the house, and *Mahonia japonica* and clipped yew for architectural statements. Against this background the conversation runs:

[from Sonia Cubitt, 2 September 1973] I have staked out two lots of narcissi in the Park ... if I wodge the 'Spellbinder' together again I think they'll look too overpoweringly solid – so would prefer to put more 'Tête à Tête' between the two groups of 'Spellbinder'.

[from Lanning Roper, 11 September] Your idea of breaking up the solid squadge of 'Spellbinder' is a good one, but I think 'Tête à Tête' is not the right daffodil ... it is not more than 9 inches tall with clusters of miniature trumpets poised on the stems. I think it will be lost ... therefore I have ordered 150 of a rather pretty jonquil hybrid called 'Waterperry'. It's fairly early and has clusters of charming flowers, which are ivory white with a pale buff-apricot cup. I think they will be ideal ....

[S.C., 29 June 1974] Big shrubbery (N. end) I would much rather have a 'Dusterlowe' [sic] rose here than 'Cerise Bouquet' ....

[S.C., 10 July] Neither in Murrell's nor Mattock's catalogue can I see any mention of the German shrub roses ('Dortmund', 'Erfurt'). Can't one get them now? If I can't get 'Dusterlowe' can I get 'Dortmund'? ... I do want a red single shrub rose if possible ....

[L.R., 16 July 1974] 'Dusterlohe' seems to have disappeared from all the rose lists and I think we ought to try 'Altissimo', which is a single red climber, very beautiful ....

Hall Place: the west front of the house with a lawn flanked by raised flower beds.

[S.C. 14 July] Following my letter of July 10 – I think you are quite right that 'Cerise Bouquet' would be the best rose ....

[L.R., 16 July P.S.] Your letter about 'Cerise Bouquet' has just come. Would you rather have 'Altissimo' or 'Cerise Bouquet' ...?

[S.C., 20 July] My dear Lanning – Yes, I would definitely like 'Cerise Bouquet' please.

[L.R., 24 July] I will order 'Cerise Bouquet' ... and also five of a very beautiful new clear yellow floribunda rose with a beautiful shape called 'Freesia'. This is to go in the yellow and blue border to reinforce it.

[L.R., report, 13 May 1976] *The Pavilion*: Alter the mowing in front of the parrotia bringing it out in a broad curve so that it is easy to walk around it. Cut back Rose 'Erfurt' and I will order another from Murrell's ... the daphnes are particularly effective with the pink forget-me-not and we should make every effort to increase the pink forget-me-not in this area, along with whites, and exclude the blues. I will send seeds of white. They are lovely and would be most effective in this area ....

    The Pasture: ... the docks are getting a hold. Either the farmer should take action against these with a selective spray when the cattle have been removed ... or the area should be mown regularly ....

Hall Place: the terrace on the south front, planted by Sonia Cubitt and Lanning.

[S.C., May 1976] Thank you for your report. I have forcibly removed out Silk's [the farmer] cattle and Michael [the gardener] is spraying the docks tomorrow .... This last weekend I went to ... Cranborne gardens and Wilton on Sunday morning. *What* a feast! I ordered three standard honeysuckles [standard honeysuckles are a feature of the entrance court at Wilton House] from the Cranborne Garden Centre to come in the autumn and thought we could re-do the north facing bed in the rose garden with these and with your new shrub rose 'Sparieshoop' in the middle of it – do you agree?

[L.R., 1 June] I'm so glad you went to Cranborne. It really is the most enchanting garden and I have always loved my visits. I'm glad you ordered three standard honeysuckle as they are so attractive. Peggy Munster has them in her garden (you should see it [Bampton Manor] some time as it is one of the prettiest gardens I know) and I'm very keen on them.

[L.R., report, 20 July 1979] The garden is in excellent shape and roses have never been better. How I wish I could see 'Kiftsgate' in full glory and 'Francis E. Lester' [a single pink-flowered hybrid musk] is now a dream. The River Walk is so beautifully kept, as is the whole place ... what a happy day and what a beautiful garden ....

[S.C., 19 July 1980] Wednesday Aug 13 will do beautifully [for you to come] ... I have so much to ask you and have taken some risks on my own! viz 'Pompon de Paris' has straggled heroically under *Ceanothus dentatus* and has really done wonderfully. So I have hacked back ceanothus (I hope at the right time) to give PP de P a chance ....

Hall Place: the orangery designed by Jeremy Benson, for which Lanning created a bower of roses and lavender.

Hall Place: the grass steps to the south lawn, a part of the garden which Lanning deliberately kept serene.

After Lanning's visit on 13 August his next report is dated the 15th; he approved of cutting back the ceanothus and suggested a little more trimming. The rest of his report covers details they discussed and then shows how, sometimes, harsh decisions have to be taken in the cause of good gardening:

[L.R., report, 15 August 1980] South bank of the river: I would remove the catalpa and tall leggy philadelphus behind it. You'll get a pretty vista, and I really don't think the catalpa is in good enough condition to warrant spending a lot more money on it . . . I have ordered a *Daphne* 'Somerset' for you, for which I enclose a cheque . . . .

[S.C., 19 August] It is too kind of you to give me a *Daphne* 'Somerset' . . . I'm not too sure about the catalpa . . . (second thoughts) I'll fell it, and then see whether I might plant another . . . .

[S.C., 21 October] Gardening is a nightmare at times. All five poplars down by the river have got honey fungus . . . .

166

Being a lady of spirit, Mrs Cubitt was undeterred; they were grubbed out, the area treated and planted with colourful maples. Lanning was both sympathetic and congratulatory, but he was too busy to visit that autumn, or the next spring. His final visit was paid in mid-July 1982, with the greatest accolade:

[S.C., 17 July 1982] It was a real delight to see you at last – and, as usual, order seemed to follow chaos when you appeared on the scene . . . .

It was to be Lanning's last visit to Hall Place, and his last report. Over the years the correspondence between him and Sonia Cubitt was brief and to the point on gardening, and only occasionally touched on other subjects, for example when Lanning gave some help and advice towards the publication of Mrs Cubitt's second book, on Lady Holland. Mrs Cubitt, though, was something of a fairy godmother to Lanning, and her lavish appreciation of him was to have repercussions elsewhere, but that is a later story.

When Lanning started officially at Hall Place in 1973 he was already working for Sonia Cubitt's daughter Rosalind, and her husband Major Bruce Shand, at their garden at Plumpton, north of Brighton. They lived in a rambling brick and flint house on the Downs which they had bought in 1951, but it was not until 1967, when their children were growing up, that they asked Lanning to help them do something with their garden. The Laines, as the house is called, could never have the classical serenity of Hall Place – it is in a completely different vein – but Rosalind Shand had designed a pretty summerhouse attached to the garden front, and a flint-walled swimming pool room in the open air; the Shands were also prepared to be more adventurous, and less classical, in their planting.

Lanning's first report, dated 4 September 1967, is a model of how he approached his tasks and his clients with optimism and vision, a certain openness of mind which gave them choices, but also with firmness on some matters. He began by saying: 'I like the site and the way you have taken advantage of the view over the countryside and to the Downs. On the whole, I think colour wants to be largely concentrated in the walled garden and treat the main lawn as a simple one, really resembling parkland except for bulbs and flowering shrubs on the right-hand side.'

There was tremendous vision in this first report he did. These photographs, taken by Jonathan Gibson to illustrate the *Country Life* article Lanning wrote about the garden of The Laines[3], show how it became a garden based on a complete harmony of his visionary ideas and the Shands' tastes.

The main lawn was cluttered with bumps and lumps, odd trees and an oval shrubbery; Lanning saw it smoothed and sloping – taking great care with trees they wanted to keep, such as the Scots pines – with cool vistas and patterns of light and shade allowed to sweep and curve with the planting. A little to the right, where the land sloped to a thick bank of shrubs, he proposed *Viburnum tomentosum* 'Mariesii', shrubby veronicas, *Senecio greyi*, purple berberis, purple rhus, golden elaeagnus, philadelphus, buddleias and hypericums. For the sweep of lawn beyond the shrub bank he cut a smooth path through rough grass, proposing to add 'one day, a big seat at the end'. In the rough grass he planted 'Cerise Bouquet', rising from the grass in the way he had learned from Barbie Agar at Beechwood, also on Sussex chalk.

The Laines: the summerhouse seen from the entrance court. Lanning immediately realized that the summerhouse needed to be linked to the garden and the house with careful shrub plantings.

The Laines: the east terrace, which affords a magnificent view over the Downs. Lanning made the terrace important in its own right, and planted it generously with phlomis, santolinas, potentillas, roses and good wall shrubs.

Rosalind Shand's pretty summerhouse was in place when Lanning arrived. He was very sensitive about what he called 'mean' terraces, and he ordered subtle adjustments to the paving, which made a proper setting for the summerhouse, gave him space for his Versailles tubs, and allowed his shrub planting to smooth the junctions between terrace, summerhouse and the original house.

The Laines has a second terrace on the east front, with an amazing clear view of the Downs and the sky framing one splendid holm oak at the end of the lawn. Because this terrace had such an important view, Lanning saw that it also had to be treated importantly in its own right; it was largely bare and supported only by a few straggling and unhappy roses. The phlomis, potentillas, bushy santolinas and generous plants on the house walls were his solution. He ordered generous brick-paved landings for the steps down from the terrace, and for other steps in the garden, for he hated patches of bare worn earth at the tops and bottoms of steps. He also made a small but important alteration by linking the brickwork of the two terraces, so that brickwork wrapped around the house on the south and east sides. *Phlomis fruticosa* marks the junction.

The pretty swimming pool enclosure, with its masses of roses, and the *jardin potager* were both developed by the Shands with Lanning's unending encouragement and advice. The triumph of the roses on the chalk is the happy result of lessons well taught and well learned. The *potager*, though more bosky and less formal than many of Lanning's other *potagers*, sports his signatures of clumpy alchemillas, lavenders and helichrysums beside the paths; he also recommended the value of parsley and wild *fraises de bois* as edgings, or using the space between the path and espaliered fruit as a

The Laines: the swimming pool garden, the outcome of the happy partnership between Lanning and Rosalind Shand.

The Laines: the south lawn, subtly remoulded by Lanning without threatening the roots of the Scots pines in the foreground. Many old and ineffective shrubs were removed and he planted several mounds of shrub roses over old stumps or directly into the grass.

Opposite] The element of surprise at The Laines – the path down from the east terrace.

narrow nursery border, 'for herbs and lettuces and growing on seedlings such as polyanthus, wallflowers or nicotiana . . . it is always useful to have narrow borders for this purpose'.

For Lanning, watching the garden at The Laines grow over the years became inextricably mixed with memorable visits to Glyndebourne for the grand opera he so enjoyed, and for the company of friends. There were so many of them in this part of Sussex, including Lady Birley at Charleston Manor, the Askews at Bentley, the Gibsons at Groombridge and Lord and Lady Rupert Nevill at Horsted Place.

From Bruce and Rosalind Shand at The Laines, Lanning was 'handed on' to their friends, Christopher and Dinah Bridge in Firle, where he was already friends with the Gages at Firle Place. The Bridges' garden at The Old Vicarage illustrates yet another variation on the theme of chalk gardening in the southern counties; I make no apology for including another chalk garden, for Lanning spent a great deal of his time

170

in Sussex and Hampshire, and it is in his familiarity with this working environment that the variety of his solutions and his appreciations of the subtly differing 'spirits of a place' can be seen. If Hall Place personified a classical Queen Anne kind of elegance, and The Laines was pretty and a little Victorian, then The Old Vicarage comes somewhere in between – it is a serene rendered house with Regency charm, set high up on the exhilarating Downs. The scudding clouds and spectacular sunsets were its glories, with the high winds and extremely alkaline soil rather less glorious.

The house faces south across the lawn to the marvellously close curving Downs. The feeling for its landscape setting mitigated against an enormous wrap-around south-facing terrace (which many a designer would have found irresistible). Instead, a tiny paved area made from the old kitchen flooring was tucked into the corner outside the drawing-room, the paving planted with thymes, lavenders and cistus and the walls hung with jasmines, roses and honeysuckles. A 'Nevada' rose was effectively trained as a wall shrub on the pale apricot coloured house, together with *Cytisus battandieri*, with silvery leaves and pineapple scent.

For days other than during a heatwave, or for balmy evenings, there is the walled garden room on the south-west corner of the house. This also has a terrace paved against the house, with pots of agapanthus and a border of roses, fuchsias, hebes and lilies. From this garden room there is a grass walk to the swimming pool enclosure, one of the prettiest of such places, with a wide band of grass around the pool surround and a pink and white flower border of roses, pinks, rock roses and deep blue lavenders. Behind them, on the wall, are 'Albertine' and 'New Dawn' roses and the clematis 'Perle d'Azur'. At the opposite end of the pool is a yellow and blue border – daylilies,

In contrast, the walk to the swimming pool garden – completely sheltered and flower filled.

ceanothus, the golden pea-shaped flowers of *Spartium junceum*, artemisias, stachys, santolinas and the white-flowered *Escallonia iveyi*.

Back on the lawn, the wall of the garden room makes a backdrop for the grandest border in the garden, south-facing to the view of the Downs – a great sweep of roses, escallonias, phlomis and ceanothus as the basis for perennial flowers – eryngiums, achilleas, anchusas, mallows, phlox, irises, peonies, rock roses and arabis.

The Old Vicarage has, within three and a half acres, an ample supply of fruit, vegetables and flowers, that pretty swimming pool, a tennis court and sunny sitting places. But it has above all, as Lanning said in his *Country Life* article about it, 'the superb views to the Downs that make this vicarage garden in the heart of an attractive Sussex village so unusual and satisfying'.[4]

The fifth garden has a house of similar period, another relic of the palmier days of country parsons, but its setting is in strong contrast to the other four. It is The Old Rectory at Orford in Suffolk, next to the Romanesque parish church which was the original place of performance for Benjamin Britten's *Noye's Fludde* and other 'church' works. At first it was a country retreat for William Servaes and his family, who bought the house in 1967 and for whom Lanning started working soon afterwards. When Bill Servaes became general manager of the Aldeburgh Festival and settled in Orford, Lanning began visiting again, usually mixing music with the gardening. The work of Benjamin Britten occupied a place akin to that of modern architecture in Lanning's feelings; it was not to his 'usual' taste, that being (since those heady youthful thirties evenings at the Metropolitan in New York) for grand opera, sometimes Wagner, and the classical composers. But, being such a person of place, he also found an irresistible fascination in a performance of *Peter Grimes* in its own legendary Suffolk setting, with the aura of Britten himself all around. Also, it was very much part of Lanning's nature to fling himself wholeheartedly into the passions of his friends, and Bill Servaes became a friend.

The Old Rectory, in typical Suffolk coastal manner, had an absolutely flat garden of four acres, with a quickly drying light sandy soil. The Orford area has very low rainfall for Britain, and it is beleaguered by salt-laden winds off the North Sea. To add to the difficulties, the main belt of sheltering trees was made up of doomed elms. Lanning's priority was to create sheltered areas within the garden, so that, at least in daily usage, one could *feel* some semblance of shelter and seclusion, even if the gale howled outside. He did a massive sweep of planting along the entrance drive, using the existing basis of Scots pines, some hollies and several yews. These were bolstered with liberal use of laurustinus, particularly 'Eve Price', and of his beloved *Mahonia japonica*, prostrate junipers, cotoneasters, osmareas, viburnums, including *rhytidophyllum*, *hillieri* and *davidii*, with ivies, euphorbias and periwinkles as ground cover. By the time the Servaes family came to Orford on a full-time basis, this drive planting gave an established introduction to the house. Thereafter the priorities were for vegetables, herbs, fruits, cutting flowers and a swimming pool.

The old vegetable garden was revived in many practical ways with constant tips from Lanning, but it was not the place for one of his *potagers*. The herb garden, though, like so many of his, bursts with an exuberance that expresses the form and textures and colours of herbs, rather than confining them to neat and tidy little regular

The Old Vicarage, Firle: a grand mixed border on the south lawn – the garden's 'opposite', which equally attracts, to the stunning landscape view.

175

patches of merely culinary function. Lanning's herb gardens are all the children of Vita Sackville-West's herb garden at Sissinghurst Castle, which I think was his favourite part of that garden, and the herb garden at Orford is a great credit to him.

In the Servaes's garden at Orford the pattern of Lanning's working life came full circle. For here was another majestic 'Seated Woman' (1957) by Henry Moore needing a setting, and this time there was a work by Barbara Hepworth as well. The 'Seated Woman' was placed towards the end of the lawn, to be viewed from the house terrace; she was given a backdrop of sea buckthorn, flowering crabs and hawthorns, maple, native flowering cherries and *Rhus typhina* for autumn colour, all dominated by a hugh beech tree. In complete and effective contrast, Barbara Hepworth's bronze 'Ulysses' is set in a wild part of the garden, underneath lime trees in a carpet of wild flowers.[5]

As I said at the outset of this chapter, these five gardens – Hillbarn House, Hall Place, The Laines, The Old Vicarage at Firle and The Old Rectory at Orford – typify what was for Lanning his happiest strand of work. These were the kind of gardens he came to England for, and they represent the kind of English life he most enjoyed. Two of them are in Sussex because it was a particularly happy stamping ground; his group of friends in East Sussex has already been mentioned, and he had another coterie in West Sussex and East Hampshire, based on Parham, Hall Place, Woolbeding and Bignor Park, where he gave a little advice to Lady Mersey, herself a great gardener.

With these five gardens I have tried to indicate the flexibility of Lanning's approach, which I feel was a great key to his success. Each of these workplaces was very different, and he adjusted easily in both personal and practical ways. At Hall Place, Mrs Cubitt expected him to take a minute interest in every aspect of the garden, and she kept him up to the mark. It is rather touching that she seemed to need a gardening companion of the closest kind, and Lanning with his kindness and good humour made it all an enchanting game for her to enjoy at the end of an eventful and exciting life. She employed two devoted gardeners, whom she called 'the boys', in the last years of Lanning's time there, and he admired their endeavours and hard work; it all seemed to work very well. At Hillbarn, though, in the beginning, things were far more formal. Though Lanning later became a good friend of Lord Wilton, and worked for him at Milton Lilbourne and in his London gardens in Chester Square and Egerton Terrace, the early work at Hillbarn was more a case of formal instructions to the architects and builders. With Hillbarn's current owners, the younger Buchanans, he became wise and avuncular (it was a role he played with kindness, and secret amusement at himself, to many young gardeners and would-be gardeners), dropping in for a drink *en route* to or from another job, walking round the garden and discussing progress. He was always very sensitive about the resident gardener's hours, realizing that though he was content to give gardening advice over his dinner, they did not necessarily want to; many gardeners, however, including John Last at Hillbarn, would happily turn out at any hour to talk to him.

At The Laines, Bruce and Rosalind Shand were always completely in control of their garden and its details; but at Orford the Servaes family were very busy with

The Old Rectory: the herb garden. Its lushness of planting and careful design make it a child of Lanning's favourite herb garden at Sissinghurst Castle.

other things, and Lanning worked with Mark Rumary of Notcutt's of Woodbridge near by. Notcutt's provided the plants and the labour for large jobs within the garden, and Lanning gave the framework of design advice.

Whatever his actual role, there were certain things Lanning was very particular about, whoever he was 'instructing'. The bulk of his correspondence and reports really deals with plant and soil health; he could not bear to see damaged or diseased trees left untended, and he had a long and successful relationship with W.E. 'Bill' Matthews of Southern Tree Surgeons, who usually worked for him. Ugly or unhealthy shrubs were always rooted out, and weak nursery stock was always returned. He was persistently advocating the cleaning of soil, or the feeding, usually both, and his eagle eye never failed to spot signs of disease. This was the toughest part of his garden advice and he always dealt with it swiftly and efficiently.

These kinds of connections in garden-making in England were reflected in other parts of the country. He was happy working in Gloucestershire and the Cotswolds, where he was a frequent visitor at Bampton Manor and Lyegrove; he had worked at Valley Farm, Duntisbourne, with Lady Hollenden and for Sir Tobias Clarke at Church House, Bibury. Suffolk and Norfolk were also familiar country, where he worked for several years at Sternfield House, Saxmundham, for Lt-Col. Sir Eric and Lady Penn, and at Wickmere House and Rudham House. There were also other gardens he did more briefly in Wiltshire, Oxfordshire and the East Midland shires. His early work with Peter Wake at Courteenhall in Northamptonshire (he later helped the Wakes with Fairfield House at Hambledon, Hampshire) was about the farthest northern limit of his regular terrain; he worked in Shropshire at Lower Hall, Worfield, but went no farther west, and he made no gardens in Devon or Cornwall. Apart from his gardening with the Normanbys at Mulgrave, and brief advice for two Scottish gardens, he avoided the north because he felt unsure of the vagaries of climate. He visited Muncaster Castle in Cumbria and its rhododendrons more than once and admired it greatly, but he does not seem to have done more than that. Details of all these gardens are given in the list at the end of the book. There remains just one more aspect of Lanning's working life to be described, and that is the subject of my next chapter.

At The Old Rectory, Lanning once again enjoyed making a setting for a work by Henry Moore [*opposite*], and, in contrast, felt Barbara Hepworth's 'Ulysses' was most dramatically seen in a wild-flower setting [*above*].

IO

GARDENER
BY APPOINTMENT

APART from working in these very English gardens for people with whom he had much in common and who became his friends, and his more public work for the National Trust and in universities where he was among fellow professionals, Lanning also had a string of prestige commissions. These he treated with great discretion, which was often the reason for his success, for whether he was planting shrubs in the drizzle of an English November afternoon or walking in a garden on an Alpine May morning, he was sharing the precious private hours of princes and politicians. Lanning was a relaxing companion who gave of his own energy, enthusiasm and knowledge unstintingly, and in the end too generously, to fulfil the private gardening dreams of people who were either born to, or had made for themselves, very demanding public lives.

Lanning always regarded his work for Prince Sadruddin Aga Khan at the Château de Bellerive near Geneva as one of his most important commissions. He found that working for the Prince brought him tremendous satisfaction, largely because of his admiration – unhesitatingly expressed, even after their first meeting – for the Prince's work as High Commissioner for Refugees at the United Nations, but also because of their shared tastes and gardening ambitions. The seventeenth-century Château de Bellerive now possesses what is undoubtedly Lanning's best and most fruitful *jardin potager*, as well as wider and less tangible evidence of his skills.

It appears from the surviving papers that he first met Prince Sadruddin (possibly through his neighbour in Little Venice, Lady Diana Cooper) to discuss the proposed walled garden in the autumn of 1969. Through subsequent visits, with Lanning armed with photographs of *potagers*, the plan evolved into Lanning's sketch design which is illustrated here. This is almost the only one, and certainly the clearest, of his own sketches that survives; it was translated into a finished drawing which reveals a beautifully balanced asymmetrical layout allowing the traditionally happy marriage between function and ornament. The 'potting shed' will materialize as a gazebo with an adjacent greenhouse; these two and a wall conceal the frame yard, seed and compost beds in the vital 'working' corner of the garden. The rest of the garden is cut by straight paths through flowered edgings, including a silver walk, with ornamental iron gates, an arbour or two, a sculpture, a dipping well or cistern or an ornamental basin closing their vistas. A small garden within a garden is devoted to herbs; there are beds for asparagus, strawberries and cutting flowers, fruit bushes and espaliers around the walls, and *potager* beds for the neat arrangements of vegetables.

Though this garden is bathed in clear Alpine light, its design is essentially English. Lanning devoted much of his energy to finding, and arranging for the export of, its

Lanning by Snowdon,
May 1979.

English furnishings. The teak garden seat made by A.T.Palmer Ltd of Headcorn, in a paved bay overlooking the cutting borders, is copied from one in the garden at Sissinghurst Castle. The original, with a wooden scroll along its back like a breaking wave, was designed by Sir Edwin Lutyens; it is interesting that the Sissinghurst copy in oak cost £71 from Palmer's in 1968. The cedar greenhouse and its fittings came from W.Richardson & Company of Lambeth Road in London, and some iron gates were made by Pearce's Bredfield Ironworks at Woodbridge in Suffolk. Chilstone Garden Ornaments supplied the stone balls and their bases for the tops of the pillars of the walls; Haddonstone *jardinières* and plaited baskets followed; and even the plant labels were mostly made in England, by the National Trust's Garden Label Workshop and by Dolphin Products of Poole in Dorset.

Lanning would never have taken on this commission without the assistance of a young landscape architect, Walter Brugger, who was in Geneva and therefore on the spot. 'I am reticent about working in foreign countries where I have not special knowledge,'[1] he had written to the Prince at the outset, and he had recommended

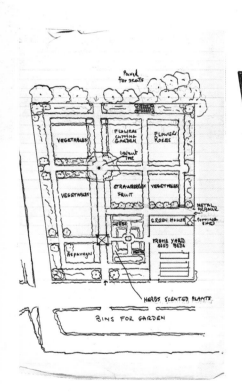

Château de Bellerive
Above] Lanning's original sketch for the *potager* design.
Right] The finished design, drawn by his assistant Walter Brugger.
Opposite] The architect's sketch for the 'potting shed'.

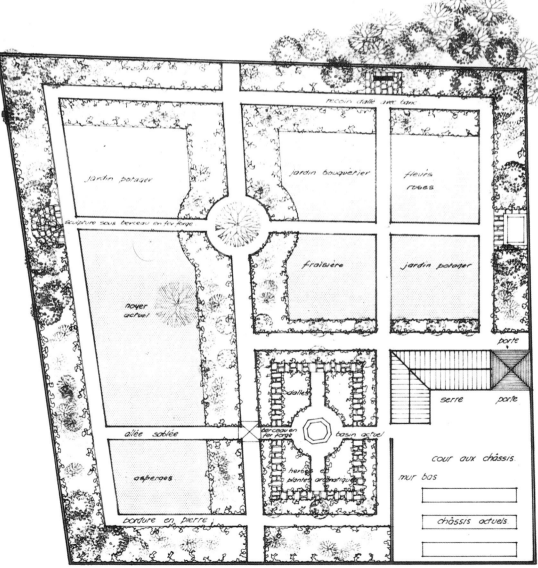

Walter Brugger, whom he met in London and who had made Henry McIlhenny's Italian garden at Glenveagh Castle, to overcome the language difficulties and also provide the required knowledge of the local climate and other variable factors. Walter and Silvie Brugger became deeply attached to Lanning, and made every arrangement for his visits to run smoothly; Walter was the constant liaison between Lanning, the Prince's household, the head gardener M. Lemery, and the job architect who built the potting shed, the arches and espaliers, and supervised the walling and paving, Marc Gignoux of Geneva. Walter and Silvie would meet Lanning at the airport and either have him to stay or arrange for him to stay at the Elite in Geneva, which he liked; later, when the Prince was at the château, Lanning increasingly stayed there. Throughout his visits in the later seventies, he and Prince Sadruddin built a friendship based on mutual affection and respect.

The planting for the *jardin potager* was lavish, and a splendid indulgence for Lanning the plantsman. His first lists were sent to Walter Brugger in the autumn of 1971, and planting was at its peak during 1972 and early 1973. Around the garden walls, peaches, apricots, apples, pears and cherries bought from Boccard Frères jostled with philadelphus, buddleias, daphnes, lilacs and forsythias sent from Hillier's in England. Lanning planned a '*bande des plantes vivaces*', a perennial border, of pinks, mauves, blues and white, for which the plan of the first version is illustrated here. Many of the plants for the Silver Walk, which sported santolina, *Thymus* 'Silver

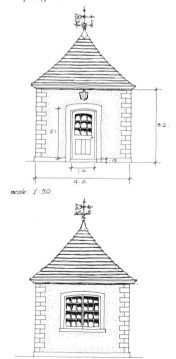

Above] The 'working' corner of the Bellerive *potager.*

183

Château de Bellerive:
'bandes des plantes vivaces'
(perennial borders) planned
by Lanning Roper, 1971.

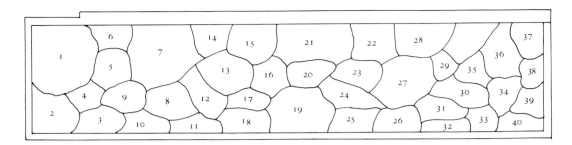

1   Box
2   *Lavandula nana atropurpurea*
3   Tulip 'Peach Blossom' and blue pansies
4   *Lilium regale*
5   Tulip 'Jewel of Spring' and blue myosotis
6   *Anemone hupehensis*
7   Rose 'Schneewittchen'
8   Achillea 'Moonshine'
9   *Salvia superba*
10 Agapanthus 'Headbourne Hybrids'
11 Helianthemum 'Wisley Primrose'
12 Tulip 'Purissima' and pink myosotis
13 Potentilla 'Vilmoriniana'
14 Lily 'Bright Star'
15 *Elaeagnus pungens* 'Maculata'
16 Tulip 'Ellen Willmott' and blue myosotis
17 Hemerocallis 'Chartreuse'
18 Tulip 'Garden Party' and pink myosotis
19 Rose 'The Fairy' and white myosotis
20 *Galtonia candicans*
21 *Senecio greyi*
22 Digitalis
23 *Ceratostigma willmottianum*
24 Hemerocallis 'First Formal'
25 *Santolina incana*
26 *Sedum spectabile*
27 Rose 'Schneewittchen Paquerette'
28 *Lavatera olbia* 'Rosea'
29 *Lilium regale*
30 Tulip 'Queen of Bartigons' and blue myosotis
31 Tulip 'Cordell Hull' and white myosotis

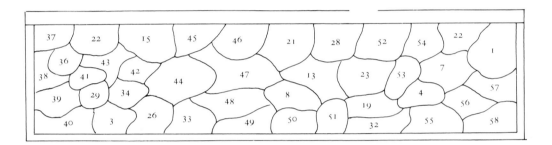

32 Helianthemum 'Wisley Pink'
33 *Ruta graveolens* 'Jackman's Blue'
34 Tulip 'China Pink' and blue myosotis
35 Artemisia 'Lambrook Silver'
36 Rose 'Blanc Double de Coubert' and *Thymus laniginosus*
37 *Rosmarinus officinalis*
38 Helianthemum 'The Bride'
39 Rose 'The Fairy' and blue myosotis
40 *Lavandula nana atropurpurea*
41 Tulip 'Lilac Perfection'
42 Hemerocallis 'Summer Chimes'
43 Ceanothus 'Topaz'
44 Rose 'Schneewitchen' and pink myosotis
45 White *Anemone japonica*
46 *Cytisus praecox*
47 *Eryngium tripartitum*
48 Hemerocallis 'White Jade'
49 Stachys 'Silver Carpet'
50 Tulip 'Palestrina' and blue pansies
51 Tulip 'Purissima' and blue pansies
52 Berberis 'Rose Glow'
53 Tulip 'Elizabeth Arden'
54 Lily 'Bright Star'
55 Tulip 'Cordell Hull' and white myosotis
56 Tulip 'Queen of Bartigons' and white myosotis
57 Hemerocallis 'Wonder Boy'
58 Lavender 'Vera'

Queen', dianthus, achilleas, eryngiums, nepetas and lavenders, came from Mrs Desmond Underwood at Chichester. Mrs Underwood's book, *Grey and Silver Plants*,[2] was published in the spring of 1971 and was received and reviewed by Lanning with great pleasure.

The cutting borders in the garden were filled with peonies, *Alstroemeria* 'Ligtu Hybrids', achilleas, campanulas, white daisies, foxgloves, crown imperials, eremurus, delphiniums, hemerocallis, sweet williams, scabious, Solomon's seal, solidago,

Opposite] Château de Bellerive: two views of Lanning's planting for the *potager* garden.

pyrethrums, gypsophila and sweet peas. Masses of tulips were planted everywhere for spring colour. The little herb beds were planted with parsleys, thymes, sages, origanum, hyssop, lavenders, balm and mints, and Lanning used standard gooseberries in the centre of each bed, though these eventually became unhappy and he suggested replacing them with *Hibiscus syriacus*, which he had noted in Paris parks. From the pictures of the *potager* it can be seen that roses were inserted at every opportunity, and so was clipped box. Lanning was amusingly avaricious about mature and healthy box – these plants were so essential to all his gardens and yet it took too much time for them to grow into soft clippable mounds, so on more than one occasion he was known to buy healthy specimens that caught his eye in a garden he was passing. Once, to the consternation of his companion, he negotiated for the resident box bushes while having a meal at a restaurant.

The final luxuriance of Bellerive's *potager* was in the greenhouse, which Lanning made great efforts to fill with a cavalcade of wonderful flowers which could also be used for the château – scented-leaved pelargoniums, cymbidiums, cypripediums, gloxinias, stephanotis, the delicious *Lippia citriodora*, tuberoses, nerines, poinsettias, *Rhododendron fragrantissima*, particularly 'Lady Alice', hippeastrums, narcissi, cinerarias, primulas and jasmines.

The *jardin potager* was Lanning's basic reason for going to Bellerive, but once the intensity of that work was over he could give his time to the rest of the garden. He slipped into a routine of visits and reports, ordering the clipping or replacing of the wisterias and hydrangeas around the château walls and of the trees that decorated the lawn. The chief glory of the garden is the view over Lake Geneva to the sunsets over the Jura, and in the careful manipulation of a view, of course, Lanning was well practised and excelled.

The Prince greatly appreciated Lanning's work at Bellerive. In December 1973 he wrote thanking him for his 'wonderful work' – and continued: 'You have performed miracles and everything you have done, particularly the walled garden, has made me much more attached to Bellerive and to nature in general.'[3] His appreciation and interest continued to grow; in April 1976 he and the Princess visited Charles de Noailles's garden at Grasse, which Lanning thought 'the prettiest garden' he had seen on the Riviera. The Prince was fired with enthusiasm and wondered if the orchid iris (*Iris fimbriata japonica*), *Melianthus major* and *Buddleia officinalis* would do well at Bellerive. Three years later he was still enjoying Bellerive's fruitfulness – the apricots, plums and peaches had been superb: ' . . . we will never be able to thank you enough for the garden'.[4]

Lanning's success at Bellerive ensured that further requests rained on him from the Prince and his family. He advised on planting for a town garden in the Rue Munier-Romilly in Geneva, and his work at Bellerive was extended when the Prince bought an adjacent estate, of which part was incorporated into the garden. However, pressure of work and a short stay in hospital made him reluctantly decide in June 1979 to withdraw from any real involvement with a project for a swimming pool and conservatory that the Prince wished to build, as he had also, reluctantly, two years earlier declined Prince Amyn Aga Khan's request for help with his garden in Paris.

For two years, from 1980 until he became too ill in 1982, he did work for the Aga

Khan at his new house, Aiglemont, at Gouvieux in France. This time he was working with an American landscape architect, Garr Campbell, who was then attached to the Aga Khan's Secretariat; even so, the size of this project, for the very large house and garden and a separate large park and garden area for the Secretariat, each with its own staff, was too much for what he knew to be his failing strength. This made him sad, for the opportunities were clearly wonderful. He listed the roses for a circular 'Rose Bowl' garden – massings of species (*R. rubrifolia,* the rugosas 'Blanc Double de Coubert' and 'Frau Dagmar Hastrup', *R. rubiginosa, R. canina, R. moyesii* and *R. paulii rosea*), modern shrubs ('Cerise Bouquet', 'Constance Spry', 'Fritz Nobis', 'Frühlingsgold', 'Max Graf', and 'Nevada'), hybrid musks ('Buff Beauty', 'Felicia' and 'Penelope'), old shrub roses ('Great Maiden's Blush', *R. centifolia* 'Cristata', 'Fantin Latour' and 'Chapeau de Napoléon', the gallicas 'Charles de Mills', 'Tuscany Superb' and 'Cardinal Richelieu'), and climbers ('New Dawn', 'Wedding Day', 'Félicité et Perpétué' and 'Adelaide d'Orléans' – these last four were always his favourites). The shrubs that kept the roses company were an equally lavish collection – deutzias, elaeagnus, hibiscus, hydrangeas, potentillas, philadelphus, rubus, spiraeas, and syringas in every variety; there was an accompanying list of trees, and he had the opportunity to include all the loveliest he knew: *Aesculus indica,* the Indian horse chestnut – 'a must', *Fraxinus ornus,* the flowering ash, golden catalpa, *Koelreuteria paniculata,* the 'Golden Rain Tree', *Laburnum vossii,* liquidamber, liriodendron, magnolias, paulownias, *Pyrus calleryana* 'Chanti-cleer', the Japanese cherries 'Ukon', 'Tai Haku' and 'Shimidsu Sakura', and sorbus galore – *cashmiriana,* 'Joseph Rock', *sargentiana, vilmorinii* and *hupehensis.* But wonderful as the ideas were, the reality proved too much, and Lanning despaired of the difficulties of managing so large an operation from so far away. I think most of his despair, which extended to a lack of confidence in both French nurseries and the gardening staff at Aiglemont, was a sad indication that this marvellous project had just come too late for him.

At home in London, Lanning's involvement in the Ismaeli Centre roof garden in the Cromwell Road came directly from his work for the Aga Khan and particularly from Prince Amyn, who was in overall charge of the project on behalf of his brother. The Ismaeli Centre is already a well-known London landmark on its island site opposite the Victoria and Albert Museum. It was designed and built by Casson, Conder & Partners, with Neville Conder and Kenneth Price as the partners in charge of the project. The building, of a design strongly reflecting Islamic traditions, has three floors, with most of the second floor taken up with a prayer hall able to accommodate over 1,000 people; above this, the top floor has meeting rooms, offices, and the roof garden. The roof garden design and implementation was the responsibility of Sasaki Associates of Watertown, Massachusetts, with Don Olsen as the partner in charge, but Casson, Conder & Partners retained some involvement as the architects for the building. Lanning became involved as planting consultant when Garr Campbell, now a firm friend, had to drop out because of ill health; the landscape contract would be in the hands of Craigwell Nurseries, the design and contracting company started by Charles Funke, who had already successfully taken over the control of Geoffrey Jellicoe's garden designed for Sutton Place in Surrey.

This weighty design team was concentrating on a very small garden, trapezium-

shaped, 50 feet wide and 55 feet deep at a maximum. After much referral to Sylvia Crowe, Sheila Haywood, and Susan Jellicoe's book *The Gardens of Mughal India*,[5] the garden materialized as a roof court, with a floor of patterned and polished granite paving surrounded by planters, and the traditional four rills, symbolizing the four great rivers of the world, crossing the paving in black marble channels. The mechanics of the water flow, between the four small fountain jets at the head of each rill and the central jet, had been solved by Guthrie Allesbrook before Lanning arrived. All that remained was the planting, but this was of course equally important and historically complex.

Throughout 1981 there were complicated changes of view about the planting. This time most of the people involved were working in a 'strange land'; the design implications (Don Olsen's priority) had to be balanced with the costs (Neville Conder's); the micro-climate of a roof in London, which though sheltered was on a

Opposite] The Ismaeli Centre: a small garden designed with tradition in mind. It is essentially a marble-floored court crossed by four water rills representing the rivers of the earth. Lanning joined the design team as planting consultant.
Above] Lanning's planting, amongst the towers of the Victoria and Albert Museum, photographed in 1985.

level with the dome of the Victoria and Albert Museum and the tops, the very tops of earth-bound plane trees was Lanning's concern, and the availability of plants – particularly such things as 'matched pairs' of gateway trees, for which cypresses, junipers, yews and bays were considered – was the province of Charles Funke. Over and beneath all was the Islamic tradition, lucidly and feelingly explored in a letter written by Prince Amyn, who had read Elizabeth Moynihan's *Paradise as a Garden*[6] and Vita Sackville-West on Persian gardens, and who summed up his preference for 'weepers, fruit trees, aromatic herbaceous plants, peonies, (lilies and irises) and bulbs or rhizomes that naturalize, with kalmia, choisya, skimmia and an abundance of roses . . . .'[7]

In the end Lanning wrote the specification for the planting conditions for most of the planting to take place in the autumn of 1982. *Laurus nobilis,* six and a half feet tall, was chosen for the 'gateway trees', to be underplanted with periwinkles and dwarf bulbs including *Cyclamen europaeum, C. neapolitanum* and *C. coum, Leucojum vernum,* dwarf narcissi, *Iris reticulata* and *I. histroides major.* Tulips, chionodoxas, scillas, anemones, hyacinths, more dwarf narcissi – including 'Tête à Tête', 'Beryl', 'Dove Wings', 'Silver Chimes' and 'Jenny' – with profusions of lilies, were to be planted beneath the choisyas, camellias, *Mahonia japonica,* jasmines and rosemary that made up the evergreen 'grove' planting of the garden. Summer colour would come from pots of scented-leaved pelargoniums, fuchsias, agapanthus, heliotropes, marguerites and geraniums with *Helichrysum petiolatum,* and *Cineraria maritima* with chrysanthemums for the autumn. Most of the plants came from a list of those mentioned in *The Gardens of Mughal India* and were thus appropriate; the only exclusions, for practical reasons, were the fruit trees, and about these (sadly) Prince Amyn did not have his way.

Lanning's last job for Prince Sadruddin, in the autumn of 1982, was to visit the estate in Virginia which he had bought as an American home. Lanning found it lovely – it was high in the Blue Ridge Mountains, and it pleased him that the Prince and Princess had found a home in his native land. He looked forward greatly to the kind of landscape work – the care and attention to existing trees and the disposition of new plantings – that he enjoyed most and found so rewarding. While he lay in hospital during the periods of treatment for his fatal cancer in that autumn, he occupied his mind with making lists of the trees and shrubs that would do well and happily in Virginia. But he did not live long enough to see them planted.

In happier times he had started work at Thenford House in Oxfordshire for Michael Heseltine, then Secretary of State for the Environment in Mrs Thatcher's government. Michael Heseltine, as it can be imagined, was another person who had very definite ideas about what he wanted to do, but needed Lanning's encouragement and technical knowledge to set it all in motion. He wanted to make a lake by damming a stream which fed a series of ponds that were not on his land. Lanning – on his first visit to the Heseltines in mid-July of 1977 – confirmed the siting of the lake, then recommended that Stephen Hawes of Aldeburgh (who had worked for Lord de Ramsey on the lake at Abbots Ripton in Huntingdonshire) should take on the project. This was done.

Lanning's concern was rather more with the immediate surroundings of the lovely

Georgian house, which was of perfect classical layout – with the drive entrance to a turning circle on the north front, and the terrace and view on the south front and more intensively gardened areas on either side. His report, submitted after his first visit, was, as usual, optimistic: 'Years of neglect have created various problems but these can be sorted out.' Lanning's role at Thenford, as it appears from the correspondence, became that of the cautionary, wise adviser; he went patiently around the estate marking up the good plants that were worth saving, even if they were moved elsewhere; he kept emphasizing that things that seemed minor, such as subtle changes of levels or regrading of levels, were actually vitally important; he repeatedly insisted that everything could be brought to nought by unsympathetic maintenance. He was privately worried that Thenford was also very cold – his experience at nearby Aynho for Lady Ward had warned him of this – and that the clay soil took a long time to warm up. Though rhododendrons were present and the Heseltines wanted a lot more, Lanning was concerned about the alkalinity of the clay; he suspected that it was variable and that the tests they had made were of limited value. He wanted to try some rhododendrons, camellias and heathers, but to see how they fared before ordering too many; the Heseltines clearly adored all these plants and wanted to order them *en masse*. Michael Heseltine didn't like box (Lanning's absolute favourite for eighteenth-century settings); and his enthusiasm led him to the delights of *Eucryphia milliganii*, *Phormium tenax variegata*, the tender New Zealand flax, and one of almost every interesting sounding and invariably tender tree in Hillier's catalogue. Lanning and his very old friend Harold Hillier had quiet talks, adjusted the tags on the planting stakes which marked where the trees were to go, and compromised as best they could. They were both old and wise enough to know that the pace of gardening and the pace of politics were rather like the tortoise and the hare.

At least Lanning had three years, 1978 to 1980, with only minor setbacks to his health, which gave him enough energy to enjoy the wonderful opportunities of Thenford House. He rationalized the immediate setting of the house by eliminating fussy bits of grass and using elegant, evergreen shrubs which were complementary to the colour of the stone. On the south front he made a border of the correct size to complement the scale of the house, with choisyas, cistus, daphnes, hebes and laurustinus to bolster up roses and hydrangeas. He made a hydrangea walk and revived the formal rose garden; he came up with ingenious mixtures of shrubs and old roses, with some clumps of essential perennials (achilleas, bergenias, *Campanula lactiflora*, *Dictamnus fraxinella*, euphorbias, hardy geraniums, penstemons, salvias, sedums and hostas), which made it possible to retain the old herbaceous borders long gone to seed. He advocated the planting of a shady grove to the west of the house, through which a path led to the church and the village, with exactly those 'flowery incidents' that Miss Jekyll wrote of: under the yews and hollies there were to be patches of polyanthus, foxgloves, columbines, ferns, variegated ivies, honesty and Solomon's seal, with sunny glades for martagon lilies and roses. *Rosa filipes* 'Kiftsgate', 'Rambling Rector', *R. longicuspis* and 'Wedding Day' were to climb into the trees, and *R. rubiginosa*, 'Lady Curzon', and *R. macrantha* to be used for covering stumps.

Out in the park there were the extensive landscape plantings that he loved. He realized the importance of screening, shelter and planting to harmonize with the surrounding landscape. The new lake, which had settled in well by the summer of 1980, had two islands, Anne's Island and Michael's Island. They were planted with their owner's choices – Anne's with red-stemmed cornus and weeping willow, poplar and sophora, Michael's with *Cornus alba sibirica*, *Spiraea* 'Anthony Waterer', alder and *Salix caprea* 'Kilmacurragh'.

Lanning found working with Michael Heseltine rewarding and exhilarating. They were action-packed days, and there was never time enough to talk through all the ideas and start everything moving in the right ways. Their relationship was strictly apropos gardening: on their working days they stopped only for lunch, and although the conversation might turn to politics, when Lanning was there Michael Heseltine was only too glad for his own passionate enjoyment of gardening to take priority. Compared to many of Lanning's more leisurely and complex gardening friendships, this one was exacting, exciting and perhaps astringent; it was, with hindsight, rather a pity that it did not occur just a few years earlier in his life.

From working for the person some tip as a future prime minister, there was only one way for Lanning to go, upwards – to work for the future King of England. In every way the commission to work for the Prince of Wales on his new home in Gloucestershire, which came Lanning's way in January 1981, was the high point of the achievements of his career.

Lanning's relations with the British Royal Family had always been good. His work was particularly admired by Queen Elizabeth the Queen Mother, from those early days when he was writing with such enthusiasm about the late King's gardens at Windsor. After that he met her fairly often, always at the Chelsea Flower Show and at the Garden Society, and frequently at the houses of friends. Also in those early days he had known many of the Princess Margaret set, and when she married the then Anthony Armstrong-Jones Lanning already knew him via his mother, the Countess of Rosse. Lanning remained friends with Lord Snowdon, and between 1978 and 1980 he helped with a green bower garden for his London home in Kensington. Lord Snowdon was quoted in *Vogue* as saying that asking Lanning to do such a small garden was 'like asking Capability Brown to come and do a window box'. It was a small undemanding commission which Lanning enjoyed completely, especially as Lord Snowdon's taste allowed him to indulge his own sense of theatre in a garden; there were some lovely pieces of statuary and ornament to be placed and surrounded with planting, and pretty 'regency' aspects to the building. Complete seclusion was necessary, and already existed from lime trees, which were clipped to make a tighter edging. Lanning surrounded the small lawn with mahonias, ferns and bergenias, with climbing hydrangeas, roses, honeysuckles, jasmines and wisterias on all the surrounding walls. Beneath these, the ground was carpeted with ivies, periwinkles, euonymus and St John's wort, which sprouted naturalized bulbs in spring – 'Nothing is prettier than a few Poet's Narcissus among periwinkle,' wrote Lanning. He was emphatic that in such a small and crowded garden the flowers should be of small scale, and he ordered small varieties of narcissi, *Iris histrioides*, chionodoxas, scillas and lily of the valley. There were to be pots of white flowers – marguerites, agapanthus, and

Lord Snowdon's green bower garden in Kensington, which Lanning enjoyed planting because he could indulge his own love of the 'theatre' in gardening.

Highgrove, Gloucestershire, at the time of its acquisition by HRH The Prince of Wales. Lanning gave advice in 1981 for the development of what he felt 'could be the most beautiful garden', but then regretfully had to withdraw because of ill health.

white hydrangeas for the summer. Everything grew very well and quickly, and the various ivies scrambled everywhere; on the days when the sun sparkled through the leaves in that special London way, it must have brought back to Lanning vivid memories of that other bower garden at Park House.

When the news broke that Lanning was to design Prince Charles's garden at Highgrove, he was surrounded with congratulations and good wishes. But it was to Camilla, wife of the Prince's friend Andrew Parker Bowles, that he wrote his thanks, for he knew that the combined good opinions of Clarence House and the Shand family had won the day (Camilla Parker Bowles is the daughter of Bruce and Rosalind Shand at The Laines). He found the Prince's first letter when he returned from a trip to America in early February 1981; Lanning immediately went down with an infection which confused his diary, and with a visit to Aiglemont pressing, it was not until May that he paid his first visit to Highgrove.

The house, as the Prince acquired it, seemed to have no garden at all, or at least nothing Lanning would call a garden. Farmland hustled the square Georgian stone house on two sides, there were extensive stables, a kitchen garden and the farmyard to the east of the house, and to the south was a large area of mown grass with some fine trees (one especially magnificent cedar) crossed by a straight gravel walk. Lanning's first impressions were recorded on 26 May 1981 in his report:

The site is a good one with some fine trees, which are a principal feature of the landscape. My instinct is to emphasize the feeling of informal parkland, altering fence lines, especially near the house, designating areas of mown lawn, rough mown grass and grazing areas, and planting forest trees of character both as additions and as feature replacements. Unfortunately the lie of the land is relatively flat with no glades or natural dells for variation, nor is there a stream or lake. It is possible that a water feature could be developed at a future date. Shrubberies and garden areas should be developed near the house and in the pool area. There will be a natural tendency to gravitate towards the stable and the pool complex. The pool in summer is to the garden what the fireplace is to the house in winter. We should anticipate the possible need for a tennis court; a croquet lawn presents no real problem.

His advice in this first report was very general: 'Go slowly and try to live in the house for a year, so as to see the landscape in all seasons before making major decisions.' He emphasized the practicalities – the number of gardeners that he thought would manage the garden well, the circumstances in which expert advice would have to be sought (for example, for tree surgery), and how it might be worthwhile to set up a plant nursery in one of the walled areas while the main planting was in progress.

He made a second visit in June, walking around for a day and a half with Tim Gray, the agent from the Prince's Duchy of Cornwall office in Bath. His recommendations were very definite – the lawn to the south of the house must be balanced up by being extended into the field, the central path and its golden yew blobs removed, trees and shrubs were to be cleared to make room for flower gardens between the south front and the swimming pool, the kitchen garden must be prepared to receive the many plants that were being offered as wedding presents and should eventually become a *jardin potager*.

By this time, of course, the wedding was less than a month away. Prince Charles was writing enthusiastically to Lanning about his willingness to accept 'the challenge' of his garden, and he had already taken some moments of relaxation to work there. Lanning in turn was inundated with requests for advice on 'garden' wedding presents, from family and friends, from the Althorp Estate staff, and from public establishments – the Borough of Torquay wanted to give a summerhouse, the City of Chester wondered what would be advisable. There were more meetings and letters; Lanning was concerned about the 'chain of command' and also that the vast amount of work by various contractors, for the stables and farm buildings and for the garden should somehow be co-ordinated. It was a great challenge, the greatest of his career. And sadly he was not up to it. Even before the wedding (to which he declined his invitation), Lanning wrote to the Prince's private secretary with his neurologist's report and opinion that he must do much, much less. He had written first of all to the Prince of Wales saying that he felt it would be unfair both to him and his new Princess, and to Highgrove, that he could not give what could be the most beautiful garden the attention it deserved. The Prince, who had already warmed to Lanning's enthusiasm and kindly wisdom, expressed his regret. The regrets were on both sides.

II

AT HOME

The garden of
29a Clarendon Gardens,
Lanning's home for nearly
twenty years.

THE LIST OF COMMISSIONS that follows this chapter records some 170 garden and landscape schemes, some very large and time-consuming, which Lanning worked on from about 1965 until his death in early 1983. The uncertainty in the starting date, 'about 1965', stems from my conclusion that he never had room to keep the papers from the time he was living and working at Park House. Some of his first jobs were probably never recorded in letters or reports, and the only evidence I really have for his work in the early sixties comes from the memories of those who worked with him and from a few, very few, sketchy scraps of paper. I am sure that there are other gardens that I have not recorded. However, 170 schemes in virtually eighteen years, far more than could be squeezed into this book, is a considerable achievement.

It was during 1965 that Lanning had to come to terms with his separation from Primrose, and I feel he decided that work would take her place. It was in keeping with his nature that he would have rather a romantic image of womankind, but not really understand the more talented and spirited of them. In Primrose he had found his romantic dreams fulfilled; she was the beautiful, cultivated, artistic and amusing companion that he expected her to be. His days were filled with her aura as well as the making of his career, which meant trying conscientiously to fulfil the demands of some very demanding people. That they were not always Primrose's kind of people would not have mattered in many marriages, because they would have been confined to office life. But, as Lanning's schedules became busier, so his time, in and out of office hours, was filled for months in advance, and there was little room left for the spontaneous gatherings of friends that she loved. After careful deliberation, I feel this must have been a major reason for the breakdown of their marriage.

But, of course, it is impossible for me really to know; I can only listen to the memories of their friends. Without exception Lanning's friends recall his shock at the departure of Primrose. She actually packed and left their Trebeck Street flat while he was away working, with no warning, and her letter of explanation was mislaid. But Primrose's friends only wonder that he did not see it coming.

For Lanning, it was unlikely that there was ever any idea of replacing Primrose; perhaps he hoped it was all a bad dream and that one day they would be together again. When he did accept it, neither his pride nor the mores of his New England inheritance made the idea of another marriage likely. It also has to be remembered that he was a stranger in a strange land; English eccentricity sometimes perplexed him, and being a guest of perfect manners and an unselfishness that was sometimes self-effacement, he would choose silence or a joke rather than press for explanations.

For him, life in England, doing what he wanted, always retained a dream-like quality. For a moment the dream was shattered, but it could and would be rebuilt. Remember all those generations of survivors behind him – who had often survived in spite of the English. That must have counted for something. The garden flat in Clarendon Gardens that he found for himself in late 1964 was his retreat for quiet, reflective moments; it was compact and self-contained, but it was mostly literally a *pied-à-terre* between France and America or Sussex and Scotland. It was not large enough for another person with any degree of comfort, but he would share it unreservedly (which meant, for him, sleeping on the sofa) when the need arose, as when his brother and sister-in-law, Crosby and Laura, were in London on holiday. The paradox to this expression of his private self was that he longed for glamorous company, amusing and artistic company, and a certain elegance and expansiveness of lifestyle. It was his work that provided this.

He continued to see Primrose over the years, though she lived in France during the winter. She died in April 1978 and is buried at Walton with her parents and her sister. A close friend, Freda Berkeley, arranged a memorial service for her in St Mary's Church, on Paddington Green. Lanning was very grateful for this because by this time he had returned to church-going and become very much a part of the St Mary's community.

His flat at 29a Clarendon Gardens was rented on short renewable leases from the Maida Vale Estate of the Church Commissioners, beginning in January 1965. He had a sitting- and dining-room, with a small kitchen, and his 'office' was on a higher level with the bedrooms, one for himself and a minute spare room which could take only a single bed and a mirror. From the sitting-room, French windows opened into an area and steps led up to a small garden. Lanning had both the area and much of the garden paved when he moved in, and both were almost always filled with pots of colourful and scented flowers. The garden was also a staging-post for boxes of seedlings or cuttings *en route* from one of his gardens to another.

Before he moved in he had the flat completely repainted and wallpapered, for the princely sum, in labour terms, of £118. Betty Hussey introduced him to her decorator friend, Merlin Pennink, who then had a shop in The Pantiles in Tunbridge Wells. Merlin found the wallpaper and fabrics and made the curtains and covers for him, but the choice was entirely Lanning's; he chose Cole's dragged blue Jaspé wallpaper, with blue linen curtains trimmed with orange braid, for his sitting-room. There were comfortable chairs and a sofa in a William Morris print in blue and orange, and natural corded carpet was scattered with needlework rugs, some old, some bought from Merlin. He had some small pieces of antique furniture and lots of pretty china, and, always, pots of flowers. The whole effect was of an English country sitting-room.

The atmosphere was completed by his books and pictures. If he had ever had the room he could easily have become a collector of books with botanical illustrations for these fascinated him. He did own Miss Willmott's *Warley Garden in Spring and Summer* (1909), number 778 of the edition of 1,000 of Sir George Sitwell's *On the Making of Gardens*, illustrated by John Piper, and R. Thompson's *The Gardener's Assistant* (1859), with hand-coloured plates. And there were many books by his

29a Clarendon Gardens:
two details of Lanning's
own garden.
Above] Pots outside the
French windows.
Below] Spring in the tiny
border.

friends, Christopher Hussey, Sylvia Crowe, Geoffrey Jellicoe, Patrick Synge, Christopher Lloyd and Wilfred Blunt, and by and about an absent 'friend', Gertrude Jekyll.

Except for the *Temple of Flora* plates, from which he was never parted, his pictures were mostly small, and they too were either by his friends or had special associations. There was a watercolour of mountains in France and another of children in a poppyfield by Bridget 'Biddy' Hubbard, little views of Venice by Lavinia Smiley, Scotney Castle by Primrose, the courtyard at Park House by Adrian Daintry, a small still life by Mary Cohen, gardening tools by John Ward, some small pastels by Wilson Steer, and a wonderfully cheerful John Nash print of a woman with a cat and red geraniums. There was also the pencil sketch of Lanning as a young man by Henry Lamb which appears as the frontispiece of this book; it was one of a pair, the other being of Primrose, which the artist gave them as wedding presents.

Lanning's home life was brief, but stylish. That is to say, he gave himself few evenings quietly at home – he was a member of the Garrick Club, there was the Garden Club and other Royal Horticultural Society committees, events and lectures, and a constant stream of friends from abroad in passage through London, as well as the dinner parties of friends. He loved, though, to return the hospitality with his own small dinners, for which he would get up at dawn and shop and prepare, do his day's work, then act as cook and host with consummate ease. On some occasions Biddy Hubbard helped him. He loved simple food, but that too had style. He could have written a useful cookery book for a busy person's entertaining, for his was almost a 'minimalist' approach, which depended first on simple cuts of the finest quality meat or fish and then on a gardener's knowledge of the advantages of the seasons. He took part in a series of Radio 3 talks produced by Pamela Howe in which he described July's assets: the thinnings from a row of beetroot, leaves, stalks and baby beets, lightly cooked, chopped and served with butter and black pepper; a soup made of young whole peas, boiled in chicken stock with mint, onion and parsley, sieved and thickened with a roux, thinned with milk, and served hot or cold; and baby broad beans, served hot with butter and a liberal sprinkling of crispy bacon pieces and a dusting of fine thyme. He loved globe artichokes, boiled and served cold with vinaigrette sauce, celeriac shredded raw with a highly flavoured mayonnaise, Swiss chard boiled and served with white sauce; he used sorrel as a substitute for spinach, especially the two mixed as a purée base for poached eggs. Alpine strawberries, which he had been planting in gardens for years for the value of their heavily serrated leaves had, he felt, no peer for their flavour, especially the fruits of 'Baron Solemacher' and 'White Pine'; he would serve them with lemon and orange juice, 'cream was a mistake'.

Lanning's delicious offerings were often written down for his friends, and he gave this recipe for kipper pâté to Jill Griffin:

Take two large packets of frozen kippers and cook as directed. Pour juice and skinned fish into a liquidizer, and when the mixture cools work in 8–10 ounces of unsalted butter and lots of freshly ground black pepper, the juice of half a lemon and garlic to taste. Pack into a terrine and chill. It is best taken out well before being served with toast or biscuits.

I have found the following recipe, for asparagus soufflé, among Lanning's papers:

Drain two tins of Epicure Green Asparagus, saving the liquid. Boil the liquid, reserving a little, with one chicken stock cube. Remove from the heat and add one tablespoonful of powdered gelatine dissolved in cold water, stir thoroughly and put to cool. Put the asparagus into the liquidizer with a little liquid, reduce to a purée, and stir into the warm gelatine mixture. When it is beginning to thicken add a great deal of freshly ground pepper, a generous half pint of whipped double cream and fold in three stiffly beaten egg whites. Chill for at least eight hours. This makes a creamy soufflé; if you want it stiffer, or have to use it quickly, use more gelatine.

He would buy the flowers for his parties with the same care as the fruits and vegetables, and his skill at putting them into a vase was totally natural. He liked mixed spring flowers in pale colours, but tulips in rich riot, especially shaggy and striped parrots and the shaggy peony varieties. It amused him to emulate the *Temple of Flora* plates, with lilies, orange or white, not mixed, a posy of auriculas if he could possibly find them, or orange nasturtiums tumbling and trailing over a small polished table. But he also liked simpler and wilder flowers, and a cloud of white daisies or cow parsley, gathered from a road verge on the way home, would often greet his guests. On one occasion, in July 1980, he 'arranged' the whole garden at Argyll House in Chelsea for a Normanby family party, with masses of potted and tubbed white marguerites, nicotianas and petunias, and sixty old wine bottles holding *Lilium candidum* and cream and pale lavender delphinium spires buried in the shrub borders. As the dusk gathered and the floodlights made the flowers gleam, the effect was stunning.

Lanning's home was also his workplace. He finished off *The Sunday Times Gardening Book* there, and it was published in 1967.[1] He treasured H. E. Bates's review of it, which appreciated Lanning's feeling for the 'theatre' of gardening. It was his last book, there not being really the room nor the time to write another one. He did ask Harry Smith and Ernest Crowson to take photographs of many London gardens, both those of his friends and those he had worked on, for a projected book on town gardens, but this never materialized. I think this may have been because Susan Jellicoe and Marjory Allen's *Town Gardens to Live In* appeared in 1977.[2] The same fate had probably befallen his earlier project, planned with Barbie Agar, for a book on cottage gardens: Margery Fish's *Cottage Garden Flowers* was published in 1961,[3] while Lanning was still gathering pictures for his project.

So in later years he was a gardening journalist, sitting down to his typewriter for his weekly *Sunday Times* piece; he wrote over 600 altogether, and the last one was published on 21 March 1976. His column was at its best in the years 1965 to 1968, when he wrote with enthusiasm and plenty of literary and travel allusions about his favourite flowers and vegetables; his coverage was very wide, with his annual Chelsea Flower Show highlights published most usefully the Sunday *before* the show. He was on the RHS show committee and therefore had the advantage of his fellows. And in December 1968 he gave high praise to the newly published *Pulbrook & Gould Flower Book*,[4] from his favourite London florist. From 1969 he shared the column, with Brian Walkden doing the more practical side, but even so, during the seventies Lanning's pieces became rather prosaic. There were long series on the basic practices of vegetable growing; though he was wholly practical, Lanning's gardening

somehow never went with diagrams of boots on spades. He was much more at home when he could be inspirational, with illustrations by Eliot Hodgkin, whose 'July fruits' and auriculas were used as part of a lovely series on his favourite plants that Lanning did for *The Sunday Times Colour Magazine* in late 1969. As usual, his favourites were lilacs, 'The Fickle Lily',[5] tulips, magnolias, peonies and old roses. I think these were really his deepest loves.

But in 1974 he did write of other plants, having been asked to name those that he felt were 'his signature tune'. He named *Mahonia japonica* and *M. bealei*, the skimmias – *S. japonica*, *S. j.* 'Foremanii', *S. j.* 'Nymans' and *S. j. repens* 'Rogersii', *Viburnum tinus* and *V. farreri*, *Prunus subhirtella autumnalis*, *Cotoneaster horizontalis*, *Iris unguicularis* (that horrid name newly given to lovely *I. stylosa*), and jasmine.[6]

Lanning always continued to write for *Country Life*, though he gave up his earlier philosophical pieces on 'architecture', 'mystery', 'colour', and 'tidiness' to concentrate on descriptions of gardens, and shared the magazine's coverage with Tony

Venison, the gardening editor, and Arthur Hellyer. Lanning wrote only about gardens he knew really well; these were not always gardens he had worked on, but they were always gardens he admired. His last published piece, I think, was about Merlin Pennink's garden around her weatherboarded Wealden farmhouse near Tunbridge Wells, published on 20 December 1982. They had discussed gardening as a result of planning the decorations for his flat together, and her lovely garden was the result.

When Lanning was not sitting at the typewriter, the seat was occupied by his devoted secretary Anne Terry, who worked for him for the last eighteen years of his life. She went in every morning in the week to deal with his post, so she was always aware of his comings and goings, of problems when they arose and when he would be able to deal with them. Often he dashed in from Heathrow, hastily dictated reports, replies and plant orders, and left her to continue after he had dashed out again. She is the gentlest and calmest of persons; I don't imagine that she could or would have raised her voice in irritation or panic, however irate and impatient the client, and she was the rock of Lanning's work organization.

Anne Terry also sent out Lanning's accounts. He was never, nor did he want to be, a very rich man and he really disliked dealing with money. In 1977 he quoted his fees as £120 per day, with travelling at 'the old AA rate' of 10p per mile, and £15 an hour for work done on the client's behalf in his own office, ordering plants and writing instructions. I think these were his top rates. In the sixties he had charged £40 a day for working in a garden, and this rose to £80–90 in the early seventies; for a long time he retained his National Trust rate at £50 a day. In his will he distributed his precious pictures and other gifts among his friends, and left the residue of his estate, as he had long intended, towards the upkeep of the garden at Scotney Castle.

A little information on the nurseries he used is scattered throughout the book, but it may be interesting to sum up. He was extremely loyal to his business associates, but meticulous in maintaining his independence and right to complain by never taking any commissions. Over long years he asked advice and discussed trees and shrubs with Harold Hillier, and Hillier's were his main source for trees. He also bought shrubs from Scott's of Merriott, whom he admired, Notcutt's at Woodbridge and Bloom's of Bressingham. He used all three for herbaceous plants as well. If he wanted something rare or special in the rhododendron line he asked John Bond at Windsor Great Park; his good relationship there was maintained after Sir Eric Savill's time, through Hope Findlay to John Bond. For roses he usually recommended John Mattock at Oxford or Murrell's Portland Nursery at Shrewsbury; for an older or rarer rose, for Sonia Cubitt for instance, he would try Peter Beales or David Austin, the old rose specialists. He ordered bulbs from Walter Blom or de Jager. He also worked very hard at keeping good strains or varieties in 'his' gardens, and always kept his eyes open for surplus seedlings or cuttings from one garden that would suit another. For years he bought herbaceous plants and seedlings from Peggy Munster at Bampton Manor, and from Bob Poland's nursery at Ardingly. Though orders went out for new and striking flowers after many a Chelsea Flower Show that his clients had visited, these nurseries were his standbys and regular suppliers.

Throughout the years Lanning did employ assistants in various capacities; in the

Left and opposite] Lower Hall, Worfield, one of Lanning's last gardens, where he was delighted to be the 'Christmas present' that Christopher and Donna Dumbell gave to each other.

early days he often needed someone to draw for him, and he liked to give work to or advise anyone who wanted to follow in his footsteps. In his later years he was glad to hand over the physical work and garden maintenance to a younger person, and he was particularly happy with the work of a young New Zealander, Christopher Masson, who continues to look after several of Lanning's London gardens in just the way he would have wished. Basically, though, Lanning always prized his independence; he did not want anyone dependent upon him, becuase he would have been less free to choose the work he did or did not do. I suppose it was the clients who counted, rather than the gardens; there was one gentleman, who shall be nameless, whom he politely refused year after year – on the other hand, there is the delightful story told by Donna Dumbell in her letter to me.[7] She had heard Lanning lecture at the RHS and had gone home, to Lower Hall, Worfield, in Shropshire, singing his praises to her husband, Christopher: 'the upshot was that we decided to give Lanning to each other for Christmas, and he was so delighted to be a Christmas present, that he accepted what for him must have been a very small commission'. His influence on the Dumbells' garden in Shropshire is illustrated here, and he wrote about it in *Country Life*.[8]

He hated it to be thought that he only did grand gardens, and Lower Hall, Worfield, is a case in point. He loved to give advice where he felt really useful, and I think it was a fault of the system that he does not have a string of welfare housing and hospital projects to his credit. These things rarely go to those who care, and are seldom unleashed from the tentacles of local authorities unless it is to huge multi-disciplinary practices. The current spate of private health sector building might have brought him more 'useful' opportunities, for where he felt it was necessary he was glad to work and give of his valuable time for little or no fee. I believe he advised on a scheme for the King Edward VII Hospital for Officers, and he certainly advised on the Clement Attlee Memorial at Toynbee Hall in East London.

I know more details of two other schemes. He planned a roof garden for Margaret Pyke House, the Family Planning Association's headquarters in Mortimer Street, and this garden was finished in 1974. It was in memory of a particular friend, Mrs William Mure, 'Parsley' to her friends, who was a great gardener and whose garden in Selwood Place he much admired and had had photographed for his projected town gardens book.

The second project was also close to his heart, for it was for Lisa Sainsbury, whose Sainsbury Family Charitable Trust had donated a considerable sum towards the refurbishment of the Hostel of God, now known as Trinity Hospice, on Clapham Common. Lanning first looked at the garden – or rather the combined gardens of two houses on Clapham Common Northside, in February 1980. They were very dilapidated as gardens, but there were some good trees – a catalpa, a mulberry, a weeping ash, planes and a cedar. His first care was for the trees which needed attention, and he arranged this; a purple beech which had to be felled was replaced by one planted by HM Queen Elizabeth the Queen Mother, Patron of the Hospice, in 1981. The work on the gardens was then delayed while alterations were made to the buildings, and Lanning never had the chance to do much more.

His illness finally caught up with him in the autumn of 1982. He became very weak from periods of intensive radiotherapy treatment, and by the New Year of 1983 he was confined to the Lindo Wing of St Mary's Hospital, Paddington. From there he kept up his battle, sending flurries of letters in thanks for flowers and visits which still contained garden instructions. Even when very weak he discussed the progress on the Ismaeli Roof Garden with Charles Funke, and he gained much pleasure and comfort from a book on the mysteries of Persian gardens which Prince Sadruddin sent to amuse him. But most of the time he was too weak to do anything but muse on and remember his gardens in his mind's eye; he thought of 'the beauties of Bellerive', of the gardens he had seen in Persia on a memorable visit with the de Ramseys, of his days planting roses with Freya Stark in her garden at Montoria. His thoughts seem to wander far away, and for a great deal of the time they wandered home. He planned lists of trees for Prince Sadruddin at Woodlawn, and he thought of the old garden at Mirador, not far away in Greenwood, Virginia, the home of James and Jeannie Scott, which he had visited the previous autumn. By a strange turn of fate this was the garden that Nancy Lancaster, then married to Ronald Tree, had made in the 1920s, and the Scotts wanted Lanning's help with its restoration. He had helped with the Trees' famous Ditchley Park, and then he had advised and encouraged Nancy Lancaster at Haseley; what was more natural than that with memories of her to inspire him he should enjoy the restoration of Mirador? Perhaps he knew it would never be, for he wrote the Scotts a long report, three times longer than any of his usual reports, setting out the choices for Mirador's future in the greatest detail.

I think it best to leave him with his own memories of home. Just before his last Christmas, he had been looked after at Buckhurst Park, Peter Palumbo's country

206

home, where he had started working on the garden over fifteen years earlier. He had been able to consider the planting of a woodland walk at the Farnsworth House, and he sent a long list with his ideas to Mrs Lilian Cannon, a friend in Chicago, who would take charge of the planting. Part of his accompanying letter, dated 24 November 1982, reads:

> The Blue Ridge Gardens catalogue has arrived and I am thrilled with it. It takes me back to my boyhood on the Palisades above the Hudson River where there were miles of woodland to roam, and I knew where hepaticas, Dutchman's Breeches, alpine columbines, Lady's Slipper, trailing arbutus and all the other wonderful wild flowers grew ... I have listed the plants I would like to use ... but I am a little confused on violets. I have marked *rotundifolia* and *cuculata*. We used to have enormous white ones, I think called the Confederate Violet, and another one called *septentrionalis* but I don't seem to find them listed. Another wonderful plant of my youth, which I adored, was *Asclepias tuberosa*. This is a wonderful orange, with flowers like milkweed. I always found it very difficult to transplant as a child and I was seldom successful .... Calycanthus I would like to grow. When I was a little boy I always took one of the flowers tied in the corner of my handkerchief to get me through the long church service on Sunday mornings ....

The memorial service for Lanning was held at St Mary's Church on Paddington Green on Thursday, 21 April 1983. The church was crowded, with a very English congregation, who heard the music of Handel and Orlando Gibbons and the comforting, quiet words of Bunyan, Donne and Cardinal Newman. But they sang 'The Battle Hymn of the Republic'.

And the gardener who had no real garden of his own now finds himself with three. The garden at the Trinity Hospice is finished and flowers because of the donations of his friends; it has been named the Lanning Roper Memorial Garden, and it will be regularly open each summer for the National Gardens Scheme. The woodland walk at the Farnsworth House now bears Lanning's name; and at Scotney Castle a streamside walk to a chalybeate spring has been added to the garden for Lanning, at the request of Mrs Hussey and with the help of the eminent landscape architect Dame Sylvia Crowe.

Trinity Hospice, Clapham, London: a corner of the Lanning Roper Memorial Garden.

209

NOTES

INTRODUCTION

1. Lanning Roper, 'Landscape Design', lecture to the Royal Horticultural Society, 24 September 1968.

1 BEGINNINGS

1. Laura Wood Roper, *FLO, A Biography of Frederick Law Olmsted*, Johns Hopkins University Press, 1973, p. 67.
2. ibid., p. 68, quoting F.L.Olmsted, *Walks and Talks*, I, p. 99.
3. ibid., p. 68.
4. Unfortunately, father proved right: Hartwell became involved with a strict religious sect and was estranged from his family. He died in January 1954, aged forty-seven.
5. Lanning Roper, notes in Roper Papers, Royal Horticultural Society, Lindley Library.
6. Citation for award of Gold Star in lieu of a second Bronze Star medal to Lieutenant Lanning Roper U.S.N.R., signed by Admiral H.K.Hewitt, commander 12th Fleet; copy in Roper Papers, loc. cit. See also Samuel Eliot Morison, *The Invasion of France and Germany 1944–45*, Vol. XI of *The History of the U.S. Naval Operations in World War 2*, Oxford University Press, 1957, including illustration of Lanning's old command 412 landing troops, facing p. 149.
7. Nevil Shute, *Requiem for a Wren*, Heinemann, 1955, pp. 82–3.

2 ENGLISH ATTACHMENTS

1. Margery Fish, *We Made a Garden*, Collingridge and Transatlantic Arts, London and New York, 1956.
2. Obituary of Margery Fish by Lanning Roper, *The Times*, 28 March 1969.
3. Lanning Roper, 'Superb Planning at Tintinhull', *Gardening Illustrated*, January 1951.
4. Lanning Roper, 'A Romantic West Country Garden', *Country Life*, 7 April 1960.
5. Calum MacRitchie, letter to author, 6 March 1986.
6. Lanning Roper, 'Exotic Plants in a Scottish Garden', *Gardening Illustrated*, January 1952.
7. ibid.
8. Lanning Roper, 'A Garden for Reflection', *Gardening Illustrated*, November 1953.

9. Lanning Roper, 'Spring in Cornish Gardens', *Gardening Illustrated*, June 1950.
10. Lanning Roper, 'Colour in Garden and Landscape', *Country Life*, 29 October 1953.
11. ibid.
12. Lanning Roper, 'Problems of Garden Ornament', *Country Life*, 6 May 1954.
13. Lanning Roper, 'The One-colour Garden', *Country Life*, 28 July 1955.
14. Lanning Roper 'Mystery in Garden Design', *Country Life Annual*, 1959.
15. Lanning Roper, 'What Makes a Good Garden?', *Country Life*, 10 December 1953.
16. Lanning Roper, *Royal Gardens*, Collingridge and Transatlantic Arts, London and New York, 1953.

3 PRIMROSE

1. Lanning Roper, 'Favourite Flowers Revalued', *Country Life*, 9 April 1959.
2. Lanning Roper, 'The Delight of Foliage', *Country Life*, 11 November 1954.
3. Lanning Roper, 'Green Flowers Old and New', *Country Life*, 6 January 1955.
4. See Wilfred Blunt, *The Art of Botanical Illustration*, New Naturalist Series, Collins, 1950.
5. ibid.
6. ibid.
7. Lanning Roper, 'Madeira: Island of Crafts and Flowers', *Country Life*, 3 November 1960.
8. Lanning Roper, *Successful Town Gardening*, Country Life, 1957.

4 EARLY GARDENS

1. David Green, *Gardener to Queen Anne*, Oxford University Press, 1956.
2. Lanning Roper, *The Gardens in the Royal Park at Windsor*, Chatto & Windus, 1959, p. 80.
3. ibid., p. 81.
4. Norah Bourke married Lieutenant-Colonel Harry Lindsay in 1895 and made a wonderful garden at the Manor House, Sutton Courtenay. She was the aunt of another of Lanning's close friends, Humphrey Whitbread.
5. Lanning Roper, 'In the Cottage Garden Tradition', *Country Life*, 2 December 1976.
6. Lanning Roper, 'Landscape Design', lecture to the Royal Horticultural Society, 24 September 1968.

7. John Martin Robinson, *The Latest Country Houses, 1945–83*, Bodley Head, 1984.
8. Lanning Roper, 'Going to Town with Plants', *Country Life*, 15 November 1979.
9. John Fowler (1906–77), decorator and arbiter of taste, partner in Colefax & Fowler, who restored many eighteenth-century houses for the National Trust.
10. Lanning Roper, 'A Plea for the Unmown Lawn', *Country Life Annual*, 1958.
11. Lanning Roper, 'Can a Garden be too Tidy?', *Country Life*, 7 May 1959.
12. Lanning Roper, 'Skilful Planting in a Berkshire Garden', *Country Life*, 15 September 1960.
13. John Cornforth, *The Inspiration of the Past*, Viking, 1985.
14. ibid., p. 151.
15. Lanning Roper, 'Off-white Magic', *The Sunday Times*, 7 June 1970.

5 IRELAND

1. Lanning Roper, letter to Michael Downing, Roper Papers, Royal Horticultural Society, Lindley Library.

6 AMERICAN ALLEGIANCES

1. Laura Wood Roper, *FLO, A Biography of Frederick Law Olmsted*, Johns Hopkins University Press, 1973, p. xiii.
2. Lanning Roper, 'Perfection in Detail: The Garden of Dumbarton Oaks, Washington D.C.', *Country Life*, 3/10 January 1974.
3. Robert W. Patterson, 'Beatrix Farrand 1872–1959: An Appreciation of a Great Landscape Gardener', *Landscape Architecture*, Summer 1959.
4. Eleanor McPeck in Diana Balmori, Diane Kostial McGuire and Eleanor M. McPeck, *Beatrix Farrand's American Landscapes*, Sagapress, New York, 1985, p. 61.
5. Diane Kostial McGuire in ibid., p. 2.
6. Lanning Roper, 'The Making of a Great Garden', *Country Life*, 6 July 1972.
7. See Michael Straight, *After Long Silence*, Collins, 1983.
8. Lanning Roper, 'American Shrubs in Britain', *Country Life*, 26 April 1979.
9. Lanning Roper, 'American Wild Flowers for British Gardens', *Country Life*, 19 May 1955.
10. Lanning Roper, 'Sculpture in a Broad Landscape', *Country Life*, 21 April 1977.
11. George Cecil, letter to the author, 9 December 1985.
12. Anne Sidamon-Eristoff, notes in Roper Papers, Royal Horticultural Society, Lindley Library.
13. Lanning Roper, report on Ananouri, 23 July 1976, in Roper Papers, loc. cit.
14. Lanning Roper, *The Sunday Times Gardening Book*, Thomas Nelson, 1968.

7 GEORGIAN GARDENER

1. Lanning Roper, 'The Future of Great Gardens', *Country Life*, 1 June 1967.
2. *The Times*, 29 September 1977.
3. John Cornforth, *The Inspiration of the Past*, Viking, 1985, p. 132.
4. Lanning Roper, report on Ickworth, 21 July 1970, Roper Papers, Royal Horticultural Society, Lindley Library.
5. Lanning Roper, 'A Garden of Vistas, Folly Farm', *Country Life*, 15 May 1975.
6. Lanning Roper, *The Gardens of Anglesey Abbey*, Faber & Faber, 1964.
7. Merlin Waterson, letter to Lanning Roper, 8 November 1982, Roper Papers, loc. cit.
8. Lanning Roper, 'The Future of Great Gardens', *Country Life*, 1 June 1967.
9. Notes for National Trust guide, *c.*1979, Roper Papers, loc. cit.
10. Lanning Roper, report on Scotney Castle, 23 July 1979, Roper Papers, loc. cit.
11. Lanning Roper, report on Scotney Castle, 20 June 1980, Roper Papers, loc. cit.
12. Lanning Roper, report on Scotney Castle, 19 July 1982, Roper Papers, loc. cit.

8 SETTINGS FOR MODERN BUILDINGS

1. Ada Louise Huxtable, *New York Times*, 2 February 1966.
2. ibid.
3. William S. Paley, statement on Paley Park in Roper Papers, Royal Horticultural Society, Lindley Library.
4. Lanning Roper, report on St Pancras churchyard, 8 July 1975, Roper Papers, loc. cit.
5. Lanning Roper, letter to Peter Palumbo, 19 May 1978, Roper papers, loc. cit.
6. Ada Louise Huxtable, 'The Making of a Master', *New York Times Book Review*, 1 December 1985
7. Lanning Roper, letter to *Country Life*, dated 29 March 1982, Roper Papers, loc. cit.
8. Colin Amery, 'Architecture at Work', Award brochure, *Financial Times*, 1982.
9. *Architects' Journal*, 5 April 1978.
10. Foster Associates, letter to Lanning Roper, 27 June 1977, Roper Papers, loc. cit.

9 FIVE GARDENS

1. Sonia Cubitt, *Edwardian Daughter*, Hamish Hamilton, 1958.
2. Lanning Roper, 'Gardens by a Hampshire River', *Country Life*, 5 September 1974.
3. Lanning Roper, 'Suncatcher below the Sussex Downs', *Country Life*, 23 September 1982.
4. Lanning Roper, 'A Sussex Vicarage with a View', *Country Life*, 25 September 1975.
5. Lanning Roper, 'A Coastal Garden of Contrasts', *Country Life*, 7 April 1977.

10 GARDENER *BY APPOINTMENT*

1. Lanning Roper, letter to Prince Sadruddin Aga Khan, 20 October 1969, Roper Papers, Royal Horticultural Society, Lindley Library.
2. Mrs Desmond Underwood, *Grey and Silver Plants*, 1971.
3. Prince Sadruddin Aga Khan, letter to Lanning Roper, 17 December 1973, Roper Papers, loc. cit.
4. Prince Sadruddin Aga Khan, letter to Lanning Roper, 5 August 1979, Roper Papers, loc. cit.
5. Sylvia Crowe, Sheila Haywood, Susan Jellicoe, *The Gardens of Mughal India*, Thames and Hudson, 1972.
6. Elizabeth Moynihan, *Paradise as a Garden*, George Braziller, New York, 1979.
7. Prince Amyn Aga Khan, letter to Neville Conder, 18 May 1981, Roper Papers, loc. cit.

11 AT HOME

1. Lanning Roper, *The Sunday Times Gardening Book*, Thomas Nelson, 1967.
2. Susan Jellicoe and Marjory Allen, *Town Gardens to Live In*, Penguin, 1977.
3. Margery Fish, *Cottage Garden Flowers*, Collingridge and Transatlantic Art, London and New York 1961.
4. *The Pulbrook & Gould Flower Book*, 1968.
5. Lanning Roper, 'The Fickle Lily', *The Sunday Times Colour Magazine*, 2 November 1969.
6. Lanning Roper, *The Sunday Times*, 15 December 1974.
7. Donna Dumbell, letter to the author, 12 June 1986.
8. Lanning Roper, 'A River Site Transformed', *Country Life*, 3 March 1977.

LIST OF COMMISSIONS

This list of Lanning Roper's gardens is compiled from surviving correspondence (the Lanning Roper Papers, now in the Royal Horticultural Society's Lindley Library) and with additional information from the memories of his clients and friends.

The list requires a word of explanation. The names in brackets after the name of the house indicate Lanning's clients, though in many cases they are no longer the owners. The words 'garden design' and 'planting design' are self-explanatory and are used to indicate a short-term commission. Lanning's preferred way of working was to tend 'his gardens' over a period of years, and I have adopted the word 'advice' to describe this. 'Garden advice' means that he oversaw a substantial rearrangement of the garden, or part of it; 'planting advice' means that he mainly adjusted and carried out progressive changes in planting only. In the places where he was mainly the planting consultant I have named the architect or other designer who may have been involved. But the situations were infinitely variable, as my book explains, and this list can only give a brief guide, though it does help in assessing his work. An asterisk ★ beside the name of the garden indicates that there is a file of correspondence in the Lindley Library; CL indicates that Lanning wrote an article in *Country Life* about the garden, and these can be found by referring to the published index of names of houses and gardens; n.d. indicates that the date of the work is unknown.

ENGLAND

BEDFORDSHIRE

HOWARD'S HOUSE, Cardington
(for Humphrey Whitbread Esq.)
Garden design in 1969 and 1982

BERKSHIRE

BAGNOR MANOR, Newbury
(for Billy Wallace Esq.)
Garden design including riverside lawn, terrace, flower borders and swimming pool surround, with the architect John Griffin, 1960–1 CL (see Chapter 4)

THE OLD VICARAGE★, Bucklebury
(for Sir Robert and Lady Sainsbury)
Garden design, including setting for Henry Moore sculptures, and continuing planting advice, 1962–74 CL
(see Chapter 4)

LITTLE BEAR★, Pangbourne
(for Mr and Mrs C.B. Goulandris)
Garden design and continuing planting advice, 1965–82
(see also LONDON: 37 CHESHAM PLACE)

THE OLD MILL, Woodspeen
(for Jean, Lady Ashcombe)
Garden design, 1964–6 (see Chapter 4)

RIBBLESDALE PARK, Ascot
(for J.R. Hindley Esq.)
Garden and planting design with William Wood & Son, 1966

BINFIELD LODGE, Newbury
(for Mr and Mrs H.J. Heinz)
Garden and planting design with William Wood & Son, 1966
(see Chapter 4)

BUCKHURST PARK★, Ascot
(for Peter Palumbo Esq.)
Planting design and continuing advice, 1966–82

FOLLY FARM, Sulhamstead
(for Hon. H.W. and Mrs Astor)
Planting advice for the Lutyens/Jekyll garden, 1971–7 (see Chapter 7)

FARLEY HALL★, Farley Hill, near Reading
(for Hon. Mrs Peter Samuel)
Garden design and continuing planting advice, 1975–82

ENGLEFIELD HOUSE★, near Reading
(for Mrs W.R. Beynon)
Garden and planting advice, 1975–80

WICKHAM HOUSE★, Newbury
(for General H.S. Hashim)
Garden design, 1976–7

RIDGE HOUSE, West Drive, Sunningdale
(Kenneth Wagg Esq.)
Garden advice, especially on siting of pool and tennis court, 1974–81

THE MANOR HOUSE★, Yattendon
(for Lord and Lady Iliffe)
Garden advice, 1977–81

MILTON HILL HOUSE★, near Abingdon
(for W.H. Smith & Son)
Garden and planting design, 1978–81

YATTENDON PARK★, Yattendon
Brief planting advice, 1979–80

AVINGTON MANOR★, Hungerford
(Lord and Lady Howard de Walden)
Garden advice, 1979–82

BASILDON HOUSE★, Lower Basildon
(for Lord and Lady Iliffe)
Brief planting advice, 1982

ASCOT PLACE, Ascot
Planting around the temple
with William Wood & Son, n.d.

BUCKINGHAMSHIRE

WADDESDON MANOR, near Aylesbury
(for the National Trust)
Planting design with William Wood & Son for The Aviary garden, 1964
(see Chapter 7)

HORSENDEN MANOR, Princes Risborough
(for Mrs Gourlay)
Planting advice in two reports, n.d.

CAMBRIDGESHIRE

ANGLESEY ABBEY★, near Cambridge
(for the National Trust)
Planting maintenance advice, 1982
(see Chapter 7)

CHESHIRE

TATTON PARK, Knutsford
(for the National Trust and Cheshire County
Council)
Planting advice for flower borders,
early 1960s CL (see Chapter 7)

LITTLE MORETON HALL★, Congleton
(for the National Trust)
Brief garden advice, 1970 (see Chapter 7)

CORNWALL

ANTONY HOUSE★, Torpoint
(for Richard Carew Pole Esq. and the National
Trust)
Brief garden advice, 1982 (see Chapter 7)

ESSEX

FOLLY FAUNTS HOUSE, Goldhanger, Maldon
(for Julian Jenkinson Esq.)
Brief garden advice, 1970

GLOUCESTERSHIRE

DAYLESFORD HOUSE, Daylesford
(for Lord Rothermere)
Planting for formal garden with
William Wood & Son, c. 1960

BOURTON-ON-THE-HILL HOUSE,
Bourton-on-the-Hill
(for Colonel Head)
Planting advice with architects
Benson & Benson, 1962

CHURCH HOUSE, Bibury
(for Sir Tobias Clarke)
Garden and planting advice (file survives but
has been returned at client's request), 1970s

THE BARN?
(for Mrs Guy Holland)
Brief garden advice, 1971–2

VALLEY FARM, Duntisbourne, Cirencester
(for Lady Hollenden)
Continuing garden advice, 1973–81

KINGSMILL HOUSE, Painswick
(for Mrs June Keith)
Brief garden advice, 1977

CIRENCESTER PARK, Cirencester
(for Lord Bathurst)
Brief garden advice, 1979

STANCOMBE PARK, Dursley
(for Mrs Gerda Barlow)
Planting advice, 1981

HIGHGROVE, near Tetbury
(for HRH The Prince of Wales)
Garden design and planting advice, 1981
(see Chapter 10)

HAMPSHIRE

EGBURY HOUSE, St Mary Bourne
(for Mrs Daphne Watkins)
Brief planting advice, 1966

NORTH END HOUSE★, Mottisfont
(for Mrs Gilbert Russell)
Garden and planting design, 1972–4
(see Chapter 7)

THE OLD SCHOOL HOUSE, St Mary Bourne
(for Dr Peter Johnson)
Brief garden advice, 1970

FAIRFIELD HOUSE★, Hambledon
(for Mr and Mrs Peter Wake)
Planting advice, 1970–80 CL
(see also NORTHAMPTONSHIRE:
COURTEENHALL)

HALL PLACE★, West Meon
(for the Hon. Mrs S.R. Cubitt)
Continuing planting advice, 1973–82 CL
(see Chapter 9)

TAYLOR'S MEAD★, Sparsholt
(for Lady Ivor Spencer-Churchill)
Garden and continuing planting advice,
1978–82

HERTFORDSHIRE

MACKERYE END, Harpenden
This is one of the early gardens for which
no records remain, only a few slides
of work done, c. 1967?

HUNTINGDONSHIRE

ABBOTS RIPTON HALL, Huntingdon
(for Lord and Lady de Ramsey)
LR was a frequent visitor and he admired the
design work of Humphrey Waterfield in the
garden; he helped with planting design
around the lake in the 1970s CL

KENT

CHARTWELL, Westerham
(for the National Trust)
Garden and planting advice, from 1966
(see Chapter 7)

SCOTNEY CASTLE, Lamberhurst
(for the National Trust)
Garden and planting advice, 1970–82
(see Chapter 7)

PENSHURST PLACE, Tonbridge
(for Lord De L'Isle)
Planting advice, n.d.

LEICESTERSHIRE

STABLE HOUSE★, North Kilworth
(for Mrs Paul Hyde-Thomason)
One visit, plan and planting advice, 1969

LONDON
(including the former Middlesex)

House in PELHAM CRESCENT
(for Humphrey Brooke Esq.)
Plan for town garden (one of the gardens
which backed on to Park House) with
William Wood & Son, 1960

10 HOLLAND PARK, W11
(for Lord and Lady Blakenham)
Garden and planting design with Ian Mylles,
his assistant at the time, and William Wood
& Son, 1962 CL   (see Chapter 4)

96 CHEYNE WALK, SW3
(for Gerald Hochschild Esq.)
Garden design and planting design with
William Wood & Son, 1963
(see Chapter 4)

THE AVIARY★, Southall
(for Whitney Straight Esq.)
Garden design and continuing planting advice,
1965–79   CL   (see Chapter 6)

37 CHESHAM PLACE★, SW1
(for Mr and Mrs C.B. Goulandris)
Garden design and continuing planting advice,
1965–82 (see also BERKSHIRE: LITTLE BEAR)

30 CHARLES ST, W1
(for Mrs Cynthia Fraser)
Planting design for a roof garden, 1968

1 HYDE PARK SQUARE, W2
(for Mrs D.L. Irwin)
Planting design for a roof garden, 1968

St JOHN'S, Smith Square, SW1
Planting around the church with
William Wood & Son (planting
plan only survives) Oct. 1968

HARROW SCHOOL
(for Mrs Edward Malan)
Brief garden advice, 1969–70

9 HAMPSTEAD HILL GARDENS, NW3
(for Mrs Michael Bowater)
Brief garden advice, 1970

1 SWAN WALK, SW3
(for the Hon. Michael Astor)
Garden and planting design with
William Wood & Son, 1970s
(see Chapter 4)

MARGARET PYKE HOUSE★, Mortimer Street, W1
(for the Family Planning Association)
Design and planting advice for a roof garden
in memory of Mrs Mure, 1970s (see Chapter 11)

31 MAIDA AVENUE, W2
(for Mrs Regester)
Shrub planting with Clifton Nurseries, 1970

CREWE HOUSE, Curzon Street, W1
Brief garden advice, 1970 (see Chapter 7)

113 DOVEHOUSE STREET★, SW3
(for Mrs John Carter)
Brief garden advice, 1971

28 WARWICK AVENUE, W9
Brief advice on garden pavilions, 1972

11 ABERCORN PLACE, NW3
(for Esteban Cerda)
Brief garden advice, 1972

14 HAMMERSMITH TERRACE★, W6
(for Jonathan McCreery Esq.)
Brief garden advice, 1973–4
(see also SOMERSET: STOWELL HILL)

47 CHESTER SQUARE, SW1
(for Lord Wilton)
Brief garden advice, 1974
(see also 27 EGERTON TERRACE and
WILTSHIRE: HILLBARN HOUSE)

NORTH MYMMS PARK
(for Mrs W.S. Morgan Burns)
Planting advice, 1975   CL

CITY CHURCHYARDS★: ST PANCRAS,
ST BENET'S SHEREHOG, ST SWITHUN
STONE, and ST STEPHEN'S WALBROOK
(for Peter Palumbo Esq.)
Design and planting advice, 1975–82
(see Chapter 8)

MANSION HOUSE SQUARE★ (project)
(for Peter Palumbo Esq.)
Landscape and planting for new city square,
1975 (see Chapter 8)

49 VICTORIA ROAD★, W8
(for Mrs Mark Bonham Carter)
Brief garden advice, 1978
(see also SUSSEX: RIPE MANOR)

27 EGERTON TERRACE, SW3
(for Lord Wilton)
Garden design and advice, 1978–82
(see also: 47 CHESTER SQUARE and WILTSHIRE:
HILLBARN HOUSE)

ARGYLL HOUSE, Kings Road, SW3
(for the Marquis of Normanby)
Brief garden advice, 1980–3

3 AUBREY ROAD★, W8
(for Lady Daphne Straight)
Garden design and advice, 1980–3
(see also THE AVIARY, Southall)

11 KENSINGTON PALACE GARDENS, W8
(for the French Embassy)
Brief garden advice, 1981

23 BLOMFIELD ROAD, W9
(for Sir Edward and Lady Ford)
Brief garden advice, 1981

13 ELM PLACE★, SW7
(for Miss Annabel Palumbo)
Garden design, 1981–2

TRINITY HOSPICE★, Clapham Common, SW4
(now the Lanning Roper Memorial Garden)
Preliminary garden and planting advice,
1981–2 (see Chapter 11)

ISMAELI CENTRE, SW7
Planting consultant for roof garden with
architects Casson, Conder & Partners and
landscape architects Sasaki Associates,
1981–3 (see Chapter 10)

GARDEN IN KENSINGTON, West London
(for Lord Snowdon)
Planting design, 1982 (see Chapter 10)

LONDON SCHOOL OF ECONOMICS, WC2
(for the University of London)
Planting design for containers for Houghton
Street and Clare Market pedestrian precinct
with Armstrong, Smith & Barron
Partnership, 1982–3

5 COTTESMORE GARDENS
(for Lady Iveagh)
Brief planting advice with
architect Vernon Gibberd, 1982

125 OLD CHURCH STREET, SW3
(for Mrs Peter Chance)
Plan of design for town garden, n.d.

47 EGERTON CRESCENT, SW3
One garden report, n.d.

NORFOLK

THE GLEBE, Bayfield
Brief garden advice, 1970

LETHERINGSETT HALL, Holt
(for the Hon. Beryl Cozens-Hardy)
Brief garden advice, 1970–2

THE MANOR HOUSE, Great Cressingham
(for Mrs Chapman)
Brief garden advice, 1970–1

WARHAM HOUSE, Wells
(for Lady Mary Harvey)
Garden advice, 1971–2

CHURCH FARM, Little Barningham
(for Mrs Walpole)
Brief garden advice, 1972

SAINSBURY CENTRE FOR THE VISUAL ARTS★,
University of East Anglia, Norwich
Landscape and planting consultant to
Sir Robert and Lady Sainsbury, with architects
Norman Foster Associates and landscape
architects Feilden & Mawson; also consultant
for interior planting design, 1975–82
(see Chapter 8)

WOOD HALL, Hethersett, Norwich
(for the Vice-Chancellor of the University of
East Anglia)
Brief garden advice, 1976–7

RUDHAM HOUSE★, East Rudham
Garden design and advice, 1976–82

STERNFIELD HOUSE★, Saxmundham
(for Lt.-Col. Sir Eric and Lady Penn)
Garden advice, 1978–82

WICKMERE HOUSE★, Wickmere
(for Noel Bolingbroke-Kent Esq.)
Garden and planting advice, 1979–82

BAYFIELD HALL, Holt
(for Brigadier Douglas Phelps)
Brief garden advice, 1982

NORTHAMPTONSHIRE

COURTEENHALL, Northampton
(for Mr and Mrs Peter Wake)
Garden design and planting advice, early 1960s

OXFORDSHIRE

STANTON HARCOURT
(for Lord Harcourt)
Garden and planting advice, 1960s

BRUERN ABBEY, Bruern
(for the Hon. Michael Astor)
Planting design with William Wood & Son,
1960s (see Chapter 4)

HASELEY COURT, Little Haseley
(for Mrs Nancy Lancaster)
Garden advice and planting design, 1968–70
CL (see Chapter 7)

TURVILLE GRANGE, Turville Heath
(for Princess Lee Radziwill)
Planting design, with plants from
Mrs Desmond Underwood, 1969

BROUGHTON CASTLE★, Banbury
(for Lord and Lady Saye and Sele)
Garden advice, 1969–71 (see Chapter 7)

GREY COURT, King's Sutton
(for Leo D'Erlanger Esq.)
Brief garden advice, 1970

DITCHLEY PARK★, Enstone
(for the Ditchley Foundation)
Garden consultant, 1973–6 (see Chapter 7)

FRIAR'S WELL★, Aynho
(for Viscountess Ward)
Garden and planting design, 1976–8   CL

THENFORD HOUSE, near Banbury
(for the Rt. Hon. and Mrs Michael Heseltine)
Garden and planting advice, 1977–82
(see Chapter 10)

SHROPSHIRE

LOWER HALL, Worfield
(for Mrs and Mrs Christopher Dumbell)
Garden design advice, 1980–1 (see Chapter 11)

SOMERSET

STOWELL HILL, Templecombe
(for General McCreery)
Brief garden advice (one report), 1969
(see also LONDON: 14 HAMMERSMITH
TERRACE)

SUFFOLK

THE OLD RECTORY★, Orford
(for William Servaes Esq.)
Garden design and continuing garden advice,
1967   CL   (see Chapter 9)

ICKWORTH★, near Bury St Edmunds
(for Lord Euston and the National Trust)
Garden and landscape advice, 1970
(see Chapter 7)

48 CHURCH STREET, Orford
(for John Trew Esq.)
Brief planting advice, 1971

METTINGHAM PINES★, Bungay
(for Lady Lloyd)
List of plants, 1971

SURREY

CHERRY HILL, Wentworth
(for Mr and Mrs J.H. Whitney)
Planting advice, c. 1959–61 (see Chapter 6)

ROYAL HORTICULTURAL SOCIETY GARDEN,
Wisley
Planting scheme for new formal garden by
Sir Geoffrey Jellicoe, 1969

DENBIES★, Dorking
(for Lord Ashcombe)
Planting advice, 1972–80

TELEGRAPH COTTAGE★, Warren Road,
Kingston
(Mrs Alexander Keiller)
Garden advice, 1972–82

SUSSEX

THE LAINES★, Plumpton
(for Major and the Hon. Mrs Bruce Shand)
Garden design and continuing planting advice,
1967–82   CL   (see Chapter 9)

PENNS IN THE ROCKS★, Groombridge
(for Lord and Lady Gibson)
Garden and planting advice, 1967–82   CL
(see Chapter 7)

HORSTED PLACE, Uckfield
(for Lady Rupert Nevill)
Advice on azalea planting, 1968–70

THE OLD VICARAGE★, Firle
(for Mr and Mrs C.C. Bridge)
Garden design and continuing planting advice,
1969–82   CL   (see Chapter 9)

FORESTER'S COTTAGE★, Coleman's Hatch
One brief report on planting, September 1969

BIGNOR PARK, Pulborough
(for Viscountess Mersey)
Brief garden design advice, 1969

BENTLEY★, Halland
(for Mrs Askew)
Brief garden advice, 1970

HIGHFIELD HOUSE, Slindon
(for Mrs James Bowes Lyon)
Brief planting advice, 1970

MARTINS, Thakeham
(for Mr and Mrs Robin Marlar)
Brief garden advice, 1970

RIPE MANOR, Lewes
(for Mrs Mark Bonham Carter)
Brief garden advice, 1970
(see also LONDON: 49 VICTORIA ROAD)

WAREHEAD HOUSE, Chichester
(for Mrs Evan-Jones)
Brief garden advice, 1971

WOOLBEDING HOUSE★, Midhurst
(for the National Trust)
Garden and planting design and continuing
advice, 1974–80 (see Chapter 7)

PARHAM HOUSE, Pulborough
(for Mrs Tritton)
Planting design for one border, 1975
(see Chapter 7)

SANSOME'S FARMHOUSE★, Rudgwick
(for Mrs More O'Ferrall)
Garden and planting advice, 1977–81

WILLINGHAM HOUSE★, Ringmer
(for Ian Askew Esq.)
Brief garden advice, 1981

WILTSHIRE

RAMSBURY MANOR, Ramsbury
(for Lord Wilton)
Garden advice, pre-1958
(for Lord Rootes)
Planting design for formal garden by
Sir Geoffry Jellicoe, 1967

HILLBARN HOUSE★, Great Bedwyn
(for Lord Wilton)
Garden and planting design with architect
John Griffin, 1958–62
(for Lord and Lady Bruntisfield)
Garden and planting design including
layout of *jardin potager* with architect
John Griffin, 1962–71
(for Mr and Mrs A. Buchanan)
Planting advice, 1971–8   CL   (see Chapter 9)

HAVERING HOUSE, Milton Lilbourne
(for Lord Wilton)
Brief garden advice with William Wood & Son,
1963

MANOR COTTAGE, Rushall
(for Mrs Wyett Larken)
Brief garden advice, 1970

LOWER MOOR FARM
(for Mrs Chance)
Brief garden advice, 1971

COMPTON HOUSE★, Compton Chamberlain
(for John Newman Esq.)
Garden and planting design and advice, 1975–9

THE PARK SCHOOL★, Wilton
(for Lady Glendevon)
Brief planting advice, 1976–8

ALLIED DUNBAR CENTRE★, Swindon
(formerly Hambro Life Centre)
Planting around new building and courtyard
(roof) garden with architects Peter Carter,
and Yorke, Rosenberg & Mardall, 1977–82
(see Chapter 8)

HAMBRO LIFE TRICENTRE (project)
Planting consultant in early stages, 1980–3

MILKHOUSE WATER★, Pewsey
(for David Allford, partner in Yorke,
Rosenberg & Mardall)
Brief garden advice, 1979–80

LIDDINGTON MANOR★, near Swindon
(for Mr and Mrs. J. Joffe)
Brief garden advice, 1980 (see Chapter 8)

KNOWLE HOUSE★, Froxfield
(for Brian Henderson, partner in Yorke,
Rosenberg & Mardall)
Brief garden advice, 1980–1

RAINSCOMBE PARK, Oare
(for Lord Clanwilliam)
Garden advice, 1980–2

OLD CONOCK MANOR, Devizes
(for Derek Johns Esq.)
Brief garden advice, 1982

SCOTLAND

GRAMPIAN REGION

ESTERSKENE HOUSE★, Aberdeen
(for Lord Cowdray)
Planting advice, 1978–80

STRATHCLYDE

CAMERON★, Alexandria
(for Mrs Telfer Smollett)
Brief garden advice, 1979

NORTHERN IRELAND

CO. FERMANAGH

CASTLECOOLE★, Enniskillen
(for the National Trust of Northern Ireland)
Landscape and planting consultant, 1967–78
(see Chapter 5)

CO. DOWN

CASTLE WARD★, near Downpatrick
(for the National Trust of Northern Ireland)
Landscape and planting consultant, 1967–78
(see Chapter 5)

EIRE

CO. DONEGAL

GLENVEAGH CASTLE
(for Henry P. McIlhenny Esq.)
Garden design and continuing planting advice,
1959–82   CL   (see Chapter 5)

AUGHAWONEY LODGE, Kilmachrenan
(for Mrs Nash)
Brief garden advice, 1970s

MARBLE HILL★, Port na Blagh
(for Mrs D. Jobling-Purser)
Garden design and continuing planting advice,
1971–9   CL   (see Chapter 5)

DUBLIN

FARMLEIGH, Castleknock
(for the Earl of Iveagh)
Advice given on screen planting, c. 1960, and
subsequent garden design and planting advice,
n.d.

TRINITY COLLEGE
Landscape and planting consultant for new
Arts Building with architects Ahrends, Burton
& Koralek, and subsequently landscape
consultant for all Trinity College buildings,
1973–8 (see Chapter 5)

CO. KILDARE

CASTLEMARTIN STUD★, Kilcullin
(for Dr Anthony O'Reilly)
Garden design and planting advice, 1977–82
(see Chapter 5)

CO. WEXFORD

STRAMORE★, Bunclody
(for Mrs D. Jobling-Purser)
Garden design and planting advice, 1979–83

FRANCE

8 RUE PIPER★, Reims
(for Monsieur F. d'Aulan)
Garden advice, 1972–3

LE MANOIR, Saintes Maries aux Anglais,
Mesnil Mauger
(for Philip Lockwood Esq.)
Garden advice, 1977–80

AIGLEMONT★, Gouvieux
(for Prince Amyn Aga Khan)
Planting advice, 1980–2 (see Chapter 10)

ITALY

LA GUIZZA★, Asolo
Brief garden advice, 1971–2

MONTORIA, Asolo
(for Miss Freya Stark)
Garden advice during the 1970s.
This was not a paid commission as Lanning
and Freya Stark were firm friends, but he
frequently visited Montoria and helped her
with the garden, especially the roses she loved

SWITZERLAND

CHATEAU DE BELLERIVE★, Geneva
(for Prince Sadruddin Aga Khan)
Design and *jardin potager* with continuing
planting advice, 1969–82
(see Chapter 10)

USA

FARNSWORTH HOUSE★, Plano, Illinois
(for Peter Palumbo Esq.)
Landscape and planting advice for the famous
house designed by Mies van der Rohe, 1973–82
(see Chapter 8)

ANANOURI★, Highland Falls, New York
(for Mr and Mrs C. Sidamon-Eristoff)
Garden design and continuing planting
advice, 1976–82 (see Chapter 6)

BILTMORE DIARY FARMS, Asheville, North
Carolina
(for Mr and Mrs George Cecil)
Brief garden advice, 1978 and 1982

1 BEEKMAN PLACE★, New York
(for Mrs John Hay Whitney)
Planting advice for small city garden, 1978–9

GREENTREE, Manhasset, Long Island
(for Mrs John Hay Whitney)
Brief garden advice, 1980

POWHATON PLANTATION, King George,
Virginia (for Mr and Mrs Raymond Guest)
Brief planting advice, 1980

WOODLAWN PLANTATION★, Virginia
(for Prince Sadruddin Aga Khan)
Brief garden and planting advice, 1982
(see Chapter 10)

MIRADOR FARM★, Greenwood, Virginia
(for Mrs J.H. Scott)
One visit, 1982, to give advice on the
proposed restoration of the garden made
in the 1930s by Mr and Mrs Ronald Tree
(see Chapter 11)

PHOTOGRAPHIC ACKNOWLEDGEMENTS

The author and publisher would like to thank those listed below who kindly supplied illustrations
and by whose permission the illustrations are reproduced.

Page numbers in italics indicate colour illustrations.

Aerofilms: 194
The Aga Khan Foundation (photos Crispin Boyle): 188, 189
Cecil Beaton photograph, courtesy of Sotheby's London: 46
Lady Berkeley: 36, *39*, 40 (photo Anthony Denny), 41, 42, *43 above*
Philip Brown: *154*, endpaper
Peter Carter: 144, *145 below*
Rosamund Codling: 153
Condé Nast Publications, reproduced in *Vogue* (photo Snowdon):
   193
Country Life: 48 (photo Alex Starkey), 60, 92, *99 above*, 110, 111,
   122 below, 123, 124, *156 below*, 163, 165, 166, 170, 171, 172, 173, 174,
   176, 177, 178, 179, 203
Country Life Books: *38 left*
Valerie Finnis: *34*, 202
Margaret Morgan Fisher: 102, *103 above*, *105*, 106
Foster Associates (photos Ken Kirkwood): 149, *150*, *151*, 152
Hedrich-Blessing: 137, *147*
Illustrated London News: 70
Museum of Modern Art, New York: Photographs courtesy the
   Mies van der Rohe Archive (photos Hedrich-Blessing): 137, *147*
National Trust: 86, 88, 89, *120*, 125, 131, 133, 135
Sheila Orme: *116*, *117*, 127, 129, *158*, 164
Pieterse Davison International Ltd: 74, 81
Mrs Laura Wood Roper: 2, 14, 16, 18, *19 above*

Lanning Roper Papers, Royal Horticultural Society, Lindley Library:
   26, 35, 37, 55, *56 below*, 65, 68, *69*, *72*, *73*, *77*, *80*, 83 above, *108*, *109*,
   114 below, 138, 143 (photo John Donat), *145 above*, *156 above*,
   159 above (photo Jonathan Gibson), *159 below*, 160, 182, 183, *185*
Anne Sidamon-Eristoff: *103 below*
Harry Smith Horticultural Photographic Collection:
   24, 25, *30*, *43 below*, 44, *47*, *51*, 53, *56, above*, *57*, 58, *78 above*, *79 above*,
   84, 85, 94, 96, 97, 98, *99 below*, *113*, *114 above*, *161 below*, *196*, *197*,
   199, 204, 207
Lord Snowdon: 181, *193*
Miss Anne Terry: *19 below*, 23, 71
Trinity College, Dublin: 90
Trinity Hospice: 208 (photo Angela Heskett)
U.S. Navy Official Photo (reproduced from the
   History of United States Naval Operations in World War II,
   Vol. XI *The Invasion of France and Germany* by S.E. Morison,
   Oxford University Press, 1957): 20
Weidenfeld & Nicolson Archives: 29, *38 right*, 66, 76 (photo Walter
   Pfeiffer), *79 below* (photo Walter Pfeiffer), 82
   (photo Walter Pfeiffer), *83 below* (photo Walter Pfeiffer)

The plans on the following pages were drawn by the author and are
based on material in the Lanning Roper Papers in the RHS's Lindley
Library: 59, 61, 62, *114 below*, *118*, *122 above*, 126, 130, *161 above*, 184

INDEX